THE POPPY FACTORY TAKEOVER:
Teenage Writing

www.crazyhorsepress.com

Crazy Horse Press,
116 Bewdley Road, Stourport,
Worcs DY13 8XH
Tel: 01299 824858
email: phayden@crazyhorsepress.com
web site: www.crazyhorsepress.com

© Peter Hayden 2000
on behalf of all contributors unless otherwise stated.
illustrations © Clinton Banbury 2000
ISBN 1 871870 12 7
Cover design – Michael Hayden

This book is sold subject to the condition that it shall not, by way of trade or otherwise, be lent, resold, hired out or otherwise circulated without the publisher's prior consent in any form of binding or cover other than that in which it is published and without a similar condition including this condition being imposed on the subsequent publisher.

Printed by T. Snape & Co Ltd., Boltons Court, Preston PR1 3TY. Tel: 01772 254553 Fax: 01772 204697

Acknowledgements

All attributed teenage pieces are published courtesy of their authors.

'Help the Aged' appeared in *'Young Words'* (Macmillan Children's Books) and is published courtesy of the author and W.H. Smith Ltd.

'The New Adventures of Robin Hood' is the work of the people whose names appear in the last few lines.

'The Poppy Factory Takeover' appears courtesy of Sean Ashe, Paul Brennan, Melissa Butera, Rachel Arkinstall, Catherine Clinton, Lydia Cooper, Thomas Delahay, Andrew Dixon, James Feely, Kathleen Garvey, Luke Griffin, Katie Griffiths, Andrew Harvey, Martine Hirrell, Claire Hoban, Natalie Jones, Amber Kite, Helen Lenihan, Ben Llewellyn, Mighele Massey, Katie McGuinness, Chris Mullins, James Neenan, Lauren Perry, Jenny Pointon, Katie Smith, Peter Stirrup, Camilla Sullivan, Charlotte Sztybel, David Thompson, Adam Tibbetts, John Townsend, Thomas Westwood, and Charlotte Whittingham. It was originally typeset by Charlotte Sztybel.

The people who most influenced the writing of 'The Headmaster's Daughter' were Fay Bethel, James Colclough, Helen Chance, Vicky Raftery, James Trickett, Alex Shuttes and Sarah Bright.

The pieces from Bishops Wood are unattributed, in accordance with the wishes of the group.

'Miss Creedle Teaches Creative Writing'. Copyright © Gareth Owen 2000. Reproduced by permission of the author c/o Rogers, Coleridge & White Ltd., London W11 1JN.

'I've had this shirt…' © Michael Rosen, from *'Mind Your Own Business'* Scholastic UK '96. Reproduced by permission of Scholastic UK.

'Weeds' appears in *'Collected Poems'* by Norman Nicholson (Faber) and is reprinted here courtesy of the author and Faber & Faber.

'Wires' appears without kind permission of Marvell Press Australia, whom I have been unable to trace by any means. Please send permission form when you see this.

'With Nansen' appears in *'setting the poem to words'* by David Hart (Five Seasons Press) and reprinted here courtesy of the author and Five Seasons Press.

'After the Requested Cremation' © Alan Holden, from *'Air and Chill Earth'* Chatto & Windus '71.

A part of Chapter 6 appeared in the T.E.S. 17 Dec 99 as *'A Bit of Rudeness can Enlarge the Mind'*.

© No teenage piece, attributed or otherwise, may be reproduced without permission of the author via Crazy Horse Press.

Other books by the same author available from Crazy Horse Press:

'The Adventures of Stringy Simon'
'The Willy Enlarging Elixir'
'The Sneeze & Other Stories'
'The Day Trip'
'The Headmaster's Daughter'
'And Smith Must Score'

CONTENTS

Chapter 1: ....The Word Pile　　1
Chapter 2: ....'The Day Trip'　　11
Chapter 3: ....The Roundabout　　24
Chapter 4: ....'Happening Time'　　46
Chapter 5: ....Football　　54
Chapter 6: ....Rudeness　　67
Chapter 7: ....Poetry　　91
Chapter 8: ....The Subjective Mind　126
Chapter 9: ....Magazines　140
Chapter 10: ....Prose　163
Chapter 11: ....Horror　205
Chapter 12: ....A-Level　219
Chapter 13: ..'The Headmaster's Daughter'　241
Chapter 14: ....Bishops Wood　252
Chapter 15: ....Friendship　270
Chapter 16: ....Finale　286

*I would like to dedicate this book to
my most respectfully remembered
English teachers:*

*D. M. Thomas - yes, really - and Ratty Wheeler
from Teignmouth Grammar
and Willy Pope, Bill Lawrence and above all,
Buddy Holly, from Hove Grammar.*

A thousand thanks.

CHAPTER 1

The Word Pile

This is not the kind of book where you start at page one and finish at the end, it's one for dipping into. Eventually you might get to read the whole book, but not in any particular order. There's some brilliant writing in it (I think), not by me but by teenagers I've met/taught in schools and workshops. In between are some bits and pieces of my writing, my writing experiences, and a few of my opinions on schools and writing. Feel free to skip pages.

I'll start by saying who I am – basically an author who writes for teenagers, sometimes juniors, and who spent close to three decades trying not to be your average teacher but never completely succeeded. My real justification for the book is the hundreds of hours I have spent writing with young people in different circumstances, and printing, reproducing, publishing what they have done in dozens of ways.

Being a teacher as well as an author meant I had to devise a routine which enabled me to get my writing done without interfering with work too much and if possible without taking up all my weekends and holidays. So I decided to buy a large brass alarm clock and one Sunday night stood it ceremonially on a tin tray by the bed, and announced to the family that I would be getting up at four in the morning, four days a week until further notice.

The alarm went off and bounced round and round the tray, waking up my son, wife, next door's dog, children, and the neighbours themselves. Lights went on in several houses. I don't think I wrote much that morning, but eventually got a routine going and stuck to it for several years and about five books.

These days I don't teach any more, but spend my time writing and publishing books and doing readings and workshops in schools. In almost every school I get asked what's it like being a writer, where I get my ideas from, how long does it take to write a book, do I actually like writing (usually asked in a kind of puzzled disbelieving voice), how do you get a book published, and what is my favourite book, or, who is my favourite author. I think that's all the most common ones. There is no single answer to any of these questions - answers vary depending what mood you're in and what book you're thinking of most at the time, they are never completely true or untrue. So, although as a writer I'm somewhere in the non-league pyramid, at the end of the first few chapters I'll put the answers that seem right for that particular part of the book.

* * * * *

Have you got any idea how much writing you do at school? I read a report once (well, actually, a summary of a report, too lazy to read the whole thing), a 1979 School Inspectors' report that investigated the amount of writing kids do in their school lives. The finding was that an average year-11 pupil wrote 120,000 words in four subjects over four terms, rising to 200,000 in the case of the more able. That's going on for a fifth of a million words (I would say the average teenage paperback you would get out of the library is about 75,000 words) - and this report was done before all the G.C.S.E. long essays, short essays, projects, rewrites and so on that you have to do now, so we can reckon it's on the low side.

It's quite easy to calculate this yourself - just get an average exercise book or piece of A4 you've written on, take a few random lines and work out the average number of words you do to a line; multiply by the number of lines on the page, then look through your folders and books and work out how many pages you've done this year. All subjects - including maths, after all numbers have to be written down as well. And, bingo... Now, if you go from Key Stage 1 to the Upper Sixth and do a few speculative sums, however you look at it you're going to come to the conclusion that you write an awful lot of words in your school life. If someone could spin them into novels...

Take an average school and just think of those billions of words being secreted day in, day out. Where does it all end up? The bin, in many cases. One of my small claims to fame at the school I worked at for eighteen years was that I realised we were throwing out an awful lot of paper, and got us on the collection round of a recycling firm. I got the kids' work disposed of in a more eco-friendly way.

Before I go on let me get something out of the way. I'm not one of these people who thinks the young have a wonderful gift, a freshness that adults don't have. I only believe in young people's writing as far as I believe in anyone's writing: if you stopped a double-decker bus in the middle of the road, forced the passengers off and marched them into a classroom and made them write an essay, probably 20% would be unreadable crap, 60% might be middling to extremely boring, 15% interesting, 4% very interesting, and 1% (that is, about one person every three buses) might be so good you'd want to kiss the page. That's all. The only difference is that good adult writing has a very small chance of finding a readership, and good kids' writing has a very big chance of finding the bin.

Words are free, we speak them by the thousand, they're colourless, odourless (except in the case of a certain deputy-head I know), and bio-degradable - but when all the annual ripping up and binning ceremonies are over and done with, you don't have much to show for three-quarters of a life spent in school, do you?

The trouble is, most of the time it's so unbelievably tedious to mark. There is a certain type of schoolwork which is exciting to mark - usually containing a strong individual voice, stemming from a personal commitment from the pupil, teacher, or both, probably the outcome of several sessions of work - but apart from that, routine marking is a special kind of hell. Living with the average teacher's marking load is like running up a large overdraft at the bank: whatever steps you take to clear it, it always comes back, it drains you. Clever really, kids hate doing it, teachers hate marking it, but it trundles on, never-ending.

Along with a couple of million other teachers, I'd love to invent a kind of exercise book marking contraption: it would take up the whole back wall of the staffroom - books would be received by a pair of extendable gloved hands which would scrutinise them before feeding them into the appropriate part of the workings. It would need constant oiling and topping up with inks. If you saw a teacher you disliked on it, you could surreptitiously change the dial, say, from geography to R.E. and work on the Western Ghats would come out with comments like, 'Fair work. Remember, Jesus died for your sins. 7/10' on it.

Most staffrooms have at least one compulsive marker, who never surfaces from an endless pile of books. If the fire alarm goes, they take some outside with them and carry on, they continue on the last afternoon of term until you actually turn them off their table so that you can set out the booze. Our guy was with a class one day when several of us were free because of exams; it was summer and we were feeling a bit perky, so we raided his pile and marked all the blank pages for him. He wasn't very happy - it wasn't that he thought about his comments that much, just that he liked to leave a kind of calling card on every page of every child's book.

Most teachers have had the experience of needing to get a set of books marked in a hurry. One mate was so desperate that he dished them out amongst the rest of us, gave us a rough idea what he wanted and left us to mark them even though we knew nothing about his subject. I put 'See Me' on all of my lot.

The English in the following piece was technically weak and difficult to follow, and it was in my mind to just glance at the first and last paragraphs and put 'Fair effort' on it. But I happened to be covering for someone in the I.T. room at the time, and there was a computer going spare. 'Wonder what this would look like properly presented,' I thought, clearing the screen:

THE SPINNER

Up, down. Up, down. Continuously up, down - it used to drive me mad.

When I was ten-eleven there was a bad craze. Yo-yos - Coca-Cola, Fanta, Sprite spinners. They cost £1.75 each, and everyone walked round the playground and in lessons playing with them. I was the only one who didn't have one, for two reasons: one, I couldn't play it very well, and, two, I could not afford one. I felt like the odd one out of about three hundred kids, and believe me it was awful. As the week-end drew closer and closer all I could think of was ways to get my pocket-money and get one. I was determined.

11.30, Saturday morning.

"Mum, can I have my quid seventy-five pocket-money?"

"Oh wait a minute, will ya."

"Oh please, I need it now."

"Why?"

"I wanna get one of them yo-yo things."

"Oh bloody hell, here, have it. I'll never make any money."

"Tar mum."

I ran out of the house and legged it to the shop as fast as my bony legs could go.

As I entered the shop, my eyes had beaten my brain to it. There they were. My eyes focussed on these brightly coloured yo-yos. As I lifted one up I saw the price on the back: £1.80. Oh... I thought, my house is miles away, I can't just run all the way back for 5p. I looked at the woman at the till and cleared my throat.

"Erm, can I have one of these please?" And I placed my £1.75 on the desk.

"Yes, that'll be £1.80 please." She just looked at the £1.75 and said, "Go on then, I'll let you off."

YES. MISSION ACCOMPLISHED. I was so chuffed, I ran back home and saw my dad lying in the chair rather sloppily. I put my finger through the loop and just started moving my hands. It wouldn't work. Oh no, after all that I don't know how to do it.

"Damn," I shouted, and my dad spotted me out the corner of his eye, which was half open and half shut.

"Christ, don't I ever get any peace round here, come here, I'll show you, I used to be ace at this."

My old man was a fairly good sort of chap in his own way, and he helped me for the next hour or so. I was getting quite good. I practised all week-end and was busting for Monday to come round. When it did, I was late getting up, so I just flung some water and soap on my face, put my clothes on, put my yo-yo in my pocket and was off. As I walked through the gates with my new smart yo-yo I was doing all my tricks that dad had showed me, and all my mates came running over to me, and started watching me.

I stole the show. I was so chuffed.

Simon McKenzie

*   *   *   *   *

Nice writing by any yardstick, and it came very close to the bin. I like the way he doesn't nick the yo-yo, doesn't get it nicked by someone else, doesn't get to school and find the craze is over, etc., etc. It's just dead straight and low key. Give me that kind of stuff every time over the big action stories, they just make me yawn.

Words words words. Every so often life pokes its face in, doesn't it? I worked for a long time at the school which suffered the M40 mini-bus accident in which twelve pupils and a teacher died, and after, when the little piles of ticked books were gathered together and sent home to the bereaved families I was struck by a sense of how little there was to treasure, really. And when I spoke to the families and friends, it was always the tangible things they remembered with pleasure, things their sons and daughters had made, trips and journeys, tournaments, projects where the outcome wasn't already known in advance, where there was some excitement about it shared by the teacher and pupils.

Something that has always amazed me is the amount of their own time, on top of all the hassles and pressures, teachers will cheerfully put in if the situation is right. Sports fixtures, productions, exchanges, musicals, music practises, cooking demos, youth hostelling, outward bound, skiing, fetes, car-boots, yearbooks, anthologies, magazines, classroom decoration, animal and plant husbandry, clothes designing, theatre trips, museum trips, college lecture trips, astronomy late at night, concert trips, field trips, charity events, chess club, computer club, art club, this that and the other club - the list is endless. We all crave for that sliver of time when learning becomes a genuine teacher-apprentice thing rather than the other thing, the bloody great nationwide chain-gang, teachers at the front, kids at the back.

One of the most enjoyable lessons I taught was up in the Home Economics block once. I don't know what they call it now, it changes its name every three years: 'The Scientific Examination of Hygiene, Nutrition, and Related Subjects Department'. Anyway, I used to wind up the Head of Whateveritis's department and say, 'Call this a kitchen? This isn't a proper kitchen - where's the grease marks on the walls and stuff lying around going off?'

My chance came when a scheme of 'activity days' was put up in the school as a way of confining trips, etc. to the end of the summer term so the kids wouldn't confuse them with the proper business of desk-based learning. The scheme faded after a couple of years - too much fun - but while it was running I got them to let me hold a balti-making day and we filled the place with root-ginger, garlic and strong spices and made a bloody good mess.

* * * * *

When I take some of the children's pieces you will read here round to schools and read them, the reactions are often stunning. And then teachers come over and say, they came across a piece like that years ago and they made a photocopy, or kids come and say they wrote a piece like that once and they might still have it - and one of the things I hope will happen is that people will send in some of these copies, and I can produce a follow-up book. I'd like to do a series of them.

* * * * *

Q. What's it like being an author?

A. Brilliant, you go round schools and the kids clap you instead of playing up.

Q. Where do you get your ideas from?

A. For this book it was easy - just kept pieces of writing that kids have done in the past that I liked. I didn't think of putting them in a book at the time, just admired what they had written and asked if I could have a copy.

Q. How long does it take to write a book?

A. I was making notes for this one for a few weeks, on and off - then it took five weeks to write, so it was probably the quickest one I've ever done; but the rewrite has been quite difficult and has taken about three weeks. One thing I haven't calculated is how much time the kids' pieces took.

Q. Do you like writing?

A. I enjoyed writing this one because I haven't had a plot to work out. But the rewrite has been harder, because I wrote it for teachers originally, but wanted it to be interesting to teenagers; now I've decided it should be for teenagers, but still want it to be interesting to teachers. So I've had to keep making small changes where things don't sound right, but even now I've finished (I'm adding this bit on the read-through) I'm not sure who I've really been writing for - teachers or kids.

Q. How do you get a book published?

A. I'm publishing this one through my own company, Crazy Horse Press. It sounds like a big deal, but in fact it's easy to publish a book. It's like having alterations done to your house, you get a builder, tell him what you want, he tells you if it's possible, then you have it done. Printers are quite like builders, you've got to keep an eye on them or they cut corners - but I've been very lucky with mine and know I can trust him (T. Snape, address at front, ask for Dominic). The difficult bit comes after it's printed - book-selling is hard, much harder than book-writing or book-printing.

Q. Who is your favourite author?

A. William Mayne is the governor, no-one can touch him. I wish I could meet him, but I don't think he comes out much. Reading him is just a wonderful experience, if you can find them. 'A Game of Dark' was out of print the last time I asked, so I stole a copy I'm not saying where from, and I won't lend or part with it to anyone. Another of his, 'Gideon Ahoy!' - brilliant - was being flogged around schools by a remainder salesman when I got hold of it. I said, how many of these can you get? I'll buy all of them. Hadn't a clue what I was going do with them, it just seemed important they be rescued. But in fact it was only an odd copy. I paid my £1.20 and felt furtive as I took it, like when a bent antiques dealer blags a priceless Titian off an old dear for a tenner.

CHAPTER 2

'The Day Trip' & Other Writing

I was an urchin at school who only liked art and games, and yet I loved English - playing with the language, taking the beads off the thread, rolling them around, holding them up, rethreading them. I suppose what attracted me to it more than anything else was that it was a wasteful subject. I was at a grammar school where everything was very methodical and curriculum-driven, but English seemed to cut a bit of slack for itself - it wasn't a low-status subject, in fact it commanded great respect, but it seemed to amble, or maybe swagger, where the others just marched relentlessly on.

The teachers reflected this: a couple of them were just mildly eccentric, the rest were plain barking - but they always had this great assuredness with words which seemed to swirl around them like an aristocrat's cape and put them above the combat. They were wealthy - fabulously rich in word and expression - and no-one could touch them. They would periodically walk in with a tatty volume of something or other, and simply read to us for the whole lesson. I would be absolutely lost, they would read with such tenderness and force, I'd be gone, not at home, until the bell went years later. One old chap used to read Browning with a passion that made his cheeks fire up, he'd spit across the room, and arrive at the last line in such a state of embarrassed fulfilment that we used to speculate whether he'd climaxed himself. No matter how obscenely we mimicked him though, there was no escaping it was an experience of a very special kind.

I started my working life teaching in a junior school in East Ham, and the day would very often end with a chapter or two from a book - and it was through this experience that I got involved in trying to write for children. What happened was, 'The Iron Man' came out, and it was so satisfying to read to them, and so frustrating afterwards that there was nothing else like it, that I decided to try and copy it - I just envied and admired it, and wanted to get under its skin.

I had an idea that inspiration was important in the best writing, and that to plan beforehand or even read through before it was finished would compromise it. So I simply got myself a ream of paper, put a table by a window, and on the first Monday of the summer holiday, without forethought, started to write.

As it will never see the light of day, I'd like the satisfaction of quoting a couple of paragraphs. This is the opening:

A pair of eyes stared out of the long grass, wide and orange. And as they stared, stems withered in their path, blades of grass wilted and turned their sides to the ground. Karen looked but was blinded as soon as their eyes met, and everything got lost behind a dazzling screen of white, as it would if you stared at the sun.

A figure rose on two legs, apelike, humpbacked and heavy, and raged towards her as if drunk. Behind it the sky was red and purple, churning and reeling, and the purple and the red twisted against each other, separated and joined again in long necks, like hot fat on water.

But the eyes were always on her, paralysing, fixing her to the spot. She blinked, and brilliant turquoise quoits shimmered in her head. The ape-devil was stretching out a withered hand - but she knew that hand. She had to remember. That was the key. That would make her safe. But already it had her shoulder and she could hear her bones crack and grind together as it shook, and shook and shook, screaming a cruel out-of-control scream:

'ATE.'

It sounded like 'ate'. It was going to eat her alive. It stretched its head closer, dwarfing hers in its size. She could feel the heat of its rage, and the teeth battening against her skull and cheek.

'WHY ARE YOU LATE?'

Mr Bridges. It was Mr Bridges shaking her in a rage and shouting, his face right next to hers. She opened her eyes. But why was mum there, and what were they doing in her bedroom?

* * * * *

I look at it now, about half a kilo of quarto deeply indented by my W.H. Smith Olivetti and held together with split pins, and the feeling I have is identical to the one that used to come over me when a year nine would rush over between lessons and hand me dozens of pages of blow-by-blow accounts of rivalry over boys and that sort of thing posing as fiction, and ask if I could help get it published. (Sorry.)

What shocks me when I read my own first attempt after so many years, is the realisation that I was under the same kind of paralysis that I have seen endlessly in schoolkids and never been able to touch - the assumption that the brain has a kind of fiction department which automatically locks on the minute you pick up a pen or sit down at a keyboard. That is the supreme problem in writing: we start a story and we are immediately in a foreign place - somewhere where the rules of life don't apply, somewhere phoney, facile, unreal.

Which is probably one reason why I disliked writing books for a long time - felt the need to, but didn't actually enjoy it at all - and that only changed when I came to see writing as a way of expressing truth rather than fiction. I'm not saying that what I write suddenly became profound, but a point creeps up on you when you finally shed a skin, the skin that appears the minute you sit at a keyboard, the writing skin; and then you can start being yourself.

* * * * *

Around about this time, I came across a small news item in the Guardian, which I've still got:

ANTI-HELICOPTER DOG HUNT

Police in Derby have been asked to help to hunt for a dog which has bitten two men and women and which thinks nothing of attacking cars, and even a landing helicopter.

Rolls-Royce said yesterday that the dog, a part-alsation mongrel, rushed at a British Caledonian helicopter arriving at the Moor Lane office complex in Derby.

A spokesman said: 'The beast leapt for the scything rotor blades but crashed against the pitot tube causing an estimated £200 worth of damage. It has also chewed through at least two car tyres.'

The people bitten by the dog had to be treated at the works surgery and were given anti-tetanus injections. Rolls-Royce has called in the police. The firm is concerned that there may be further attacks in the neighbourhood, possibly on children on holiday from school, said a spokesman.

The large mongrel often leads a pack of dogs which ranges over the open spaces round the office blocks. It is believed to be living wild.

For some reason the article got to me, and I knew 'The Dog Pack' would be my next book: I would write the dogs' story.

I think because I hadn't been successful up to that point, that I decided I would have to do some serious research for this one. During the next six months I went to Rolls-Royce and talked to the people in their medical room, went round the neighbouring estate and found the family that had owned the alsation - they had it put down after the police threatened them with court, though they couldn't say for sure that theirs was the dog in question; I attended magistrates court sittings, spent a morning in a police station, went to dog training classes, spent half a day at a P.D.S.A. dispensary, watched puppies being born at a dog kennels, and went up in a little two-man helicopter.

That's serious research by anyone's reckoning, I'm amazed I ever got round to doing the book. But it pottered along O.K. It wasn't easy to write - I was trying for a dog's-eye view, which was hard, and the research got in and weighed it down a bit, like surplus baggage. You need to research, but you can't let it stop a story from evolving. But it came out in the end, and I sent it off.

I was sent a flattering reader's report, which asked, all the same, if it was suitable for children, and not too depressing. ('...What age does he intend this for? I have visions of booksellers and teachers up and down the country being besieged by parents.') I went down to the publishers who had shown an interest to discuss it. They said, yes, it was publishable, but not as a first book. I needed to get a readership together first, before floating this. Put it on one side. Write another one. Make it light.

Here is part of the chapter where pups are born on the waste land - one of these eventually becomes the leader of the wild pack:

Stan Fletcher drove slowly down the feeder road. He caught sight of an old alsation, fat-looking, ungainly, lowering itself under the gloom of battered privet that demarked the industrial park from the council houses and remains of the site, and swung round towards the floodlights. He was early: the afternoon shift wasn't away, and the car-park was full. He skirted the rows and found a wedge-shaped space at the far side, by the mesh fence. The rough ground looked more bleak and derelict than during the day. The surface was humped and hacked at, scattered with debris:

fork-lift palettes, polythene, cleansing paste drums, tyres, bottles, carrier bags of domestic garbage. Plants poked smutty leaves at angles - weeds, grass and garden flowers that had seeded from the estate. He turned the radio off and got out.

Shoney stood close in to the privet for a moment, while the engine died and the door slammed, then continued along the mesh to where there was a gap in the rough outer hedging. She was panting now, using strength that she could not spare. Clear of the factory she broke from her line, working to and fro over the clutter of dim shapes for one that might offer her the shelter she needed. Wheel-less, at a tilt (part of the back axle was embedded in the ground), a van slouched, one door wedged open. Only the bare shape remained. A tongue of earth ran along part of the inside edge, wet but not waterlogged, and some cardboard remains. It was covered and uninhabited, and the smells were long dead and suffused with ground smells. Shoney went in.

She pawed at the cardboard and lay, panting. The contractions were strong; they ran ripples down her flank so she arched her head back and let out a straining, crooning sound, the kind Sally could get from her by blowing continuously on her recorder. An occasional jar of brakes or sweep of headlight at the car-park penetrated her labour, but these were distant, and there was no breaking off. A new impulse, urgent, back legs up, spine curved, head back forcing the skin to gather, muzzle craning, the outrush of breath, almost human, and the first pup lay shapelessly in its bag of fluid. She came onto her side again, raised her leg, snouted round for the sac. Her nose found the rope of whitish gristle running from the belly of the encased pup, through the membrane, up into her own swollen vulva. With her side teeth she chewed at the cord where the membrane puckered round it. Fluid dribbled from the sac and the pup's writhings became clear. Working the cord into place, Shoney chewed it through. With the length of it still trailing from her body she tore the membrane: the pup was pink and tadpolish. The great rhythmic sweep of tongue pushed at it, working the membrane off, and the pup prised mole-like to her belly, snouting the fine fur for a nipple.

Shoney licked the discarded membrane and took it into her mouth. A spasm pulled at her and she flicked her hind leg and swallowed the half-chewn skin. Her rump was up again causing the pup to tumble away. She quivered in the contraction's grip and the glossy meat-red knot of placenta emerged and plopped to the floor, bringing the cord with it. She stood, still quivering at one foreleg, turned to sniff, then dropped and began licking it, feeling for a starting place. It was rich and limp, and she needed nourishment; the pup nestled back in and its feeble bleat subsided. There was a blare from the factory.

* * * * *

A youth crabbed his way round the far side of the car-park, trying the doors. He froze, and scanned across to the barrier. He was nervous; at school he had done the odd pub car-park with a mate and not had any bother, but now that he'd left it was another business, working alone, methodically, making what he could. There'd be no protection from social workers now - he was in it all the way. Which meant he might as well be thorough and make it worthwhile.

The door of Stan's car opened. He held it for a second, listening, then ducked in. He swept out the glove compartment and ran a hand down inside, then turned his attention to the radio. He took a screwdriver, disconnected it and wrenched it from the wires. With a glance at the back seat he bagged it and was out. It was the last in the row; if he continued he would have to work back from the fence, towards the security. He tugged up at the mesh and slid his bag under. With his weight on the diagonal he hauled himself up, over, and down on the other side.

The last pup was born now, nuzzled in with the others, and the remains devoured. Shoney growled deeply, for the footfall was light and alert - the step of a hunter or scavenger, fearsome in humans. The youth hurried on for the broken hedging at the far side, and Shoney dropped her head again, and fell back into sleep.

* * * * *

By this time I had reached a point where I was getting ideas for books quicker than I could write them, and I would keep them in a kind of mental pipeline till they could be dealt with. But the next one out was major - I sensed a long way off that it was going to chew me up, and probably go the way of the others at the end of it (i.e., left in a drawer unpublished). So I pushed it back down the pipeline.

There was a summer holiday coming up, and I thought, right, I'm going to knock something off - they want something light, they can have light - I'm going to do it in a holiday. And I did: it took about thirty full days, and a few more to revise. And, yes, you've got it - they published it.

I often say to kids this or that was fun to write, which isn't quite true - it's still work - but it was uncomplicated to write. The story sat up, and I wrote it. What I think now, is that the story wasn't uncomplicated in itself, I made it uncomplicated by deciding beforehand to put a limitation on it, and I suppose I probably short-changed myself out of a decent idea. On the other hand, it gave me a sense that I was in the driving seat. Up until then my stories always seemed to be driving me: I just assumed they kind of super-nova'd in space somewhere, and the writers duty was merely to spot them and magnify them.

I got the idea for 'The Day Trip' after a school trip to Boulogne. A hundred and thirty kids over to France and back in a day - daft idea (not mine), good fun, very tight timing. We gave them some free time and said they had to be back at the meeting point on the dot in order to get the right ferry back. Two kids were late, and bang - in that ten-minute delay, there was the story.

The time-difference was the perfect way in: the kids in my story are ten minutes late, but earlier, when the teachers are explaining to them to put their watches forward an hour, they're too busy chatting-up to notice; later they realise and change them, but now think they have to take off an hour to get the right time for the meeting point, so in fact they're ten minutes late but an hour early (if you're still with me). They charge off to the quay to catch up with the rest, are waved on board as the ferry departs, and find themselves sailing home on the wrong boat.

Here's the bit where the story is set up - a girl has lost her bag, and the four main characters are looking for it:

The car deck was wet and dingy. They each took a row and searched it, like a murder hunt in a wood. A crewman chased them off. They clanged up a deck and continued, scouring from stem to stern. Toilets, everything.

The top deck was mostly outside, but still nothing. They tapered down to the stern, where the crew tackle was, closed off: coiled ropes, capstans, pulleys, tarpaulins. France was enormous over the side. The wind whipped their words away. There was only one more level - a kind of platform by the funnel, with an iron ladder. Michael climbed it. Lee and Angela stood back in the doorway. Kerry watched, windswept.

He was round the other side.

"Hoy, Kel - here!"

She raced up. The funnel loomed like a cooling tower - it had seemed small from the dockside. He was standing there. She looked down, expecting to see the bag, then at his face.

"*Give us a kiss then.*"

"*You cheeky sod.*"

It was a mock fight. They held and pecked, and kissed. She broke away.

"*What's up? You're supposed to do it like that. That's the French way.*"

"*Give them your spit then.*"

The horn gave a blast, leaving them breathless. They tried again.

"*Come on, it must be time.*"

* * * * *

"*Voici votre itineraire: Il est maintenant neuf heures du matin - une heure plus tard qu'en Angleterre...*" *There was some fiddling with watches. Michael's head was spinning from the kiss. France came slowly towards and took him in. He looked, but saw nothing.* "*... apres ca, nous nous retrouverons au bord du quai a dix-neuf heures. Dix-neuf heures precises. Y a t-il des questions?*"

There were no questions. You had to ask them in French.

"*What was all that about?*"

"*Dunno - just follow the rest.*"

They shuffled down the gangway to France.

* * * * *

So, 'The Day Trip' became my first published book, and although I didn't know it then, it features someone quite famous. For characters I picked on two boys and two girls who were on the real trip and used them fairly loosely as my models. I picked on them because they had the right sense of fun I wanted for the book. The two girls were Amanda Hatfield and Rachel Garrad (I called them Angie and Kerry), and the two boys were Mike Tracey and Lee Sharpe, who I just called Mike and Lee because I thought their names were common enough not to be recognised. You've got it - Lee went on to play for Man United, Leeds, etc. If any of you four are reading this, don't sue me chaps, I was only funnin'.

I was taking a free-reading lesson once, and one or two of the kids had copies of the book. One stopped to have a fairly long conversation and I yelled at him. He went back to the book. I thought about what had happened, and said, in these words: 'Do you realise you've probably had a unique experience there - reading a book and being bollocked by the author at the same time...'

I remember a similar thing: a good friend had his son at the school, who at this time was sitting an A-level in a silent, packed gymnasium, when out of the blue his old man could be heard for several seconds ranting at a pupil a few classrooms away, and I remember thinking, yes, you've probably had a fairly significant experience there.

* * * * *

Q. What's it like being a writer.

A. The pits. You sit at a computer all day imagining things that aren't really happening, and write about them. You often don't talk to anyone for several hours at a time.

Q. Where do you get your ideas from?

A. 'The School That Died' - I didn't have an idea, just kept writing what came into my head, which is why it was so boring and embarrassing to read.

'The Dog Pack' - from the newspaper article: a dog-lover might read it and resolve to become a vet, the director of a fencing company would get on to Rolls-Royce and offer them a quote for a dog-proof fence, but I decided it would be a good idea for a book.

'The Day Trip' - the kids being late for the meeting point. At first I thought of some kind of dangerous adventure, but when I asked myself why they would really be late the most obvious explanation was that they had been getting off, so that was what I wrote.

Q. How long does it take to write a book?

A. 'The School That Died' - about a year to do most of it, then I got stuck and left it for four years, then I finally fetched it out and finished it in three weeks. I hadn't realised I was right near the end - I never knew where I was with that one.

'The Dog Pack' - I think about three months, but the researching took a long time.

'The Day Trip' - six weeks; it was only a short book to read as well as write.

Q. Do you like writing?

A. I didn't really enjoy writing any of these books - I was always too anxious to finish and kept stopping to count the pages. It's like when you're clock-watching at school, the more you do it the slower the lesson goes. I didn't really like being an author at that time, it was just the idea of being one that kept me going. I wanted my name on the spine of a book.

Q. How do you get a book published?

A. Luck. My lucky break was when I enrolled for the only writing workshop I've ever been on, which was run by one of my top authors (see below), Jill Paton Walsh. When it was over I sidled up to her and asked her if she'd read 'The School That Died', and to my surprise she did, she read the whole thing, properly, and wrote me a long letter of encouragement. From then on, over many years, she was the first person to read almost everything I wrote, and through her I eventually met the editor who published 'The Day Trip'.

You can also be unlucky, though. 'The Dog Pack' never did get published - the editor quit before I'd built up my readership, as he put it, and his successor turned the book down.

Q. Who is your favourite author?

A. Jill Paton Walsh. 'A Parcel of Patterns' is wonderful, so is 'Goldengrove' and the follow-up, 'Unleaving', which is brilliant, her best book. I'm not saying this because she was so good to me, but she was, all the same. I once said to her, 'You've probably read as much of my stuff as I've read of yours' - and I've read the lot - that's way above the call of duty, and I'd just like to thank you Jill a thousand times. I didn't have the kind of publishing profile you thought I would, but I've had some brilliant writing adventures, and it was you who pushed the boat out.

I got a set of 'Unleaving' into my school once and tried to read it with a keen group, but they wouldn't bite. It mentions the philosopher Wittgenstein, for one thing. But what I used to do was keep a collection of that type of book - demanding, difficult, but fabulous - in a special place in the cupboard, and when the bookish kids came to me saying they couldn't find anything decent, I'd pass one over. Like bookshop owners during the 'Satanic Verses' crisis, hiding them under the counter. I was buggered if I was going to let Point Horrors take over the whole show.

CHAPTER 3

The Roundabout

After 'The Day Trip' came out the school decided that as they'd got a proper writer on the staff they might as well get me doing some creative writing classes. We started what we called an English 'roundabout' in the second-year, year eight: one teacher was responsible only for literature lessons, one for language, one for drama, one for creative writing, and the kids would rotate between us. I think it's a good system, shakes things up a bit. So for the first time I was free just to help kids write - spelling, punctuation, grammar: not my problem. If someone was poor at those things it could be typed up and corrected. My job in the roundabout was simply to help them find something worthwhile to say.

This is not so easy. I used to spend the first month's lessons trying to prevent them from writing; if I hadn't have done this they would have all been away from the blocks in the first few minutes of the first lesson. School writing is always that way: 'Ready, steady, go - right, you've got just under forty-five minutes...'; 'Sir, I can't think of anything'; 'Pretend you're on the Titanic or something - just start.'

But imagine you've got a whole year to work on any idea you like. What's the point of charging at it?

First I would deal with the 'can't write sir, ain't got any imagination' merchants. 'Shut your eyes a minute - go on, humour me. Right, what's your favourite meal/drink/etc.? Can you picture it? Can you taste it? Can you smell it cooking? Dentist's drill - can you feel it?

'What have you got next lesson? Can you picture the teacher coming in? What kind of mood are they in? What are they wearing? What are they saying? Can you hear their voice?

'Who do you fancy most? They're on holiday - can you picture them? What are they doing? You're with them - now what are they doing?'

'Wor...'

'Right - who's good at lying? Anyone here ever told a porkie..?' A few hands go up. 'O.K., lesson on lying... ("What did you do at school today dear?"; "Geography, history, R.E., lying, games...") Key Stage 3 lying, here we go: What types of lie are there..?'

That's the way it would go. There are white lies, black lies, whoppers, little porkies, exaggerations, omissions, fantasies, hypocrisies, economies with the truth, politenesses, tales, fibs, stories; people sometimes lie out of consideration, or tell the truth out of inconsideration. And so on. It's a fantastic field to amble about in. I used to get them to write down and define categories and exceptions, with examples...

And where it leads, always, is that truth is elusive and changing: there are kinds of lying that bring you closer to it - sometimes fiction, for example, can prevent you from being blinded by trying to look too hard at it - and kinds of truth, fussy, precise little truths for example, which keep it at arms length, away from you.

This is Julian Barnes' definition of the purpose of fiction, from an Observer interview: 'It's to tell the truth. It's to tell beautiful, exact, and well-constructed lies which enclose hard and shimmering truths.'

So - I would give them time to whittle away thinking what they wanted to construct a fiction about, plenty of time, three, four, five lessons; it was like a surgery, they would come up to talk it over, and I would simply ask them questions. 'Who is this character? Is he single, married, has he got children, how many? Where do they live? Why there? Are his parents alive? How was he brought up? Has he got a job, has he always had it, how did he get it?' On and on. I used to write whole strings of them in their books - they would have to write answers. The ones who just wanted to write the story would get exasperated: 'As I have already told you three pages back...'.

But it was a good exercise. They would construct a story, rather than dive head-first into it making straight for the climax. If you think about it, the story of the Titanic can be told very quickly. There are some people on a ship which hits an iceberg and most of them drown; two of them fall in love, he dies but she doesn't. Unless it's constructed properly, no-one gives a damn who dies and who doesn't, nor what happens in the first place.

So, it's O.K. to knock off a story (i.e. a lie, a make-believe) in a forty minute English lesson, it's just a task the teacher sets. But if you're going to spend a whole year on it (or in my case, a lifetime), you need to ask yourself some questions first. Like, why are you doing it, why make stuff up? Is it to get off on all the things that won't happen to you in real life? No problem. Is it because composition lessons are a doss? No problem. But if it's because you need to get things out of yourself to understand them better, to give them different shapes and positions, I think it helps if you realise that.

That's how it is with me - things seem easier to get at if I put them into fiction: if they seem more believable one way and less believable another, I feel I've achieved something, like I understand life a tiny bit better. I think it might help in writing (or any other kind of art) if you feel you don't really understand life in the first place...

If you know your real reason for writing is to fiddle about with truth, then you can never 'use' a character. You're god - you bring characters to life, you give them good or bad luck, get them off with their dream lover, win them the lottery, kill them, cripple them, do whatever you like, but you shouldn't use them. Especially evil characters - it's very satisfying to have a bloody good hate figure in a story, especially at the climax when the hero needs someone to beat up or blame. But where does it get you? Bad guys have histories and childhoods too, they were probably just as excited on Christmas Eve as anyone else once.

In other words, whatever you do, your characters must have rights: you gave them life, let them speak to you, listen to them.

One activity I have found quite fun to do to focus on character is give out questionnaires. There's a good one every week in the back of the Guardian Weekend magazine, for example: 'What is your idea of perfect happiness? What is the trait you most dislike in yourself? Who or what is the greatest love in your life?' Etcetera. You make up answers for your characters. It's good, it gives you clues. You can also draw the character's bedroom, or his/her house; round the edge draw all the particular things that are important to that character and their family - just do what comes into your head, don't think too much. When you're done, start asking yourself questions: 'So that's a saucepan and some spices? He likes cooking, then, does he? Or does he have to do it because no-one else does? So how did he get interested in cooking in the first place?' Given that choice of character is mainly intuitive, what you are doing is exploring your intuition a little, exploring what basically caused you to make that choice - and this process can often improve fictions surprisingly.

And so the roundabout progressed. I have good memories of it. Many stories were written, some twenty and thirty thousand words long. It was like a surgery, I would be their adviser rather than teacher, my job was to ask the right questions.

There was a team of parent typists - kids paid for the typing in wine, chocolates and flowers. I made copies for the authors and spares for reading in class. Kids used to fight over them - particularly the ones that hinted at sexual awakening, or sly genetic experiments in school labs - but also quite quietly written and undramatic ones, too.

They would take them home, and also steal them. That's not bad - we're talking schoolwork here - and I thought I might be able to get some extra copies run off, sell them and give the authors a royalty. But the finances didn't work out and it wasn't done.

If you're going to ask a schoolkid to write a book, you have to believe it's possible for it to become a book, I think. If not, what you're saying is that there's a real world and a writers' world, or a real world and a classroom world, and you deserve everything you get for having chosen the wrong one.

I sat on the idea for years, and eventually decided to form my own press and have some printed commercially. I picked out four from the mass I had collected over the years, approached the writers and their families, contacted four pupils/ex-pupils that I knew could illustrate, put them together in a room and went off and made tea. When I got back they had sorted themselves out, and Crazy Horse Kids' Press was founded.

As they are still available (details at back...), here's one I didn't publish at the time, simply because it had won a prize in the W.H.Smith Young Writers awards, and they claimed the copyright:

CHAPTER ONE

I was really sick of school, so that's why I joined 'Help the Aged' or H.T.A. for short. I was assigned to help Miss Evelyn Hancox of 32 Wood Grove. I missed Maths on Tuesdays and Thursdays so why not?

I set off for Wood Grove and found it was a very small road and very exclusive but 32 was a very old house. Should be knocked down I thought. It was a big house with roof windows and about four floors. I walked up the long path leading to the large grey steps. A rusty boot scraper nearly tripped me up as I knocked at the door.

"Who is it?" came a croaky voice from inside the house.

"Mrs. Hancox? I'm from St Joseph's School up the road. I've come to help you," I replied.

"I want some identification," the voice came again.

"I have my bus pass," I said, and I posted it through the letter-box.

The old lady peered through the letter box and said, "Well it looks like you."

"That's because it is me," I replied.

"Don't be cheeky, I won't have cheeky people in my house," she snapped.

"Alright, alright," I said, "I was only pointing out the obvious."

"Well you better come in then, I suppose," the voice said.

The person who opened the door was very different from the voice. She was old, bedraggled, withered almost. She had pure white hair and brown skin. Her face was small and not very wrinkled. She stood up almost straight but she had very thin legs - like matchsticks. She wore a faded pink cardigan with a repulsive blue flowery dress, and black tasteless shoes.

"Come in then," she said.

I stepped into a long corridor with doors leading off it. Each door was padlocked except one which was open. The whole hall was covered in dust and I spluttered. Animals in glass cases were sitting miserably.

"My late husband's collection," she said, "I'll show you all of it later if you like."

"I'd love to see them," I lied. "Why are the doors padlocked?"

"Well you can't be too careful these days," the old lady said.

CHAPTER TWO

"This way," she said, and I followed her into the unpadlocked room. Inside was a very, very old kitchen. It had an open fire with a black grate and a big copper kettle hanging over it. The room was warm and friendly.

"Fancy a cup of tea?" she asked.

"Yes please but I'm meant to be helping you," I said.

"Well you can start by doing the washing-up," she said. I walked over to the big sink and turned the taps on.

"Where's the Fairy Liquid?" I asked:

"Fairy Liquid, Fairy Liquid! I don't waste my money on that stuff!" she shouted, "here, use this."

"What is it?" I asked.

"It's home made soap," she said and dumped a green blob on my hand. It was cold and slimy.

"Euuhh," I said and deposited it in the water.

When I had done the washing up I began to drink my tea. It was cold and full of tea leaves.

"Do you like it?" she asked.

I was fed up with all the questions, so I exploded, a very unsensible thing to do.

"No!" I shouted, "it's cold, and full of tea-leaves and I believe you put salt in it."

"*Oh,*" *she said quietly.*

"*I'm sorry,*" I said.

"*Its all right,*" she said, "*I can be annoying in a way. It was a test.*"

"*A test?*" I asked.

"*Yes, a test to see if you are truthful. Here, have a nice cuppa,*" she said.

CHAPTER THREE

I was taken aback by this old woman and all her possessions.

"*Do you want to see my late husband's collection?*" she asked.

"*O.K. then,*" I said.

"*This way.*"

We left the kitchen and went into the hall with padlocked doors. She unlocked one of the doors with an enormous key. The door creaked as she opened it.

"*My late husband was a taxidermist,*" she said.

"*Oh I see.*"

The walls were lined with glass cases filled with birds and animals in impossible poses.

"*Do you want one?*" she asked.

"*One what?*" I asked.

"*One of these,*" she said, and she turned to a small chest of drawers and opened it with a small silver key, Inside were tiny mice in little glass boxes.

"*O.K. then,*" I said.

"Don't force yourself," she said. She opened a glass box and a small stiff mouse fell onto my hand.

"Thanks," I said.

CHAPTER FOUR

When I got home my mom immediately asked all about it, exactly what I had done, if she worked me too hard, if she was rich, etc. Honestly, she never stops. I said it was O.K., she was very nice, she was an old lady who was a bit eccentric but very good-natured.

"Don't let her take advantage," she said.

I wish my mum wasn't quite so stupid because how could an 84-year-old woman take advantage?

I went upstairs to go to my room but I was ambushed by a red Indian and a cowboy closely followed by Batman. It was the twins and Peter.

"We got you!" they said together.

"Get lost," I said, "I've got to do my homework," which was a lie because I didn't have any.

"Oh, can't you play with us, please?" Peter said.

"No, I can't, I've got other things to do."

Peter is the boy from next door. He's six and the best friend of my twin younger brothers, Sam and Darren, who I am not too keen on at the moment because they killed my newts by picking them up by their tails and waving them about until they were so dizzy that when they dropped them in the water, they drowned.

I also have an older brother called Jeff who is O.K. at the moment. He is 16 - two years older than me.

Anyway, getting back to the point. I went to the meeting about our first visit to our old people. It was on Wednesday. In the beginning the H.T.A. was a 6th-Former's idea.

We met in a private room in the Youth Club. I don't think I'll go again because it was a complete fiasco from start to finish. It was only Dominic who made it possible. He is the 6th-Former who thought up the idea.

There was also someone else. I had never seen him before but he looked somehow familiar. I asked my best friend, Christine, she said he was a new boy in her form. His name is Andy Fields. He is very nice. He has dark tanned skin and black hair down to his neck, with brown eyes and a deep mellow voice.

"He comes from Greece, Cathy," Chris said.

"Oh, how old?" I asked.

"Fifteen," she replied.

"Who did you get?" I asked, quickly changing the subject.

"Mrs. J, Harrison," she said, in a posh voice.

"I got Mrs. E. Hancox," I said in a posh voice.

I walked home slowly, I didn't feel like going home.

Then I saw him. He was walking home. I shouted, "Hey, Andy, wait for me!"

He waited, I ran over to him, "Hi, Andy," I said. "I saw you at the H.T.A. meeting, remember?"

"Oh yes, I remember, your name is Cathy isn't it?"

"Yes it is."

"I'll walk you home if you like."

"O.K. then."

"We'll go through the park," he said.

"O.K. then."

The sun was just setting and there was just enough light to see him.

"Let's go and sit on the swings," I said.

"I'd rather sit on a bench," he said.

"If you like," I said.

We chatted for half an hour, then he asked me if I had a boyfriend. I hadn't and he said: "You have now."

Then we kissed and he said he'd better get back because it was getting late. Then he walked me home and kissed me at the door.

"'Night," he said.

"'Night," I said.

I walked upstairs and fell into bed.

CHAPTER FIVE

"I saw you yesterday, running off with Andy," Christine shouted across the classroom.

"Whoo!" everyone shouted.

"It's no use going red," Christine said.

"Shut up," I said. "What lesson have we got now?" I asked, changing the subject.

"Geography, Room 33, Mr. Sandwell," she said.

"Oh no," I said. "I haven't done my homework."

"Why don't you copy Andy's?" Chris said.

"He wouldn't let me," I said jokingly.

Then the bell went, and we all went round to Room 33 for Geography.

* * * * *

I had been visiting Mrs. Hancox for a couple of months when one day I was cleaning the porch when the postman came.

"Good morning, there's a letter for Mrs. Hancox," he said.

"Shall I take it in to her?" I asked.

"O.K. then, here you are," he replied.

"Wait a minute, this is from the Council," I said.

"Is it now. 'Bye," he said, shutting the gate behind him.

I went into the house. "Mrs. Hancox, it's a letter from the Council."

"Thank you," she said, snatching it out of my hand. She opened the letter. Then her expression changed, as she read it.

"Oh no," she said.

"What's wrong?" I asked.

"It's the Council, they're coming to knock the house down."

"But they can't do that, the house is yours."

"Yes they can, the house is my husband's brothers and he's on the Council, so that's all there is. I'll be living in a chicken coop - a council-flat. You've got to stop them."

"I can, my dad's on the Council, he'll help us."

CHAPTER SIX

"It's just out of the question, I can't help you save a clapped out old woman who wants to keep her home. It needs to be knocked down. It's not my fault."

"But, Dad...."

"But Dad nothing. I can't help you and that's final. Now go to your room at once."

"But Dad...."

"GO!"

"O.K., O.K., I'm going; 'Night Mom," I said as I went upstairs.

Later on, Dad came up to see me. He explained about the house, and the need for ground to make more posh houses, and how she would be dead soon, so it didn't matter.

"If it doesn't matter, why not wait until she is dead?"

"Look don't ask me, it's not my idea, it's John's."

"Don't you know it is important to me, and her?"

"Yes I know it's important to you, but I can't do anything about it. I'm not on the Housing Committee. I'm on the main Council and I was outvoted when the vote for it came up."

"How many of you were there?"

"Six out of the fifteen on the Council. Me, Jake, Bob, James, Steve and Brian."

"I've got to do something. Can you help me form some protests?"

"I'm a member of the Council! I can't go round lying in the middle of roads, forming picket lines etc., etc!"

"O.K. I'll have to do it by myself. Good night, Dad."

"Goodnight, love, and don't do anything I wouldn't do," he said, shutting the door behind him.

CHAPTER SEVEN

"So you see Christine, I've got to help her. She's my responsibility."

"You know I'll help you. I'll do all that I can, and I'm sure

Andy will help you."

"What can we do?"

"Well first, we'll have to put up a notice to see who wants to help. We'll put it up in our form room."

"What will it say?" I asked.

She drew a rough sketch for me

CALLING ALL H.T.A. MEMBERS
CATHY BANKS IS HAVING PROBLEMS WITH HER OLD LADY
THEY'RE COMING TO KNOCK HER HOUSE DOWN!
IF YOU WANT TO HELP, COME TO HER HOUSE ON TUESDAY - 5.30 P.M. ONWARDS, 56 CRESCENT CLOSE.

"That's really good, I hope it attracts a lot of people," I said.

*   *   *   *   *

"So are we all agreed?" I asked.

"Yes!" nineteen people shouted.

Our first plan was to get up a petition against the knocking down of her house.

If it didn't work, our second plan was to lie in the middle of the main road to stop the car flow with several banners.

If that didn't work, our last plan of action was to lie in front of the bulldozers and all the other machines like that.

CHAPTER EIGHT

On Saturday morning, we all set off to ask the people shopping to sign our petition. At the end of the morning we had collected 23 names including ours - 3 excluding ours!

"It hasn't worked - we'll have to put our second plan into action......"

That didn't work either. The only thing we gained was two days in the local Police Station lock up.

"I've got a cold," somebody said.

"And I've got chilblains," another said.

"Well we'll have to do our last plan. They're coming to knock the house down next Saturday."

CHAPTER NINE

Saturday morning we met outside the Youth Club with banners, signs and other things like that. We set off when everyone was there. It took us a quarter of an hour to get there. When Mrs. Hancox saw us all, she nearly had a fit. They had to take all her stuff to a warehouse. It took four lorry loads.

We spread out over the house, some on the roof, some down stairs, some upstairs, and some on the floor outside. The house was to be demolished at 9.30 a.m. precisely and at 9.15 a.m. the bulldozers came.

Andy was near to me, lying on the floor. He whispered to me, "All great lovers die together!"

"Thanks a lot," I whispered back.

Then, all of a sudden the machines were turned on, so we all started singing "We shall not be moved...."

I was lying near a bulldozer and its 'jaw' started to come down on top of me. It was just about to touch me. My heart was beating fast. There came a cry, "Stop, Stop, Stop..." and a small man came running down the road. He had a piece of paper in his hand and he was waving it. "So so sorry..." he said, stuttering slightly. "Wrong house. Mr.

Johnson said Woods Grove, not Wood Grove. Mrs Hancox's stuff will be brought back - so sorry."

I sighed with relief and brushed the mud off my clothes.

* * * * *

CHAPTER TEN

It had been a year since I helped Mrs. Hancox and I had been so busy with Andy that I had forgotten her.

One day it struck me that I hadn't been round to visit her for ages so I went round.

When I knocked on the door, a middle-aged woman opened it.

"Hello," I said cheerfully. "Is Mrs. Hancox in, I'm her helper."

"You're Cathy Banks aren't you?" she said. "You haven't been round for ages. I suppose you had better come in."

She took me into a large room which had been locked before now. A large cat posed on a post in the centre of the room.

"Sit down and I'll explain," the woman said. "I'm the old lady's daughter. I'm living here because she died of a heart attack a couple of weeks ago. She left the house and everything to me except this, and this." She pointed to a piece of paper. The piece of paper said:

HOME MADE SOAP

TAKE:-

3 spoonfuls of carbon paste

2 spoonfuls of soap powder

1 spoonful of water

1 cupful of mixed herbs and a pinch of salt

Stir thoroughly until a green slimy mixture.
USE IMMEDIATELY!

I took the cat and the recipe home, and cried myself to sleep.

Lucy Williams

*   *   *   *   *

The roundabout had more miles to go, but not in the same form. As you know, not all kids like writing long stories or poems; as you get older a lot of you go for the bread-and-butter side of writing - comic-strips, photo-stories, sit-com sketches, fanzines, newspapers and so on - and I eventually managed to get a 'Writing Skills' course with a certificate set up in the year ten and eleven options, where they could do that kind of thing.

I always avoided calling it 'Creative Writing'. When I hear the words creative writing I get this involuntary picture of a teacher urging the kids to use words like saffron instead of yellow. Have a read of this, it's a scene from the all-time pits of a creative writing lesson (from the book 'Song of the City' by Gareth Owen):

MISS CREEDLE TEACHES CREATIVE WRITING

'This morning,' cries Miss Creedle,
'We're all going to use our imaginations,
We're going to close our eyes 3W and imagine.
Are we ready to imagine Darren?
I'm going to count to three.
At one, we wipe our brains completely clean;
At two, we close our eyes;
And at three, we imagine.
Are we all imagining? Good.

Here is a piece of music by Beethoven to help us.
Beethoven's dates were 1770 to 1827.
(See The Age of Revolutions in your History books.)
Although Beethoven was deaf and a German
He wrote many wonderful symphonies,
But this was a long time before anyone of us was born.
Are you imagining a time before you were born?
What does it look like? Is it dark?
(Embryo is a good word you might use.)

Does the music carry you away like a river?
What is the name of the river? Can you smell it?
Foetid is an exciting adjective.
As you float down the river
Perhaps you land on an alien planet.
Tell me what sounds you hear.
If there are indescribable monsters
Tell me what they look like but not now.
(Your book entitled Tackle Pre-History This Way
Will be of assistance here.)
Perhaps you are cast adrift in a broken barrel
In stormy shark-infested waters
(Remember the work we did on piranhas for R.E.?)
Try to see yourself. Can you do that?
See yourself at the bottom of a pothole in the Andes
With both legs broken
And your life ebbing away inexorably.
What does the limestone feel like?
See the colours.
Have you done that? Good.
And now you may open your eyes.
Your imagining time is over,
Now it is writing time.
Are we ready to write? Good.
Then write away.
Wayne, you're getting some exciting ideas down.
Tracy, that's lovely.

Darren, you haven't written anything.
Couldn't you put the date?
You can't think of anything to write.
Well, what did you see when you closed your eyes?
But you must have seen something beside the black.
Yes, apart from the little squiggles.
Just the black. I see.
Well, try to think
Of as many words for black as you can.'

Miss Creedle whirls about the class
Like a benign typhoon
Spinning from one quailing homestead to another.
I dream of peaceful ancient days
In Mr Swindell's class
When the hours passed like a dream
Filled with order and measuring tests.
Excitement is not one of the things I come to school for.
I force my eyes shut
Kicking ineffectually at the starter;
But all I see
Is a boy of twelve
Sitting at a desk one dark November day
Writing this poem.
And Darren is happy to discover
There is only one word for black
And that will have to suffice
Until the bell rings for all of us.

* * * * *

The Writing Skills option was the furthest I got in establishing writing as a subject in its own right. It only lasted a year before being squeezed out by the national curriculum, and from that point on I knew that I would have to find another outlet if I wanted to continue working with children's writing. But it was a good scheme while it lasted. One of the memories I have is of a pupil who had basically opted for the course because he thought it would be a doss. I asked him what he wanted to write; he shrugged his shoulders; I asked him what his interests were; he shrugged. At length I managed to narrow him down to birds of prey. Did he have an idea how he might approach birds of prey in writing? Poem. O.K., fine. Not long after, he brought me one. It rhymed, except where it didn't rhyme, started with a stanza and finished in a block. It said nothing.

I thought about this, and after much difficulty managed to get funding for him to spend a week at a falconry centre. What I want to say is that from there on his writing took wing, soared, hovered, swooped; but in fact he skived three of the days and wrote no more afterwards than he had before.

Life just won't fit into the bloody plot.

*　　*　　*　　*　　*

Q. What's it like being a writer?

A. Good, you can make anything you like happen; you create the universe and rule it how you want.

Q. Where do you get your ideas from?

A. Deep inside.

Q. How long does it take to write a book?

A. I don't know, but it takes a long time to start one sometimes. The next one I want to do is the story of a girl and her horse: it's an idea I've had for a couple of years but I'm petrified I'll mess it up, so I still haven't even got round to researching it never mind the writing.

Q. Do you like writing?

A. It's the best way I know of telling someone exactly what you want them to hear. You can go over it as many times as you like before giving it or sending it to them. If I have a row with a person, or tell a joke, I get my words wrong. I hate those situations and spend ages afterwards thinking what I could have said. So, I'm happier to write it. You don't often get to see the look on their face, though.

Q. How do you get a book published?

A. Hard. No-one's good enough to find a publisher any more, they're dwindling in number and their schedules are blocked in for years ahead. It's no longer a question of being a good writer, you've got to be a flipping genius - but not too much of one or you'll be more than eighteen months ahead of your time and they won't want you.

Put yourself in the position of a junior editor in a big publishing house - they're regarded as the lowest of the low, especially in young fiction which is still seen as lollipop stuff, they're paid next to nothing and they're moved on frequently. They've got hundreds of scripts a week to get through. They have probably been told to eliminate immediately anything involving hospitals, police, football, animals, school, grumpy pensioners and a couple of other things.

They might read the first and last page (on a good day). After the thousandth 'Boofy & Biffy Build a Nest' their minds are too pickled to pick up on anything decent, and their seniors probably don't care anyway, it would only give them a headache if something did turn up, they'd have to find a place for it in the schedules. They are told not to respond to anything personally, just send it back with a covering letter and get the pile down. I'm not saying they're always wrong, just that balanced judgement must be difficult in those circumstances, and anyone who sends something to a publisher expecting to be judged on merit is probably being, let's say optimistic.

So my answer is, if you want to get a book published get a job in publishing yourself or marry an agent.

Q. Who is your favourite author?

A. Alan Garner. You know how you wake up the first morning after something life-changing has happened to you - someone dear to you has died, or you have fallen completely in love? You wake up and it hits you straight away, but you can't remember what it is for a few seconds? I felt like that the morning after I finished Red Shift.

CHAPTER 4

Happening Time

The book that I really wanted to write had been gnawing at me for about a year, but I still wasn't game to write it. I had an idea some very primary material was going to go in there, I mean stuff from my heart, which once released would never be recaptured. Now I don't see it like that: you need a good relationship with your heart to be a writer - it doesn't work if you think you're going to blow yourself apart every time you pick up a pen.

Anyway, I started on a different one. I was helping kids with their plots in one of these roundabout classes, and came across a girl with a good idea. She didn't realise it was good, and wasn't keen to go with it, but it appealed to me, and I suppose because of that I spent some time helping her put it together. She wrote something else. I said, if you're not using that idea, I'm going to. She said help yourself.

It was about the relationship between a radio D.J. and his listeners. It's possible she was thinking of that late night D.J. drama series on T.V., but I don't think it had started then. I'd say this was about 1984.

I chose to write in a girl's voice, possibly because that's how the idea came up in the first place: she's a girl who's reluctant to make the jump out of childhood, one of those who seems to retreat into herself while all around her classmates are getting on with it. Basically, I put her through a series of ordeals and sorted her life out for her. Quite a satisfying job, writing. Her name is Georgia, and 'Georgia On My Mind' turns out to be the theme tune of a local phone-in radio show, 'Teen Chat'.

She dares herself to phone the show one day, and before she can stop things she is on air. She gives a false name, but when she tries to collect her free stickers and tee-shirt in person her real name comes out. The D.J. wants a publicity shot with her, because of his theme tune - 'Popular D.J. Finds His Georgia' - and as a result she meets his two sons. She is dated by one of them, and when this gets round at her school some of the girls start to take an interest in her for the first time. She gets asked to be a model for the sister of one of her new friends in a hair-styling contest.

The results are spectacular, but land her in a lot of grief. She is dumped by the boy but noticed for the first time by his brother, who happens to be better looking.

A fascinating incident occurred when I was researching, at the preliminary stages of a hair-styling contest: the model, who was a very quiet schoolgirl, suddenly realised what they were doing to her hair, jumped out of the chair and ran home crying. I couldn't believe my luck, and of course gobbled it up and spat it straight out in the book - it becomes one of Georgia's ordeals.

I also made a major discovery about 'using' characters, that I referred to before. I wanted a nerd to be the first boy Georgia dates, so that she would be able to dump him and gain a bit of confidence. I asked myself what his hobbies might be, and came up with the idea of a model railway enthusiast. So I invited myself to a model railway club meeting for research. I'm there like a predator - I'm stealing up on them, working out how to mimick their habits. And what you find is, wherever people gather for the love of something, whatever it is, you will find great care, attentiveness, devotion to the final detail: and it's difficult to disrespect that.

So I had a tussle with myself - my attitude to the nerd was changing, but I still wanted to use him and chuck him out of the plot. And by the time I came to write the section where he dates Georgia, I still hadn't resolved it, and where Georgia is supposed to be dumping him she starts to feel sympathy for him instead. I should have stayed with that and let the plot rewrite itself, which is what all writers tell you to do, but I couldn't let him do it, I didn't have the confidence to let him pull me about.

In fact I think it came out alright, but to me it reads like a series of episodes rather than a story that evolves through a relationship, which would probably have been better. The working title was 'Georgia Gets Stuck In', right up until the day the four-year-old daughter of a friend of ours turned away from the mirror and said to her mum, 'Will I have boobies when it's happening time?'

I might have thrown away a character, but I caught the title cleanly. 'Happening Time' it had to be.

This is part of the hair-styling episode: the stylists are all trainees and Chris is the lecturer on their course; they are half-way through and have stopped for a lunch-break. Georgia has got swept along with the excitement and doesn't really notice how drastic her new style is, until her friend Angela drops in - her sister Sharon is Georgia's stylist.

They came into the cafeteria in their towels and gowns, and colonised a row of tables, spreading out the picnic from Chris's box. The shutters were down; it was empty apart from a knot of students smoking, and some teachers on a course, seated neatly, nibbling at snacks from the vending machines. The clatter and fuss as they spread out - Chris had brought real plates, cutlery and glasses; it must have killed her carrying the box up - turned heads. They were the action. The wine uncorked with a pop. They cheered. Georgia took her glass and looked round her. They were all in gowns, hair wet and tousled, or towelled, rollered, or in Sarah's case still hooded, with a new, brighter growth streaming from the holes. They were all in the same half-finished state, and she was one of them. It was like being backstage, where everyone is half-someone else, so all are equal. She drank wine with them. She would be compared and judged with them. She was in the thick - she had arrived.

"Mornin' fans - how's it going? Where's Georgia...?"

Georgia recognised the voice. She turned and raised her glass.

"Oh my God... God, Georgia. What've you done Shar...?"

Angela stood on the spot. Georgia put down her glass. The other tables had gone quiet. She put her hands to her head and felt her ears, properly, for the first time - they seemed huge and fleshy - and realised what she had done. Still holding them she stood up, caught sight of the Ladies, and like a victim of shell-fire, ran.

Holding taps for support, she stared at her head. Angie was right - it was hideous. What had she been dreaming of? It was worse when she broke into tears. The mirror was too dull to send her image back properly. It was fake glass. It framed her ugliness and held it from her, forcing her to look - to see what others saw; what Angela had seen. The taps let her go, and she reeled to a loo and sat down. She took off her glasses and buried her face in the gown, and howled.

Voices from outside.

"She's my mate and I'm going in...."

"You've done enough damage for one day."

"Let go - I'm going in...."

The door clattered open. Angela was in front of her.

"Brought your bag in case you wanted a hanky...."

She gave it, and squatted down. Georgia put her glasses on and fumbled for one. A card fell out.

Angela looked at it.

"I/D card. I was going to go hostelling with a youth group."

"How old were you?"

"Only last summer. I changed my mind. Don't know why I kept it."

She put out her hand for it. It was the picture Angela was looking at.

"You look so young and gawky. You're much prettier now."

She blew like a trumpet, and sniffed. Angela handed it back.

"..... really. It was just the shock - you've been the same for the last ten years: it was a bit sudden, that's all. I'm getting used to you now. You look better - more mature."

Georgia looked at it. It was a photo-booth job, a mug-shot. Was that who she'd been making all the fuss over? She looked at Angela and smiled.

"Mature? Look at the pair of us..."

They got up. The mirrors glowered. She still looked puffy faced and shriven, but what did it matter? It didn't bother Angie. She threw the picture in the bin.

The others turned as she came out, and waited for the worst.

"Are you alright?" It was Sharon, standing. "You've been crying, haven't you?"

"I was saying goodbye to someone... Is that my wine?"

* * * * *

So, unlike the girl where I did my research, Georgia sticks it out.

At this point, something happened that affected my future very significantly. I finished 'Happening Time' and sent it off, but before it was properly redrafted and done I took a run at the book I was busting to write and started it, and from then on I was in so deep, there was no way I was coming out until it was finished. I met and discussed 'Happening Time' with my editor - yes, it would be published. We sorted the terms quickly, shook hands on it, and that was that.

Some time later, I got a letter saying it needed a bit of rewriting. It did. I got a deadline for three months ahead and thought, good, it'll only take a week, I'll see if I can finish the other book first. Not long after, I get a phone-call: What about the rewrite? You said October. Yes, but we thought you'd have had something to show us by now. I can't now, I'm busy on something else.

Within a couple of months my editor had left and I was up the creek without a proper contract. There will be a short unscheduled chapter break while I go and find a quiet corner to weep in.

* * * * *

Q. What's it like being a writer?

A. For me, it's like being a gambler, you always have that hope you might hit the jackpot one day. But if you're on a losing streak (i.e., your books don't sell, or they keep getting rejected) it can be depressing.

Q. Where do you get your ideas from?

A. As I said, I pinched the starting idea for Happening Time from a pupil. I gave them a lot of ideas too, though. But it's not the start of an idea that's the tricky bit, most people can do that, it's the plot you develop afterwards that I think people really want to know about - how do you turn an idea into a massive plot?

We have an advanced computer at home, with so many functions and programmes that only my son can use it properly. I do simple things on it, like this script, but I know I have a basic fear of it and I panic when I can't get it to do what I want. I don't know why, but I know that fear blocks me from learning new tricks on it. Pathetic, don't you think?

My son has learned to love computers, and can't wait to get his hands on them, and so he learns quickly and easily if there's something he can't do on one. It's not a problem for him. I learned to love making up fiction when I was young, and it's not a problem for me - therefore I don't get blocked by fear, therefore I don't have many problems in the first place. If I have a decent idea, I work out calmly who I want to be in it and roughly where I think it should go, and how I want to get out of it. I ask myself what interests me about it, because that might give me some ideas on how to approach it. I don't rush to shape a plot, I try and let my intuition do a bit, and jot things down even if they don't make sense.

I sit on it for a while, and turn it over in my mind, or let it lie there quietly. I don't usually talk to other people about it, because I'm afraid they might suggest things that throw me off the scent, and I may not be able to pick it up again.

There comes a point where I think I can see some of the separate scenes - maybe chapters, maybe not - and that's when I try to set it up in a definite sequence. When I'm reasonably happy with that, I take the first scene and try and magnify it so I can see what bits it will need. Then eventually, I try and write one of the bits. Something Jill Paton Walsh once said that I always remember, is that once you know for sure you've got your first sentence, your book will fall into place.

[You can't just go round thinking of sentences though, hoping a book will write itself round one - it only comes if you work from the big idea and narrow it down, down, down until at last, if you're on centre, the first sentence will appear. Then the book is probably ready to be written.]

Q. How long does it take to write a book?

A. Happening Time took from July 23rd 1984 to 30th Dec 1985, and I can't believe this but I made two hundred and thirty-eight pages of notes before starting, some only notebook pages but even so, I'm staggered - can't believe I put that much work in. The first sentence was 'Stu Grant's studio is a cockpit', by the way.

Q. Do you like writing?

A. I like finishing. It's like decorating a room, you don't do it because you like it, you do it because you want to see the transformation at the end.

Q. How do you get a book published?

A. This one never got published. But now I've taken it out of the drawer again and had another look after all these years, I wonder if I should update it and bring it out through Crazy Horse. There were some good scenes in it. Why should I let someone in a publisher's office flick through five pages and tell me it's no good, after that much work.

Q. Who is your favourite author?

A. Jan Mark is brilliant, she has the most wicked warped sense of humour of any writer, but has also written books like 'The Ennead' and 'Divide and Rule' which are incredibly bleak and serious. Try 'Feet and Other Stories' if you want to dip in and get the feel of her style.

CHAPTER 5

Football

Football is responsible for more bad writing than you can wag a stick at: the topic only has to raise its head and sound judgement flies out of the window. I can't think of a single piece of good football writing by a schoolkid, although it gets churned out by the cartload, mostly featuring kick by kick commentry of fictitious or actual games climaxing in last ditch victory and the lifting of a trophy. And when I came to write And Smith Must Score... the same thing happened to me. My brain went and sat in the away end.

The only interesting class activity I can ever remember football generating was a brief, glorious kind of poetry slam, that took off when I stuck the following on the wall:

I'd like to celebrate, and with good reason
About the way we're playing this season -
With Savo, Yorke and Tommy J.,
We're scoring goals home and away.

I think that Macca's really great
But so are Yugo and Gareth Southgate.
Wrighty, Charles, Townsend and Taylor
Will keep us safe from any failure.

Add Draper, Bozzie and the rest of the crew
And you'll see why I'm a Villa fan through and through.

Nathan Whatley

This sparked off a fusillade of low-grade replies. I can only find a couple now - one of mine (wanker, I joined in), and one other:

Up the Blues, up the Blues,
And all the different songs,
That's all you can hear on a match day at the Blues,
Fans cheer as the Brummies come out of the tunnel.

The match has just got underway,
Trevor Francis shouting on the touchline,
Posh people sitting in the executive boxes,
And normal people like me in the Tilton.

The away fans sit in the railway end,
They sing as loud as they can, and then
The loud Brummies start to sing
And overpower the small amount of away fans.

The Blues score,
The crowd roar,
We all look at the clock with one minute to go...
The final whistle - a Blues win again.

Stuart Pawelczyk

It was a pleasant springtime evening
With just a touch of sun.
Behind our goal it was heaving
As the Baggies were thrashed three-one.

How come they're called the Baggies?
What's wrong with just the Old Bags?
If they were Scots they'd be called the Haggis,
Their shots hit the corner flags.

Next week we play the return game
Up at the Hawthorns stadium,
It'll probably be three-one again
Same as the first time we played 'em.

So if you're a Baggies supporter
And the Seagulls have made you feel blue,
Come south with the lads by the water -
Brighton's the team for you.

Footballing Greats I Have Taught: Lee Sharpe (Torquay, Man Utd, Leeds, Sampdoria, Bradford City), John Sharpe (Man City, Exeter), Vince Bartram (Wolves, Bournemouth,

Arsenal, Gillingham), Darren Wassall (Forest, Derby, Man City, Birmingham), Steve Guinan (Forest, Darlington, Burnley, Halifax, Cambridge). I've probably taught a few murderers, rapists and general felons by now, too, but you can't check up on them each week in the teamsheets. Lee is responsible for my having once worn an F.A. Cup winner's medal and a European Cup-winners Cup medal - he brought them in on one of his visits. My friend who took him for games and P.E. said to him in a fatherly way, 'Have you thought about resitting those G.C.E.'s like I said, Lee?' Good advice to a bloke who could have bought him out ten times over before he was out of his teens.

I was lucky to work with a staff full of football nutters. The staffroom before a big weekend, for example F.A. Cup third round, was electric - phone-lines blocked as blokes rang home trying to blag tickets, announcements at staff briefing ('Staff and pupils are invited to a short prayer meeting in the chapel this lunch-time; the theme for our invocations will be Arsenal Football Club, who face armageddon at the hands of Bristol Rovers F.C. this weekend. Children are encouraged to bring prayer books, rosaries, incense sticks, candles, lucky charms and join hands in supplication for the Arsenal in their hour of demise. That's: Pray For The Arsenal, twelve-fifteen, in the chapel. Thank you.'), Jocks turning up on the Friday in full tartan - the lot. In fact, a very good mate in the technology department wore full tartan the day before we dumped them out of the world cup one year, and I was in quite early on the Monday and spotted him in the office having a cuppa with the caretaker; so I barged in, dropped my trousers and said, 'Kiss my arse, you great Scotch toe-rag,' and without hesitation he got down on his knees and planted one on the cheek. That's what I call rubbing their noses in it.

The Arsenal man, by the way, was head of religion and a very very 'umble man. He would take boxes of books home to mark every weekend; on the Monday you'd skip up the stairs with your paper in your pocket and meet him trying to steer himself and his boxes in through the door, and he'd back out again, hold it open for you with his foot and say sorry to you as you went through. Somehow it was just right that he chose the week of the Heysel Stadium disaster to take his family on holiday to Belgium, I bet he apologised to the entire nation individually.

He was the man responsible for my first ever cup final, 1980, Arsenal-West Ham. He knew I had lived and taught in East Ham for a number of years, and offered me his second ticket.

In my enthusiasm, I overlooked the significance of this bloke being a lifelong Arsenal man, rummaged around and found a claret and blue scarf, Villa I think, probably confiscated it off a kid, and found myself alone for two and a half hours in the epicentre of the Arsenal end wondering what a knife-blade in the back would feel like. (He said sorry afterwards.)

Years later came that fabulous night when they nicked the championship at Anfield with almost the last kick of the season. I went in the next day, thumped him on the back, shook his hand, spilt his tea - 'Fantastic mate, brilliant, you must have had a hell of a night...' 'Not really Pete, I've stopped supporting them. Colchester's my team now (his parents had moved out to Essex), they need my support more than the Gunners do...'

Every word of that is true - if anything, I've understated it. I saw him at a parent night after he left (his children still went to the school) to work at a far more difficult school in Birmingham, same money. He came up to the table wringing his hands. I said, 'How can a sad old git like you have such a stunning, intelligent daughter?' Affectionately, of course.

Incidentally, the Boleyn Ground is the only place outside non-league where I've seen a player visibly react to a

57

comment from one of his own fans - it's something you don't expect to happen with a crowd of thirty thousand. Harry Redknapp, then an orthodox winger, was receiving no service from his midfield in a difficult game, and had decided to hover on the touch-line and basically excuse himself from the play. A fan no more than two metres away from him shouted, 'Want a read of my paper Harry? You might as well, you're doing fuck-all else.' He went scarlet and moved off, pretending to get involved, which caused as much laughter as the joke.

But I digress. No I don't - hang on, just one more: in one game, a 3-3 draw against Wolves, the referee was pole-axed by a volley full in the face and went down unconscious. The ball was hoofed out to the wing, and the game continued - both linesmen seemed paralysed and unable to act. Bobby Moore calmly stepped over, released the whistle from the ref's wrist, put it to his lips and looked up. The West Ham attack was still developing, in spite of a few unchecked fouls. He waited until it broke down and then, grinning all over his face, stopped the game. He was the most commanding player I ever watched.

My daughter was born on Cup Final Day 1985 (Man Utd - Everton, 1 - 0, Whiteside 110th minute, Moran sent off, can't remember her weight unfortunately). I've been there at the births of all three of my children, but if she'd been born on that special Cup Final Day of 1983 where would I have been then - hospital, or Wembley? My lips are sealed.

* * * * *

Brighton has not always been a basement club. There was a time when things were very different, and those wonderful, delerious, poignant days of 1983 were the subject of the book I couldn't write, 'And Smith Must Score...'. It wasn't really a football book at all, it was a story about a boy who manages to fiddle the national savings lottery, the Premium Bonds - in fact it started off with the title The Great Premium Bond Swizzle.

It took two years to work myself up to starting it, by which time I had boxes full of cuttings, outlines, plans, chronologies, god knows what - and finally, in the February half-term of '86 I started it. By the summer I was seriously underway, and into the early morning stints. During the long holiday I shut myself in a room all day and only came out for tea, bleary-eyed and smelling of tension. My wife said if I didn't do something with the kids she'd leave me. I did a couple of small things, my mind miles away all the time. We had a showdown, so I said I would start getting up at four in the morning again and work through to lunch-time, so I could spend afternoons with the family. I got up at four and worked through till the evenings anyway.

Why? Why so hard? All I can say is, I lived every line of the book. When I was writing it, I would be adrift in an emotional place miles away from land. I was deep in my childhood, and as close to the hole of despair that dominated it as I could have got without falling in. And yet the style is actually light and quite comical, and it is as near to pure fiction as anything I have written.

The year went on, and I carried on into and through the next summer, writing, if anything, more manically than before. My wife took the children on holiday by herself (don't think I'm indifferent to this - I feel sick reading it); on the day they went, I had just cleared the decks and got started when a friend dropped round: he said later he had never seen me so fired up in his life, my tension drove him away. That was the day I wrote the semi-final chapter, I remember it.

Here's a sampler. The main character, called Percy (which is one of his problems in the story), or Cy for short, has moved up north with his father. In this chapter he is spending the half-term week back home in Brighton; he's gone round to his friend Jeffo's house to try and organise a plan for getting to the semi-final. Jeffo has two sisters, one teenaged and one a little Downes girl, Belinda:

CHAPTER TWENTY-FOUR

It's Angie who answers, what a knockout, I have been away, been away years, she's grown up. She greets me like her best friend. In the right places too, god her shape, she's in this immaculate ice-blue boiler suit. I get this intuition that the Spurs game's not going to come off for some reason, and a stronger one, that I don't really care.

Things are shifting. There is a dangerous shifting of the ground.

"Cy. You're back home. I wondered when we'd see you."

I'm standing there like a lemon. I can't get over her.

"Jeff's not here. Didn't he even tell you the pig? He's gone up north somewhere, Durham I think, with his girlfriend and her mum and dad. He's getting in awfully deep these days Cy you'll have to have a talk with him. It's one of these Shrinker Saver weekends or something. D'you want to come in? Mum's just gone to the shop but Belinda's here, she'll go mad when she sees you."

Blimey. I cross the thresh-hold. He's obviously chucked the rule-book away, I mean weekends with the parents as well.... we must have passed in opposite directions, clever really when you think we've got a major historical event to co-ordinate and only a fortnight left.

Belinda's on her rocking-horse, she's changed too but not like Angie, christ it's like Bosworth Field under my rib-cage. She gurgles at me and starts whanging away like Lester ruddy Piggott, rockers off the ground, the thing's come to life, she'll be over his head at the next fence. Angie crouches to steady her, she'll make a fantastic mother, I go round and put my foot on the back runner and Belinda lifts her face *right back till she can see over her shoulders. I move from side to side trying to find the point where she has to straighten up again, but her little upside-down eyes follow me everywhere, swivelling her head like a baby owl.*

This is all very well, but someone's got to do something about the tickets. I try to ascertain the extent of the damage with Jeffo, though it looks pretty obvious.

"So it's dead serious then, with Jeff and Nicky....?"

She looks puzzled.

"Who, Nicola Samuels, you're joking, he's not going out with her, her parents won't let her see him any more, trust him. It's Debby Hedges now, she's the latest. That's who he's gone with."

She smiles at the effrontery of it. Debby Hedges. She was nothing a few months ago, we used to joke about her. I can't keep up with any of it. Belinda grabs my leg with both arms and hangs on. All I know is, once Angie starts getting it sorted out with the lads I won't stand a cat in hell's chance. She unhooks Belinda for me. There's a snotty mark on my jeans, it doesn't matter but she gets her handkerchief and wipes it off. My leg melts. She stands. We're next to each other. I start slapping my pockets like a madman.

"When he gets back tell him to phone me, about the match. Tell him it's urgent. I'm staying at my gran's."

There's a felt-pen in Belinda's toys, I pick it up but I've got no paper. I feel something in my top pocket, gran's cards, I can't, it would be sacrilege. Suddenly I've got her hand I don't know what's come over me and I'm writing gran's number on her skin bright yellow not the ideal choice I go over it again and I'm holding it and when I look up I'm closer to her face than I've ever been before and her eyes are deep and she's breathing fast and I know I'm going to kiss her, she knows too her lips drop I swallow her breath and we're touching touching faces Angie my Angie the kiss.

The door.

The room lurches. There's a kind of speechless tableau like you get at the end of kids' nativity plays, all waiting for the signal to move again. Belinda runs to her, stumbles on a brick, Angie and her mum both dart forward and end up face to face about two feet off the floor.

"It's time for her bath. I'd like a word please."

They take her out, Angie glances back closing the door. I stand there useless, the archangel waiting for the scene to change, arch prat more like. The pen's still in my hand, I look for the top without actually moving from where I am, what a wanker, fancy not hearing. It's got to be somewhere. Angie's back in.

"I think you'll have to go...." She's whispering, like a favourite vase has got broken. I make several starts at speaking. I can hear water gushing.

"It's alright. She just wasn't expecting it that's all. Nor was I...." She takes the pen from me and puts the top back on the right end. I regain movement. There's a smile in her eyes. "She'll get used to it."

She leads me to the door.

"I'd better go, I'll tell Jeff to ring.... it was nice."

She colours slightly and shuts it.

Where the hell am I? It's ten in the morning and I've just kissed my best mate's sister. I've got a welly-boot full of water walloping around in my chest. It's going to be a bloody long day.

I wander down towards the seafront without really thinking, I don't even know what road I'm in, what's a road anyway they're all the same. I kissed her, christ, I thought my throat was going to seize up. A car screeches and paps at me cheers mate it was just a simple kiss no need for that fuss, *easy does it calm like the sea, get used to it she'll get used to it bloody hell. I kissed her. I kissed her.*

*   *   *   *   *

The earth turns. The tide reaches in, kisses the pebbles, grey, serene, lingers, recedes, a wet kiss. There's been a meal somewhere and a telling-off. I think it was today. I'm on the groyne with the fishermen like it's always been, where else would you go when your life's just rearranged itself without asking? A distant roar drifts past us and dies at sea, and a few minutes later another. They've won. Two goals in the last eight minutes, from the jaws of defeat.

Damn it. We're two of a kind, me and Jeffo. Lovesick. You can't just moon up to Wembley in a lovesick daze and ask them to let you in for the game. We're going to mess this up. Worse, we're not even going to care.

One of the anglers strikes and starts to wind in. It's dusk, infinite, peaceful. A few gnats on an unseen string. The sea sucks and laps, breathing. We're apart from the mass of folk with their lights, drawn off, chosen by the elements. His rod bends like a whip, water runs down the line catching the last light, splashing; strands of seaweed drop. We're all riveted though it's probably only kelp he's caught, as always. The ratchet ticks, he's in no hurry, he knows, he can feel through the rod. There's a thresh from the gloom's edge, other lines are left, it's a turbot, a huge diamond of sleek white muscle, finned and gilled, a nugget of pure life brought up from the underworld. He removes the hook firmly and kills it. His face strong and peaceful. A man who knows what he came for, and got it.

I've just realised - that's the third consecutive book of mine where a main character is called Angie. Strange - I have no idea why.

Anyway, the bit you've just read is the streamlined version. But when I first wrote it I was so convinced it was the most brilliant thing man had ever written I just chucked it in a bag and sent it off without making a single change. The couple of friends who read it first tried to warn me, but I wasn't listening. At least having been published, I generally got a proper letter back rather than just a rejection slip. Here's a typical one (from Faber):

'... It's far too long. It needs to be shortened by half at least. This is the only manuscript where I find your writing too dense, too full of wanting to get in every detail, every emotion, every character. I can understand why but you need to discipline this one...'

Well, I sulked for a year, then did something I haven't ever done before: got it out of the drawer, re-read it, realised they were right, and ripped the guts out of it. Scene after scene went - mainly football trivia - and when I'd finished, it was twenty thousand words shorter. That's a lot of writing to rip up.

It did get published, at last, but I had to do it. I pillaged money from our account, saying I would pay it back with interest from the huge sales I anticipated, but I had to pay the bank back with interest instead. Was it worth it? For the reviews, yes, for profit, no. A good review would always be followed by a small flurry of orders, but what I needed was to be shortlisted for something, and that didn't happen.

Like I said, when football raises its head, sound judgement goes out of the window.

* * * * *

Q. What's it like being a writer?

A. You are always at war with yourself. One part of you wants to write nice little clever stories with a beginning, middle and end; the other part of you wants to mess them up because life doesn't come in neat little stories and it's dishonest to make out that it does. That's how it is for me, anyway.

Q. Where do you get your ideas from?

A. The basic ideas for 'And Smith Must Score...' came from life. I was a skanky little kid who used to nick things from corner shops, scrump from gardens and go carol singing with a phoney charity box. My all-time dream was to have a secret stash: to find a wallet in the street stuffed with notes of very large denominations and not hand it in - or maybe hand it in anonymously having liberated nine-tenths of the sheets first. So that's the bit where he fiddles the Premium Bonds. The football bit obviously came from life too. It's easy when you base your stories on life, you don't have to make so much up. Trouble is, it's difficult to mess with things that have actually happened. I wanted to give Brighton just one little goal to win the 1983 final, but it doesn't work that way.

Q. How long does it take to write a book?

A. I started 'And Smith Must Score...' on 18th Feb 1986 and finished 19th Sept 1987. But I did over a hundred pages of notes before that, and spent two years turning it over in my mind.

Q. Do you like writing?

A. Doing 'And Smith Must Score...' was like being fired up for the biggest exam of my life for three and a half years, all told, so I suppose the answer has to be no, really. I think I passed though.

Q. How do you get a book published?

A. Did this one through Crazy Horse, realised I had got the title and cover wrong, scrapped it, and did it again.

Q. Who is your favourite author?

A. Russell Hoban - crazy, brilliant. 'The Mouse and His Child' is typical. 'Turtle Diary' is about as sane as he gets, I love it; most of the others are off the wall. There's one called 'Ridley Walker', where the human race has gone primitive after nuclear war and almost lost language. He has very deep, fabulous mind.

CHAPTER 6

Rudeness

Love is the fart
Of every man's heart,
It paineth him when 'tis kept close
And others doth offend when 'tis let loose.

John Suckling

I have to hold my hand up here and say that I enjoy profanity (rudeness), and it annoys me intensely when people enthuse over someone like Billy Connolly themselves, but turn white at the idea that the young might simply enjoy coarseness too, rather than be irredeemably corrupted by it. I have never stopped any of my own kids watching things I've enjoyed watching myself, or using the swearwords I like to use. But having said that, it is quite difficult for English teachers. Where do they draw the line? If they encourage pupils to respond to and reflect life in an honest way, sooner or later they are going to reach the point where they have to ask themselves 'what goes?'.

I was supply-teaching in a school in Birmingham, and my fellow-supply teacher next door was an old chalk-wagger who liked to have the kids working strictly from the textbook. But he was a great bloke, with a twinkle of devilment permanently playing on his face, and one morning he decided to open the window to liberalism and let them write some play-scenes together. He was going round looking over some shoulders when he noticed the line, 'Have you shagged him yet?' He made a fuss, they complained that they needed to be realistic, he stood his ground. They went into a huddle for a while, then one of them called out, 'Will you at least accept a bit of sex, sir?' And he said without a pause, 'Depends who's offering it...' He was a funny bugger to work with.

More relevant to this topic is a year-eight drama lesson I once took, in which a group was performing an improvisation involving the crew of a plane that was about to crash. They were very well-mannered kids and I always had complete control with them. One was playing the co-pilot, and in the absence of a fuller role he had appointed himself the job of passing round imaginary cigarettes from time to time; the plane goes into free-fall and the most confident one, the captain, is carrying the whole episode, totally in role, wrestling with the controls and barking urgent orders to the others. The co-pilot thinks it's time he got more involved and offers his captain another cigarette. Without hesitation the boy shouted, 'Fuck the fags, fetch the parachutes!' There was a kind of open-mouthed second of silence, which included him as well as all the rest of the group, but he was so in role that he snapped straight out of it and carried on trying to save the plane.

There's a good book for teachers, 'The Intelligence of Feeling' by R. Witkin, which deals with this problem - the fear of things getting out of hand in creative lessons such as art, writing and drama - but identifying the problem doesn't give you a solution.

I see it as a massive issue, because most of what is being turned out creatively in schools is dangerously safe - it avoids issues that might trouble the school value system - and so I would say the passive lesson that is being taught is that writing is the tool of insincerity. Let's not fudge this. We either believe in meaning, and are prepared to go where it takes us: the only other option is to involve yourself in the concealment of meaning. Art as the highest form of deceit, or self-deceit. Choose your words nicely, pick a subject which is 'cold' to you but favourable in the eyes of your teacher, fictionalise it, give it a tidy ending: get a good grade. If you've got anything 'hot' to say, keep it to yourself, don't rock the boat.

What can anyone do? Box clever, I suppose is the only answer. People in all walks of life have to. If a doctor helps an elderly patient die comfortably, they face legal consequences - but I've no doubt it happens. If artists find themselves severely at odds with the public mood, they risk failure and financial loss. But it's a risk they might take, if they believe strongly enough in their work.

I had a girl once who wrote a long narrative piece that she wanted to have entered in the Smiths Young Writers competition. When I say long, I mean about thirty-five A4 pages. It was in draft, and she wanted me to pass it on to one of my gang of parent typists. I read it, and said I was on a spot, because although it was good it was too explicit to give to a parent (there was a bit of blouse-fumbling at a party and some swearing); there was the risk of a complaint, with consequences for her and myself. The girl took it back and returned after the week-end having handwritten the whole thing out neatly, and submitted it.

I think this is a good litmus test. If you put a fairly tricky obstacle in someone's way and they refuse to be discouraged, they are probably sincere. So as a teacher, one has to give the issue its proper weight, take a deep breath, and prepare to defend it. That doesn't mean commit suicide, it means box clever, and make sure you keep coming out of your corner when the bell goes. I think that's what kids need to see. And if you are a pupil who wants to write something real, write it, but be aware that it might give someone a problem. Don't hand it in with the rest - see your teacher separately and let them know you're on the level.

But it's difficult. Most school managements want their art meaningful enough to attract attention, but not too meaningful. They are concerned with lack of meaning.

Here's a fun poem that was given me at a workshop:

CHEESE ON TOAST

I wanted cheese on toast,
My boyfriend wanted beans.
And so to serve the idiot right,
I ripped off his jeans.

He made no attempt to stop me,
And with a smile on his face,
He ripped off my chiffon blouse,
To reveal a bra of lace.

Running round the kitchen,
Squealing with delight,
I pulled down his boxers,
And I had a fright!

Yelling for revenge
He chased me some more.
Pulling at my belt,
He threw me to the floor.

I screeched as his hands
Wandered to my breast,
Honestly, my boyfriend,
He'll never let me rest!

I fought hard against him,
Pulling at his hair.
Then I had an awful shock -
There was nothing there!

Where is your penis?
I asked him as a joke,
But I could see his face drop
Even as I spoke.

It came off in the swimming pool,
So I stuck it back on,
Oh my God, this is awful -
Where has it gone?

We searched the whole house,
Calling softly, 'dick',
But nowhere could we locate
His poor and lonely prick.

I think you'll have to face it,
Your dick has run away,
Now a castrated man
You will have to stay!

Ruth Lemiech

I haven't got anything deep to say about that, except that it was a fun poem. It was read out, and made the kids laugh and relax, but they didn't start writing filth because of it. My experience is that dirty-minded writing, as opposed to clean-minded dirty writing, is the result of inhibition, not serious expression. You tend to sense where it's coming from very quickly.

I had a pupil come to the staff-room with a friend in tow, a bit furtive, asking me to look at something she'd been writing. I felt I was being involved in a conspiracy, and my heckles went up. The piece involved a pupil and a teacher meeting secretly - not a coded message to me, but I guess a fairly well-developed fantasy involving someone on the staff - and it was detailed. I asked her what other people had thought of it, and she giggled and said she wasn't going to show it to anyone else. So I told her that if it wasn't fit to show anyone she should either start showing a bit of respect for the reader, or stick it in a drawer and write it for herself when no-one was about.

She didn't come back, and I knew she wouldn't, because she was not prepared to come clean about what she was doing. If she had have been, I would have discussed it upfront with her, and supported her in one way or another.

On the other hand, I would put myself on the line to defend the author of the following, written in 1990 for an annual Christmas poem I used to get sixth-form pupils to write - the one rule was, no clichés:

CHRISTMAS DAY

*On Christmas Day,
come what may
you have to say
We'll get our way.*

*It's lots of fun
to get a gun,
and shoot an Iraqi.
But I find it better
to wear my sweater
especially when it's parky.*

*But the gulf is exceptionally hot,
The snowy Xmas you'll get... not.
Our lads out there would enjoy getting plastered,
But they can't cos of Saddam Hussein, the bastard.*

*He's not your average Tommy's mate,
The sadistic git has annexed Kuwait,
So our boys are out there, and the Yanks
sweating for oil while George Bush wanks.*

*So let us not forget the score,
we're on the verge of a a Gulf war
but until old Saddam rears his head
we can eat lots of food and get pissed instead.*

Tony McCooey

I was doing English with a low-performance year-eight group, only about twelve in the class, finding it hard going, when one of them brought in the commercial tape of Roald Dahl's 'Revolting Rhymes' ('I like poetry sir, wanna hear this.. Why can't we do poetry like this, sir?'). I said, O.K., we'll try it. I told them to cast around for a folk story we could modernise, and after some argument they went for Robin Hood. I spent some time on prose versions, so that we could come up with an agreed story to work on. Then it came to writing the lines themselves. I gave them a photocopied outline of the agreed story in as much detail as possible, and the process was, at each point I would get them to try and write quatrains (four rhyming lines); they would read them out, and I would listen, scribbling interesting lines and turns of phrase quickly onto the board.

Some of their lines weren't in verse at all, some were relentlessly over-rhymed, hardly any scanned. But I made what I could of them, fishing out rhymes where possible, showing them how to scan them, linking with my own rhymes to fill the gaps. When they were finalised to the group's satisfaction, they would copy them down.

It was all done as a collaboration, and if they rejected lines they didn't go in - but obviously I was the conductor.

Here it is:

THE NEW ADVENTURES OF ROBIN HOOD

There was a man in olden days
Who's read about in books and plays.
He had a mum - her name was May;
She didn't like him.

Anyway,

Our story starts in Nottingham
Where this chap lives with his old mam.
(His dad was kicked out years ago -
He used to drink but now he dow;
He's on the wagon, he's gone T.T.,
But she won't have him back - he's on Ecstasy.)
He lives with his mum in a council flat,
No brothers or sisters - just them and a cat.
He hangs around, he's on the dole,
He's driving his mum round the pole.
He won't clean its tray, he's such a loafer -
The cat does its poos under the sofa.

His mum says, "Get up and out right now,
And find a job - don't be a clown,
You silly fool, you're such a prat,
Go out and earn some proper cash."
Things went flying, his mum went red,
"Try the grocers by Tesco's," she said.

So he ran a mile - he wore out his shoes -
All of that just to be refused.
The grocer, Bob, said, "You're too persistent,
Clear off - I don't need another assistant."

That was a blow - he'd been to Bob's
Looking for the easiest of well-paid jobs;
There was no hope for poor old Robin,
So he thought he'd try a bit of noggin'.

Credit cards are good and proper,
They're easy to nick and not much bother.
He went to the library and hung around
And lying on a desk he found
A leather jacket - he knocked it off
Just for a look, and sure enough
There was Visa, Delta and Access
Not to mention American Express.

*The man in the corner whose coat it was
Had found the children's section because
At home his kids, the little bitches,
Liked Roald Dahl - 'The Twits' and 'The Witches'.
He never saw Robin pilfer his jacket
And belt through the door - he made off with a packet.*

*He ran down the street, where he saw a rich dame;
He took her bag. She was a little bit lame:
"Oi, come back here you thieving bugger,
You'd take the roof off your own grandmother.
I'll fetch the police, I've got a dog,
Get back here you little sod!"*

Off he ran past Broad Street Motors
Where he saw a chap checking second-hand Skodas;
He took some cards and a pension book
From the old git's jacket up on a hook.
He runs round the corner as fast as he can
Straight into a traffic jam.
He doesn't see the roadwork sign,
And falls head-first down a massive drain.

"Poh," says Rob, "it stinks in here,
It smells like a dose of diarrhoea.
If I stay I'll smell like a skunk.
Maybe it comes out at the city dump -
I'll walk this way and see what happens -
Anything's better than being flattened
By rush-hour traffic bibbing and hooting;
Too bad a chap can't do a bit of looting."

Just then he saw Little John Smith:
"Hoi mate, what ya doing underneath
The pavement living with rats and mice -
Haven't you got a flat or a house?"
"You must be joking, I'm on the dole,
I have to live in this dirty hole.
It's not in use now, exc:ept when there's floods...
Why don't you join us Robin Hood?
They've built another lot of sewers
Since the old days when you knew us.
It ain't so bad. This is Maria,
She's my girlfriend - you'd better stay clear.
Anyway, she'd turn away from you -
You're a Larry Loner too...
Maria, this is Robin of Loxley.
Maria - Robin."
                "He's a bit poxy,
I don't like him, where d'ya find him?
If he gives me the eye I swear I'll blind him."
"Pack it up Maz... Want to see what I've earned?"
Says Little John. He got down and turned
A loose slab up - there was a stash
Of stereos, TVs, videos and cash
Nicked from houses up in the street
And stacked in a hole right under their feet.
"Cor blimey, where d'ya get all that lot from?
Can I borrow some to give to my mum?"
"No way in the world - but you can join our posse."
"Ah, smart - I swear I won't be bossy.
How d'ya nick all that John, how did ya tax it?"
"Easy peasy mate, you go through the whatsit -
Through the old sewers to the conservatories,
The ones they used for the outside lavatories -
They've knocked them down now, but the pipes are
    still there
Maria goes up and lets us in the rear.

You can come with us next time we go
And we can teach you what we know."

"Ta mate, brill, don't mind if I do -
But how do you flog it? It's not even new..."

"The market. We've got a regular spot.
We just set up a stall and flog the lot."

"Hey," says Rob, "mum needs a camcorder,
Mind if I have one to take home for her?"

But John thinks that's a bit of a joke,
There's no way he's giving stuff to the poor folk.
"Come with us next time, then you'll find
V.C.R.s and anything you like."

So off they all go together.
Maria goes up first, she's as light as a feather,
And lets them in - they nick tons of stuff -
But all Rob can think is, she's a nice bit of fluff.
He smiles a smile, an eyelid flickers,
He wants to get inside her knickers...

"Fair robbery, that, we've made a good taking,
Look at all the money we're making,"
John says after. "But if you want some gear to take home
Go out tomorrow on your own,
You can take Maria if you like -
She can squeeze inside the pipe
And let you in. There's places so posh
You'll make yourself a pile of dosh."

But Robin has ideas of his own,
Never mind nicking from someone's home
What he wants is a bit of a snog...

"I hope this place hasn't got a dog,"
Maria says as they come to one.
She starts climbing up. Cor, what a bum
Robin thinks as he gives it a shove;

He's falling head over heels in love.
"Let go! Get off, you silly dope..."
But before Maz knows it they're having a grope.

She finally breaks in overhead,
But they forget about crime and rush to the bed.
After a while the telephone rings,
Maria gets scared - they're still having their fling,
Then the door goes as well while they're at it.
Rob hardly has time to get on his jacket.

"Ooh, ah, I've lost my bra..."

"There's no time to look now,
he's parking his car!"

They clamber out
the upstairs
window
And disappear
as fast as they
can go.

John gets
mad. "Where
the hell have
you been?
And where's the
stuff? There's
nothing to be seen.
Have you two been out giving it away
To down-and-outs who've got no pay?
You've been gone over an hour,
And - hang on a minute: where's your bra?"

Maria went a blooming red:
"I think it's in the wash," she said...

John gets a funny feeling in his bones:
They've been frolicking with their hormones
He thinks, I'll get them back -

*I'll lead them both into a trap.
I'll give them another house to fleece,
They'll never guess it's the central police;
They come up by the sergeant's desk
If I'm not mistaken. What a wicked arrest!*

*So off they go, back down the tunnel
Looking for the particular funnel
John's given them, to the place above.*

*"I think it's somewhere here my love,"
Rob says to Maz. "Oh - what a drag,
I've left the diagram in my bag,
But here's one, look, on the right,
Switch on the torch a sec, let's have some light."*

*Maz thinks it looks more or less familiar:
"Come on," she says, "I'm sure it's this one here."*

* * * * *

*Meanwhile, whilst this has all been going on
The lottery's been claimed by Robin's mom;
She's won a massive rollover jackpot -
Twenty million. What a crackpot:
She's bought herself a tudor mansion
Right next door to the local cop station.
She keeps her winnings in a safe
Guarded by an ex-nark - her mate
From before, when she was in the old street.*

*A sudden noise gets him to his feet -
Rob sneaking in the house with Marion behind him.
The guard pricks his ears up and tries to find them;
The noise is coming from the kitchen -
Quick as a flash he turns the switch on
To all the lights and the burglar alarm.
They're caught red-handed, arm in arm.*

"Right, you're nicked! Down to the station!"
Rob's mum's face is filled with elation;
She's watching it all in her dressing gown.
But - wait a minute - she starts to frown:
"Oh dear, sargeant, we've got a problem -
You've just arrested my son Robin..."

"Mum! What ya doing in this pavillion?
If you're so rich, give us a million.
At least you can pay my bail to freedom..."
"Not a chance - burgling's not the way to be son."

You think this poem will never end,
But that is where you're wrong my friend.
It took us nearly all the year -
We've had a few hassles - but now it's here.
Every week down in room 6
Greg Fisher, along with Chris Fox,
Natalie Palfrey and Daz O'Brien,
Have spent their English classes trying
To sort out the story. Natalie Riddell
Did her best: she had a fiddle
(With the verses), while Mr Hayden
Wrote the words up - he made them
Rhyme - and Carleen Whittal
Came in late but still did a little.
Also Mike Driscoll and Emma Jones -
We could have written hundreds of poems,
But concentrated on Robin Hood
And kept working at it till it
*   sounded good.*

So - you really think it's never-ending?
Well it ends next week. Rob's case is
*   pending...*

The End

That was a very satisfying exercise, and I would like to make a couple of points about it.

First, I set the coarse tone (surprise, surprise...) because they began by putting up such meaningless lines, lines that were completely divorced from anything they were remotely likely to say themselves - lines that they thought were 'poetic' (i.e., ludicrous); and also, because they had brought the Dahl tape in precisely because it was a little bit rude and near the knuckle.

Second, as the process went on, the kids developed more of an ear for the lines: they were more likely to adjust them when they didn't scan, and became more capable of putting down lines that didn't rhyme and matching them up with lines by other people - or changing key words without changing meaning - so that they did rhyme. They were never brilliant, but they got hold of the idea.

Third, it took a year to do, one lesson a week, with the usual gaps for exams and so on. That's a long time, and I came close to dumping it on a number of occasions. Sometimes an entire lesson would produce no more than six agreed lines. I persisted, because it got to the point where too much work had gone into it, and to scrap it would have given more of a signal of failure than ending up with a bad poem.

Last, my impression was that it satisfied them at the end, and was something they would have remembered. I typed the whole thing up when it was done and read it through while they followed with their copies. There was a buzz after, and they were elated that they had been responsible for something that sustained and coherent. There is no question that I was the motor-boat and they were the water-skiers being dragged along, mainly on their bellies, but there were clear lines that they could identify as theirs and they were satisfied to be involved in the process. Best of all, word went round, and their friends from other sets laughed when they read it.

I will bring things to a close with a piece of rudeness of my own. It's the last one of a series of short stories for the young, entitled 'The Adventures of Stringy Simon'. In it, Stewart has just started secondary school. He dreads the showers. I don't read it in schools unless the teacher has seen it first, but when I do, it brings the house down. I have read it to quite old children, years ten and eleven, as an example of what I do for the young, and they crack up when they hear it, too.

He has just made his first rugby tackle:

THE WILLY ENLARGING ELIXIR

As a matter of fact, Patsy wasn't quite as impressed with the flying tackle as Mr Hughes had been.

'Look at you,' she said as he took his uniform off after school, 'you need a scraper to get all that mud off, never mind a flannel. Aren't the showers working?'

'Um...'

Stewart hadn't had a shower since he got there, but a feeling came over him things were about to change. If only he didn't have such a tinsy willie, he thought, it wouldn't be so bad. Imagine having to stand next to Stormin' Norman and his great big donger. It'ud be like Little and Large. Laurel and Hardy. Only worse. He looked down at it - it wasn't visible at all at that precise moment, the bath water was so muddy it looked like cocoa. He ran other one. It was nearly cold.

There was no doubt about it, sooner or later he was going to have to.

He was sitting in the religious teacher, Mr Nugent's, lesson the next day, quietly minding his own business, when a note was slipped onto his desk. Without taking his eyes off the board he nonchalantly unfolded it, and had a quick glance down.

'FOR SALE. WILLY ENLARGING ELIXER. GARENTEED. PASS IT ON.'

There was a flash and a distant explosion in his brain. Wow! He looked down again. Yes, there it was, as bright as day. His troubles were over.

A shadow passed across and settled on him. A Mr Nugent shaped shadow.

'Is that a note I see, young man. Would you be so kind...'

'Er, pardon...?' stammered Stewart.

'Please sir, haven't you forgotten the homework?' came a voice from somewhere else with just a slight edge of panic in it.

'Ah...'

As he half-turned, Stewart stuffed the note in his blazer and swapped it for some pocket-fluff. He held it out.

'Eugh. Put it in the bin, boy.'

*   *   *   *   *

Stewart went all round the playground four times before he could find him. Bertie Snodbrolly. He had aspirin bottles full of gunge-coloured paste. Looked like he'd spooned it straight off the rugby field. Talk about a potion.

'Guaranteed to work,' he said. 'Full refund if no improvement in seven days. While stocks last... Thank you, sir. Thank-you...'

It was selling like hot cakes.

'What is it?' said Stewart, looking closely. It seemed to have seeds in it.

'Old family recipe, sir,' said Bertie, 'handed down from father to son. Kindly purchase before inspection.'

It had already cost a homework. Stewart sighed and coughed up his dinner money.

'One application per day, before retiring. Cover with suitable material. Rinse off the following morning. Not to be taken internally.'

'It had better work,' he said.

'Ask my cousin,' said Bertie. 'He invented it. He's got a massive one now, it's damn near as big as an elephant's.'

The lesson buzzer went.

That night Stewart scooped some of the paste out with a lolly-stick and smeared it on. It was disgusting. He'd never smelt such a stink. He wrapped a hanky round it, put his pants back on, and got into bed. His willy was tingling already.

Wow. What if he got a gigantic one. Well, not as big as Bertie's cousin's, you'd trip over it, but one he could sort of swing a bit. It would be brilliant.

All night he tossed and turned. His dreams went crazy. Elephants, giraffes, snakes, river eels. Octopuses, storks, geese. Great hanging vines, thicker than your arm. Tarzan. Tarzan of the apes swinging from them. Swinging from tree to tree. Huge, massive great trunks you couldn't get your arms round. Erect. Penetrating the sky, spurting their great canopies of foliage high overhead. Jack - Jack and the beanstalk, huge, never-ending, nosing its way into the clouds, gigantic, FEE FI FO FUM

'HELP!'

Stewart was bolt upright in bed, sweat pouring from him. There was a merciless throbbing pain down below, burning him alive. It felt like he'd cooked it.

Oh no, he thought, in desperation, what shall I do? Um, just a minute... 'Not to be taken internally' No, um... 'Rinse off the following morning...'

Yes, of course. He didn't need a second bidding. He shot to the sink and turned the cold tap full on.

Aaah, that was bliss. It was bigger alright. As the stuff came off he could see it was almost twice its normal size. Bit pink, mind. In fact, almost purple, but bigger, definitely, there was no question about it. Wow. It was worth the pain. He sprinkled it with cool talc, and leaving his pants off this time he went back across to the bed. Yes, he could feel it, it was swinging. It felt enormous.

Next morning he awoke for the second time to the most excruciating pain. It was throbbing like crazy, making him wince every time. He daredn't even look. He daredn't let anyone else look either. It felt like it had dropped right off. He clutched the blankets when any of them came near. He was petrified.

* * * * *

Doctor Rawalpindi Rajid Kamur Singh Khazi didn't arrive till nearly lunch-time.

'Well, well, well, sir, and what have we got here?' he said, taking a little peep. 'Oh dear, dear, native uprising in the corner of the empire. Very serious indeed sir. And what is the cause of the eruption?'

Very sheepishly, Stewart passed him the bottle. He frowned and looked at it.

'"Willy enlarging elixir." Very interesting. Special prescription.'

He took a sniff.

'Goodness gracious me. It is Indian speciality. Vindaloo. You have put this on your private member's bill? Oh goodness me. With a couple of popodoms and some pilau rice it would be ready for the Maharajah's table.'

'Oh...' Stewart looked at him. 'You mean I've got a curried cock-sparrow?'

'Special recipe sir,' said Doctor Rawalpindi. 'Taj Mahal take-away.'

'But how come it worked?' said Stewart. 'Look, it's twice as big...'

87

Doctor Rawalpindi shook his head.

'Swelling is big sir, but private member exactly as before. Only very small majority.'

'Ow...' said Stewart. 'All that trouble for nothing. Now what am I going to do. It'll never get bigger at this rate.'

There was a silence, while they both looked sympathetically at his poor red, throbbing thing.

Suddenly, Doctor Rawalpindi opened his bag and fumbled inside it. He handed Stewart a magnifying glass.

'See for yourself sir. I think we have first signs of development. Just there...'

Stewart scanned the scene for himself. Yes. Doctor Rawalpindi was right. One tiny, curly little pubic hair, all on its own. His first one.

'Wow,' said Stewart. 'I never noticed. If only I hadn't ve.... Do you think it will survive?'

'One man alone, defying the might of the British Empire,' said Doctor Rawalpindi. He was beginning to get poetic. 'Soon one will be many.'

'You mean, it won't be long before...'

'It is inevitable sir, Independence Day very soon.' He pointed to the tiny whiskery hair. 'We must call him Mahatma Ghandi.'

'Mahatma Ghandi,' said Stewart, leaning back on his pillow with a deep, tranquil sigh. 'Wow... Showers, here I come.'

* * * * *

Schools can be amazing - very sensitive if I so much as hint at swearing, snogging, anything at all like that in my readings, whereas the kids themselves are all into Viz, South Park, and as we all know, much worse. It's amazing the two universes co-exist at all.

There was a headline in the Observer (30.8.98) round about the time I was writing this chapter: 'Read Naughty Books to Boys, Urges Blair'. I snatched it up and started reading: "...authors today need some of the mischief of a Roald Dahl to keep children interested; I think he was one of the first who would write in a slightly naughty way, which makes books intriguing and interesting." Not bad, I thought, maybe I should send him a copy of The Willy Enlarging Elixir. Then I noticed his recommended reading list: Narnia, Lord of the Rings, Sherlock Holmes, Pickwick Papers, Ivanhoe...

* * * * *

Q. What's it like being a writer?

A. Some people say it's like being a traitor: you use everything you see and everything you hear, whether it's private or not; you betray your best friends, your family, your work-mates, your lovers. There is no confidence or situation, however personal, you won't use for your own ends. (But I'm not like that.)

Q. Where do you get your ideas from?

A. With 'The Willy Enlarging Elixir' I just thought about what would be embarrassing for someone of his age. Young people don't believe old gits like me have ever lived, and they are often surprised when they realise we know about getting-off and things like that. We didn't all spend our teens in the Boys' Brigade.

Q. How long does it take to write a book?

A. The willy story is one of forty-five I did about a character called Stewart. Each one is about three thousand words, and I wrote roughly two a week. Actually I wrote nearer sixty, but scrapped a few that didn't turn out right.

Q. Do you like writing?

A. Yes, these were fun to write because I didn't have to worry how unrealistic they were - the dafter the better. Also, every week I had something finished to show for my work.

Q. How do you get a book published?

A. The Stewart stories (otherwise called 'The Adventures of Stringy Simon') have been done through Crazy Horse. There are three volumes so far, each containing about seven stories. They are the most successful thing I have done, and one volume is onto its third printing. What was difficult was finding the right illustrator - they were either too busy, or they didn't want to illustrate a book which didn't have a major publisher, or their style wasn't right. It took years to find Clinton Banbury; I'm glad I did though, his style is perfect.

Q. Who is your favourite author?

A. Anne Fine, she's witty and clever, and not just in her writing. I've heard some supposedly funny authors giving talks and they could bore for Britain, but she's full of vitality and wit, and she doesn't let questioners get away with anything. 'Goggle Eyes' is clever - a whole story set in a broom cupboard.

CHAPTER 7

Poetry

FRUIT PICKING

Picking is ace
Until you fall on your face
Pick a plum
Then you will say yum
After you will feel sick
My poems don't mean anything
+ they do not rhyme
Strawberries are nice
So are apples
Cockles and mussels
I love bananas
Oliver likes them too
Blackberries strawberries peaches
Apples plum kiwi
Are all nice
Unlike school.

Luis Ferreira

There are many ways of generating a full-throttle class groan, particularly in secondary schools, and one of the most reliable is to walk into a classroom saying the two words, 'Right - poetry'. Poetry has given me my most perverse lessons in English teaching, yet probably my happiest.

Let's just start from scratch a minute - if we take one meaning of poetry as words used in rhythm, we've all been into it since we were in the cot: raps, rhythms, chants, they're irresistible.

The match that put my local team Kidderminster into the Football League was the away game at Woking. Brighton were playing at Shrewsbury that day, and my son rang up and said, how about it dad, coming to Shrewsbury? And without thinking I said, you must be joking, I go to Woking, and we both cracked up just because of the rhyme. Another football one while it's in my mind: I was watching Brighton v Reading one boring day; the crowd was very quiet. The ref gave an unimportant free-kick to Reading and suddenly a bloke in front of us who hadn't said a thing all game screamed, "Brighton's ball you bald-headed bastard'.

The people around him fell about - partly because they were bored, and partly because his reaction was over the top. But also because it sounded funny, with all the b's and d's, and the double 'ball' sound. If he'd have said 'Reading's ball you ginger-haired foundling' people probably would have laughed, but not so much.

Here's a very simple poem I've often started a poetry unit with:

'I've had this shirt
that's covered in dirt
for years and years and years.

It used to be red
but I wore it in bed
and it went grey
'cos I wore it all day
for years and years and years.

The arms fell off
in the Monday wash
and you can see my vest
through the holes in the chest
for years and years and years.

As my shirt falls apart
I'll keep the bits

*in a biscuit tin
on the mantlepiece
for years and years and years.'*

© Michael Rosen

Poem. Rhymes, has verses, has a chorus line. Someone will pipe up, 'It doesn't rhyme all through...' I ask, why is that? Various answers: it's only a kids' poem; he only rhymed the lines that worked; started off O.K. but ran out of rhymes; doesn't get paid much for one poem so has to do them quickly, etc. These answers all suggest the poet isn't much good, which is always possible. So where exactly does the rhyme break down? And as one looks more closely, it becomes clear that the poem has begun to disintegrate, just like the shirt.

I have seen year tens hoot when they realise that...

Here's another one - 'Weeds' by Norman Nicholson (found it in the NEAB anthology):

*Some people are flower lovers.
I'm a weed lover.*

*Weeds don't need planting in well-drained soil;
They don't ask for fertilizer or bits of rag to
    scare away birds.
They come without invitation;
And they don't take the hint when you want them to go.
Weeds are nobody's guests:
More like squatters.*

*Coltsfoot laying claim to every new-dug clump of clay;
Pearlwort scraping up a living between bricks from a
ha'porth of mortar;
Dandelions you daren't pick or you know what
    will happen;
Sour docks that make a first-rate poultice for
    nettle-stings;*

*And flat-foot plantain in the back street, gathering more
    dust than the dustmen.*

*Even the names are a folk-song:
Fat hen, rat's tail, cat's ear, old men's baccy and
    Stinking Billy
Ring a prettier chime for me than honeysuckle
    or jasmine,
and Sweet Cicely smells cleaner than Sweet William
    though she's barred from the garden.*

*And they have their uses, weeds.
Think of old, worked-out mines:
Quarries and tunnels, earth scorched and scruffy, torn-up
    railways, splintered sleepers,
And a whole Sahara of grit and smother and cinders.*

*But go in summer and where is all the clutter?
For a new town has risen of a thousand towers,
Every spiky belfry humming with a peal of bees.
Rosebay willow-herb:
Only a weed!
Flowers are for wrapping in cellophane to present
    as a bouquet;
Flowers are for prize arrangements in vases and silver
    tea-pots;
Flowers are for plaiting into funeral wreaths.
You can keep flowers.
Give me weeds.*

© Norman Nicholson

Poem? There would always be a dispute: yes, it's in verses, the lines are arranged; no, the verses are a mess and it doesn't rhyme. What about 'lovers/lover'? Pah... 'towers/flowers'? Where? What, six lines apart?

O.K., but it's a superbly weedy poem - it's running rampant. There are lines of two and three words along with, well, if you go by the margin capitals line sixteen has twenty-four. In order, the stanzas (the verses) have two, six, five, three, four and ten lines. It's the opposite of what you would call cultivated. Clever.

So, looking at the shape of the poem before anything else: of the choices that were available, the poet chose this. Does it fit? Raiding the NEAB anthology again (no particular reason - probably just the last thing I worked with before going solo), why did a bloke who could do anything with words use such simple rhymes in 'Stop all the Clocks' (the poem that was read out in 'Four Weddings and a Funeral')? Because you don't show off how clever you are at someone's funeral, right? The metre in that poem is right, too, a real pall-bearers' metre - in fact, if you take the comma as an off-stress (strong words = stressed, weak words + comma = non-stressed), isn't the first line exactly the rhythm of the Chopin funeral march?

'Stop all the clocks, cut off the telephone'
   x - -   x - - x - - - x

dum da da dum da da dum da da da dum

I know I'm going on, but I did find it difficult when A-level students came on day one carting their attitude with them, yet having not clue about form. I'm starting from scratch with year-twelves. It's true, they often have no ear for the rhythm of a poem at all, no feel for the poetry of it. I played a dirty trick once. A year-twelve A-level girl is screwing her face up trying to work out the stresses in a poem. She looks at me in despair and says, 'How do you begin..?'

I say, you have to love the poem. They say (solidarity), is that all you've got to say? I say, let's drop it - look, I've had a bad week, my wife left me, I'm gutted, but I'm determined not to go under, I'm going to join one of these singles clubs; the only problem is, I don't know how to dance, could anyone just explain basics, just to point me in the right direction?

One or two puzzled looks (should he be getting this personal?), but they start to explain. I make out I don't get it; they get me on my feet and try to show me, I make a mess of it; they say you've got to go with the music, you have to get in tune with the music.

I say: 'Aah... Same with poetry.'

One more before I go on, by Philip Larkin, which is quite good for starters:

WIRES

The widest praries have electric fences,
For though old cattle know they must not stray
Young steers are always scenting purer water
Not here but anywhere. Beyond the wires

Leads them to blunder up against the wires
Whose muscle-shredding violence gives no quarter.
Young steers become old cattle from that day,
Electric limits to their widest senses.

Just a short poem about calves finding out the fence can give them a mild electric shock. There is a kind of rhyme but it's very bitty, and two lines end with the same word. When you look closely you realise there's actually a very definite rhyme - the lines in the second stanza rhyme in reverse to the first, like a mirror image.

That just leaves the problem of the two lines that end in 'wires'. But if you think of the calf blundering - i.e. probably bumping into it a couple of times before it realises - using 'wires' twice is the perfect choice. There's a full-stop in the middle of the first 'wires' line, too, just to underline the fact that it can't go any further. So it wanders back again, like the rhyme does.

* * * * *

Here are two poems I was impressed with, from a year eleven group using 'nature' generally as a title:

DAISIES

The sun shines - it is a good day for appearing
Above ground. A little cluster of daisies,
Innocent, snowy white and egg yellow appear
And wait, optimistically. For what?
Seven daisies. A little boy comes
And carefully counts them.

Next visitor!
The child bounds up, gurgling,
And pulls one joyfully from the turf.
A present for mommy!
She wanders away, the smiley sun
Shining from above.
Discontented, a girl wanders up and stoops,
Picking a daisy from the patch:
'He loves me, he loves me not...'
Eventually she throws the plucked daisy down
And stalks off. What do flowers know anyway?
Five left. The sun still shines.

With wagging tail and wet nose
A dog comes and paws at our beloved cluster.
Petals scatter, pollen flies, leaves fall. All is destroyed
Save for two, which bravely remain standing.
Oh poor, innocent little daisies!
The drone of the mower draws near.

Imogen Hughes

When I was typing that, I wanted to tidy it up and tone down the sentiment. But by any standard there's music in it. I love the confidence of it - the different kinds of sentences: questions, exclamations, long and short statements - I think it has a very assured and playful feel, culminating in a musical and precise last line: you could say it is a cut-off statement. There are beautiful touches everywhere - the run-on of the first/second line, for example, the 'gurgle/joyful/turf' echoes in the second verse (gurgle and joyful rhyme), the unintentional(?) pun of 'stalks off', the rich echoing sounds in lines 5 and 4 from the end, which tee up the wonderfully musical last line.

Here is the second one:

The budgie sits on his perch waiting.
Waiting for his owner to let him out.
Out into the room for a fly around.
Around in circles, round about.
About time, here she comes.
Comes to open the door to let him hop on.
On to the outstretched finger.
Finger comes out, and the budgie is gone.
Gone to the top of the curtains.
Curtains shake as he hops around.
Around about, then his head disappears.
Disappears behind the curtains look and his
        head is found.
Found peeping out at the other birds.
Birds singing, chirping and making a noise.
Noise of sparrows, robins and wrens.
Wrens and sparrows that chirp in their joys.
Joys that catch on, and the budgie hears.
Hears them and wishes he could meet them.
Them, then he could copy them, maybe he could.
Could, but sparrow, robin or wren?

Wren's too seldom, robins too. Sparrow?
Sparrow then. He could copy their chirp.

Anna Walsh

I'm full of admiration for this poem. I asked Anna why she had opted to repeat the last word of each line in that way and she said she didn't know, it just felt right, as did the full-stopping. My view is that they combine to give a tremendous sense of restriction and purposeless repetition - they cage the poem in. The last three or four lines, in which the caged bird is alerted to the wild birds outside, are more alive and muscular (I mean tighter in their use of words), more rhetorical (the kind of agitated questions and answers), and impatiently repetitive. And the last sentence is dramatic, short, full of meaning - the short 'c' alliteration also gives a sense of the caged bird's attempts at mimickry. That's my view.

But how deliberate is all this? I don't know, but I would say it was absolutely deliberate in the sense that she empathised with her subject and was rewarded with writing that fell into place with it. That is fundamental to all poetry writing, I'm sure - if you can't lose yourself for a bit while you're writing it, no matter how good you are it won't come out right.

Ted Hughes puts it this way, in 'Poetry in the Making':

'The one thing is, imagine what you are writing about. See it and live it. Do not think it up laboriously, as if you were working out mental arithmetic. Just look at it, touch it, smell it, listen to it, turn yourself into it. When you do this, the words look after themselves, like magic. If you do this you do not have to bother about commas or full-stops or that sort of thing. You do not look at the words either. You keep your eyes, your ears, your nose, your taste, your touch, your whole being on the thing you are turning into words. The minute you flinch, and take your mind off this thing, and

begin to look at the words and worry about them... then your worry goes into them and they set about killing each other. So you keep going as long as you can, then look back and see what you have written.'

This next poem was fun. I was doing a workshop with the Birmingham poet Simon Pitt, in the function room of a large pub. It worked very well - they laid on soft drinks, meals at lunch-time, and there was a garden to hand with climbing apparatus. On the last day Simon wrote the poem 'On Leading a Creative Writing Lesson in a Public House':

Today the beer stays in its barrel.
Instead: four hours of heavy thinking,
Followed by a swift outpouring
Onto paper.

Today the beer stays in its barrel
But uncorked ideas
Make us heady and merry
And ready for more.

Later, while out practising my wacky Wordsworthian walk,
I'm stopped by the poetry police.
"Excuse me, Sir - you're three poems
Over the legal limit."
The punishment is severe.
They take away my pen for a year.

© Simon Pitt

* * * * *

The best school trip I ever did came after I had read a wonderful book by David Hart, called 'Border Country: Poems in Progress'. It's an account of the first Hay-on-Wye

Festival poetry squantum - from a native American word meaning, roughly, pleasure party.

It used to be a regular event, lasting for the first weekend of the festival: five or six poets have a meal together on the Friday night and are given the title for the squantum; over the weekend, their task is to complete a poem based on the title. They meet the public in four sessions, one each morning and afternoon of the weekend, to discuss their thoughts and fragments, working towards the final Sunday session when they should be able to read the finished poem.

It's a brilliant idea which exposes the poets to an element of pressure and allows a sympathetic public to watch them squirm. People in the audience usually booked for all four sessions, and often worked on poems of their own at the same time. As far as I'm concerned it was a pleasure party, I never missed it, and it was 'Border Country' that got me hooked. Details at the back.

So I decided to give my sixth-formers some first-hand experience of the process of poetry - to them it was no more than fish on a slab, it stank. I spoke to Peter Florence, the festival director, to see if we could participate in some way, maybe as a second tier, a kind of youth tier. I wanted them to be part of it, not to simply go and be passive somewhere else instead of in the classroom. His response was brilliant: get them along, they can have the status of one poet - so when the poets stand up and offer their thoughts and fragments at each session, we can put forward one person as a representative of the group.

To cut costs, we decided to leave early on Saturday morning for the first session rather than stay over on the Friday night. So we chose a balti-house locally for the Friday night, passed on their number to the festival, and midway through the meal there was a phone-call to give us the title: it was 'Flesh'.

Hay is beautiful in spring: the whole festival is held in a series of huge summery marquees on a green site; the town is Britain's second-hand book capital, and well-pubbed. I nominated a small pub as our lunch-place and periodic meeting point, and apart from that they roamed free, in and out of Melvyn Bragg, Doris Lessing, Alan Garner, Joanna Trollope, Graham Swift, Germaine Greer... The late event for Saturday night was billed as: 'The irresistible, foul-mouthed, pencil-thin, bottle-blonde sex maniac... brassy and exuberantly offensive humour'. It was Jenny Eclair. I thought, that's what I want to take them to, just for once something with no point or educational meanings, just a bloody out and out good laugh. Afterwards, as they tumbled out, one of them said to another, 'What I liked about that was, it was so true to life...'

* * * * *

Flesh was not such an easy subject: it didn't produce a dozen little finished gems, but some hard writing got done and no-one came back with the same attitude that they went with, I'm fairly sure of that. There isn't much I'd go back to the classroom for, but I'm writing this now thinking, damn it, I'll never do that again... In fact, I know it was one of those one-offs that aren't meant to happen again - it would be wrong to hijack the event and fill it with sixth-formers anyway. We just happened to be in the right place at the right time.

I didn't get many finished pieces given to me afterwards, though as I said, there was a lot of grafting - so in this case I'll quote mine:

FLESH

My earliest memory of getting a hard-on:
A summer's day, my auntie's garden,

Her stroking my neck, that breathless trance -
My little trouser-finger doing the blood dance.

It always worked in such a manner -
The whispered heat of the barber's trimmer,
The call from below: 'Anchors away!'
I'm gone - awash in the tingling waves.

Years on, now it's you who stills me to silence
In that duvet of air lying around us;
From its furthest reaches I hear your breath
Become voice, trace the shape of your mouth.
In the cellars, blood bangs at its winery wall,
Bays for your genes - hears womanhood's call.

A cat in a window. A garden awaits him:
The skin-smells and pulses, the twang of a mating.
Sleek wetness, sun, seed drifting the air...

To make love to paper's a pathetic idea,
Like football in an empty stadium...
So fuck the poem and fuck the squantum -
Fuck every word on the printed page, fuck
The wind they make when you open their cage.

Flesh is a twosome.

A slight hangover from Jenny Eclair, maybe... It was read out at the final session, and for some weeks after the group would greet me with a wave of their little fingers.

* * * * *

In the chapter on the roundabout system (chapter 3) I was going on about how kids would take photocopies of other pupils' writing home and sometimes nick it. Well, I had a copy of 'A Modern Robin Hood' knocking around, and three years after, someone from another class picked it up and started to take an interest. Before long it had gone round, and they were pestering me to do one with them.

It turned out to be another one of the most fun classroom projects I got involved in, but you wouldn't have known that at the outset.

In the first place, it was hard to find a traditional story that hadn't been modernised and stood on its head a dozen times. Out of weariness more than anything, they settled on the three pigs - this was just done by a process of suggestion and voting. Then there was the question of whether to treat the story as a pig story, or modernise it into a people story. Then - if we change to people, there's no need to keep the house-building either, there are other ways of showing how the different personalities cope with life.

It was October, and getting tedious. I was ready to drop it. Some sixth formers came in selling remembrance poppies. We've stripped the plot back so they're lottery winners now - but can't decide what they do with the money. The sixth form sell three poppies and troop out. I know sir, they could buy a poppy factory.

Eureka. Don't ask me why. I was curious. Is there a real poppy factory? No-one knew. Maybe they're made in Korea or somewhere. Does it matter? We could invent one... There was something marginal about the idea, and I gave it the green light. I was also sick of the process, and wanted to either get started or stop.

I began by getting them to sketch out a plot in prose, and by a process of display and voting we finished the session with half a plot - enough to be going on with. In the sessions that followed, I would take a small section of the plot and tell them to write a few lines. This was a middle-range quite capable year-eight set: an average twenty-minute spell might easily produce a couple of hundred lines altogether. I would ask them to pass books round for a while, then get them to read out good lines, either their own or someone else's.

As they were read out I would single odd lines and couplets out and scribble them on the board. They got used to unreadable board work, but at the same time they were seeing a process that was genuine. I would then try and sequence what was there, and match up or adapt odd lines. They would call out suggestions. It was a bit anarchistic, and if they had have been uncooperative there is no way I could have continued. But we got off to a flier, and fairly quickly had an agreed sixteen or so lines. I wiped a hole in the board scribble and began to write them out neatly. They followed suit. Ah, peace.

When I collected the books in, I realised there were good lines that had not been read out in the lesson, and they had to be inserted later. I got into the habit of scribbling down good lines and initialling them as I went through the books, and making a few copies of my notes to share around.

I think it helped that I was excited by the process, I wasn't standing to one side guiding it towards the 'correct' outcome - I didn't have a clue where it was going to come out until we were almost there. In fact at one point it ground to halt. They got the participants to London to collect their lottery winnings, where they meet an old serviceman selling poppies and buy the lot off him for a joke - but it just wouldn't come together after that. My feeling was that we needed to go round a factory before going on, not necessarily a poppy factory, just to get some bearings. I decided to knock the writing on the head for a while and try and arrange it.

I told them this. I asked if anyone could find out whether there was a real poppy factory. By the end of lunch-break one of them handed me a phone number: he'd got the librarian to look it up for him, clever bloke.

We ended up going down to Richmond in Surrey and having an experience to remember. The British Legion Poppy Factory is a wonderful old place on the banks of the Thames; its employees are disabled ex-servicemen or their families; all the machinery is worked by hand, so, for example, it will punch out a few dozen petals at a time, but the lever that does the punching is worked by hand. There is a room where the parts are assembled into finished poppies, and here the kids had the experience of sitting and chatting with the assemblers, making some up themselves, and watching gobsmacked as someone with, say, one hand flicked all the pieces together and assembled them quicker than they could using two.

If I had set out to 'do' the First World War or whatever, I am sure what happened would not have happened. So I can only say again that all my most memorable experiences in teaching have been where I have not started out with a definite educational point in mind. I may have had an idea of what I would like to happen, but other than that I have been prepared to sit back and see how things pan out.

I hope it works after all that:

THE POPPY FACTORY TAKEOVER

Characters in this poem:

ROY - an unemployed street-performer
BOB - an unemployed newspaper deliverer from Birmingham
SUE and DERRICK (DIRK for short) and their children KIRK and SALLY - a family from Harrogate in Yorkshire

*   (all lottery winners)   *

EGBERT WITHERS - a war veteran and poppy seller
DAVE BURTON - a guide at the Royal British Legion Poppy Factory
Major JOHN HOWSON - founder of the Poppy Factory
BILL BARCLAY, IAN LINDSAY, ROY ADAMSON, COLIN BROWN, FRANK McNIFF, GERARD DU PLESSIS, SHEILA (and GRACE)

*   (Poppy Factory workers)   *

[All events in this poem are fictitious, as are descriptions of the Poppy Factory; however, members of the Poppy Factory staff referred to are genuine. We would like to thank them for an enjoyable visit to Petersham Road.]

* * * * *

Roy is working as a clown by day.
He's not so good cause the children cry.
His party act is not very clownish,
his face paint ain't bright, it's more kind of brownish.

Sue comes from Harrogate where posh people live,
her husband stays in at night as he can't drink and drive.
He got done one afternoon, he got breathalysed,
so now they watch tele till it ruins their eyes.

Down near New Street Station in the middle of Brum,
Bob lives in a flat with his sister and his mum.
He's got no job so he does a paper round,
it takes him past the Birmingham City ground.

At Sue's house they're bored. "Let's have a bash
at the lottery and win some cash."
Kirk says, "If it's after seven we've missed the deadline.....
Quick! lets have a look at the local headlines."
They all have a check - Sue give the thumbs up,
"We've got half an hour, let's pick our numbers up."

2-4-6-8
who do we appreciate,
not the king, not the queen,
but the great National Lottery machine.

Dirk, Sue, Kirk and Sally,
all sit down to have a chin waggy.
"I'm first," says Sally - "Thirty-six."
"Twenty-eight!" says Kirk, "and tootle pip!"

*Sue chews her pen and picks number seven,
and then she chooses legs eleven.
"Right!" shouts Derrick, "then to win a bomb,
I'll have 20 and 41."*

*Dirk says, "O.K. I'll get my bike..."
But Sue shakes her head: "Will you 'eckers like!
I'll ring Doris and some of the ladies,
and we'll go down together - I'll take the Mercedes.
I'll try the Esso garage down by the motorway,
you watch the kids while they play.
I'll nip in there and get the tickets
and on the way back I'll fetch some sticky cakes
    from Pritchetts."*

*Roy finished working as a clown that day,
he always did the lottery because he liked to play.
But now he's unemployed he's not very rich,
he's become a street performer, the street's his pitch.
He entertains the people with his great big feet,
then someone throws a pound down in the street.*

*Roy takes the pound off the floor,
and as soon as you know it he's at the shop door.
Not far away there's a big shopping mall,
where it is situated down by the school.
There was a little shop right in the middle,
that stood in between Asda and Lidl.
"I'll just take a Lucky Dip,
and then get home and have some kip.
36, 41 and 28,
that's the number of my garden gate.
7, good, 11 and 20,
Let's hope it wins me plenty."*

*Brummie Bob delivers the Sun
through the door of forty-one.
"Twenty-eight on Wednesbury Court,
I need to deliver a Daily Sport."
He talks to himself because he's bored,
he's saying the numbers of all the doors.
"I know! I'll use the last six houses
as a lottery ticket - there's a quid in my trousers."
He shot down to the shop like a rocket,
and back home to mum with the ticket in his pocket.*

*Saturday night, it's cold out-side,
the teles are on - Bruce Forsyth,
Generation Game, or maybe it's Cilla,
Doris from Durham is choosing a fella.
At last she goes for number 3.
"Who's going to choose?" "The girl!" says Norm.
"A holiday for two in Benidorm!"
"Wow, fantastic!" They all go bananas,
too hot to even wear pyjamas.
"Don't forget to come back chuks..."
But soon it's the lottery: mega-bucks
for some lucky devil sitting at home.
Roy the clown is all on his own
watching the Simpsons and picking his warts.*

"Roy," says Bart, "Eat my shorts!"
"What an omen," thinks Roy the clown,
"I'm glad I put my numbers down.
Fancy Bart Simpson saying that!"
He's not interested in Andrea's love rat,
or Cilla and her wedding hat.
He's not interested in Blind Date no more,
he's looking for his ticket in the kitchen drawer.
Now the lottery draw begins,
and Lancelot begins to spin.....

"Mom, all our numbers are in one line."
"We've won, we've won! The money's mine."
"Oh my god I don't believe it!
Give me that ticket, don't you leave it
lying around, we daren't lose it
or when we claim we'll never prove it."
"Mum, help, I've dropped my chips."
"Oh, who cares, we're stinking rich!"

Bob opens his window and starts to shout,
"I've won, I've won!" - his head's sticking
    out -
then he's kissing his mum and hugging
    the dog,
and ringing his Boss to chuck in his job!

Roy the clown spat out his tea,
he didn't give a damn. "Yippee!!"
he bellowed, and danced and jigged
    with his cat,
"Mystic Meg predicted that!"
"That's this weeks lottery
    over viewers,
I bet it's left you all in tears.
Never mind, there's always
    next week's..."
But our friends can't hear
    above the shrieks.

*Sue and Derrick and Bob and Roy,
are all shouting and jumping for joy.
"We've won! we've won! How do we claim?"
"Its on the back - ring Tolpits Lane
in Watford, or send them the ticket."
"You must be joking, the postman will nick it."*

*They can't get rid of their silly smiles,
they're down to London like heat-seeking missiles.
Bob's gone down to New Street Station,
he's off to take up his invitation.*

*Roy goes down by minibus,
driven by his best friend Russ.
They just get as far as Camelot Headquarters,
when - "Dear oh dear, the bus that brought us
has broken down ...." But to their surprise
they manage to get the barrier to rise.*

*Bob and Anthea hand over the cheque.
"Nine million pounds! Flippin 'eck,
I'm so happy I'm over the moon ...."
"Shut up Derrick, you stupid baboon.
Let's go out and spend, spend,spend,
until we go right round the bend."*

*So Sue, Derrick, Kirk and Sally
all treat themselves to the Royal Ballet.
But Roy and Bob catch a bus,
"I can't believe it's happened to us,
I'm going to take my share of the cash
and buy a business with the stash.
Let's go to the pub and have a round,
there's one over there by the under-ground."
"I want a holiday in Jamaica ...."
"I want to be a poppy maker -
look at that old bloke over there,
selling poppies - he's got no hair,
I bet he's been stood there selling all day,
nobody's buying from his tray.*

Why is he standing by the road?
He won't flog them there - I could sell a load.
Lets go over and have a chat ......"
"No, what's the point you silly prat."

But Bob's on his way - he's half way across,
"Good afternoon, how's trade then boss?"
"Get down, GET DOWN!!! Mortars - look out!"
He's short of the full loaf without a doubt.
It turns out his name is Egbert Withers,
and the reason he's got a bad case of dithers
is, his dad was shell-shocked in the war,
poor old sod, he was shot and all.
Not in the last war, I mean World War One -
in World War Two a hundred pound bomb
blew up half the houses in his street,
and just missed his by thirty feet.

He's had life a little to bit rough,
standing there with his old dog Wuff.
There's not much work for a war veteran
so selling poppies is better than
nothing. Roy buys twenty and puts them in his hat,
"Let's invest in poppies, I like the sound of that!"

Just then the others come back from the ballet,
they've had a good time and are feeling quite pally
so they join the rest. They like the idea,
Dirk's always fancied an unusual career.
Bert says they're made by the Royal British Legion,
the factory is somewhere in the West London region.

"It was started up by Major Howson,
now we make poppies by the thousand."

"Egbert, lets go now to your factory..."
"How will we get there?" "I'll phone a taxi!"

But they hire a Limo to take them there,
Bob's reading the map - what a scare.

"Take a right, now a left,
watch out missus! Flippin 'eck!"
At last they make it to Richmond, Surrey,
a good job they weren't in too much of a hurry
and the car was comfy, they weren't too cramped.
Egbert leads them up the ramp,
walking slowly, avoiding the mines,
shouting, "Gerry's coming behind!!!"

They huddle up, trying to get through the door,
and then stand in silence looking at memories of the war.
It all goes quiet, their tongues are stilled:
sad letters and photos of men who were killed
are displayed on the walls. Their guide Dave Burton,
looking proud with his British Legion shirt on,
says a lovely poem from days of old.
It seemed so nice the way it was told,
they all thought it was really nice,
especially the first few lines:

"In Flanders Fields the poppies blow
Between the crosses, row on row
That mark our place: and in the sky
The larks still bravely singing fly
Scarce heard amid the guns below.

We are the dead. Short days ago
We lived, felt dawn, saw sunset glow,
Loved and were loved, and now we lie
In Flanders Fields.

Take up our quarrel with the foe:
To you from falling hands we throw
The torch: be yours to hold it high.
If ye break faith with those who died
We shall not sleep, though poppies grow
In Flanders Fields."

※　　※　　※　　※　　※

All the fun of the day is forgotten,
suddenly our friends are feeling rotten.
But Dave cheers them up - he takes them round
the flats and the factory and outside grounds,
once owned by Lord Cardigan of the Light Brigade,
one of his grandsons had all of his pets laid
to rest in the grounds - dogs, monkeys and cats -
they had to rebury them when they built the flats
for the workers, who are mostly disabled....
The first ones were the people George Howson was able
to help find jobs when the war was over
and the troop ships brought them back from Dover,
back from Ypres or Essex Farm
in Flanders, minus a leg or an arm.

There were plenty of people there
who made up the poppies with lots of care:
Bill the fix-it who mends the machines,
and Ian Lindsay who makes them gleam,
Roy Adamson, he does the wreaths,
and Colin Brown, who got an M.B.E.
They met Frank NcNiff, who was a stuntman
in "The Italian Job" - that film whose frontman
was Michael Caine. Frank lent his van so that
it could be blown up ("not a lot of people know that").
They met a long-bearded chap, Gerard du Plessis
who makes little wooden remembrance crosses,
and Sheila, with her blind-dog Grace.....

There were peeling window-frames around the place
and here and there it was rusty and cold -
the factory was getting old.
"I want to help," says Sue out loud,
"let's do the place up good and proud!"
Our friends have a talk with the factory clerk:
Bob says, "This place needs some major work,
it's a multi-million dollar disaster."
He's thinking he could be the master

of renovations. "Like Challenge Aneka; Sporty Spice,
we could invite her to open it, that would be nice!"
"Yeh - let's get a band like Eternal or Spice Girls,
they would give us loads of thrills -
when we're finished they could sing and dance
oh, come on mister, give us a chance......."

"I'm sorry kids, I know you want her,
I just don't think I have the power."
"Then why can't we get Dame Edna
even though she is a fella?"

Dirk wants so much to be a director,
he has a plan. He calls the rest over.
He quietly whispers in their ears,
"Let's get machines to replace the workers!"
"We can't just let the workers go,"
says Roy, "let's hire another thirty or so.
Besides, where would we get such clever machines?"

"We've got enough money, we can buy the things
then send this lot to a caring home
surrounded with pretty garden gnomes,
put the machines in to replace them,
and then we won't have to pay' em."
"No - if we're going to become directors
let some more disabled work with us;

we've got lots of money, so here's the idea
we'll employ more disabled, they're great! Look at Sheila,
she can work as fast as the others,
we'll even take their sisters and brothers.
Don't stop now, let's keep it going -
carry on making," says Sue, "I'll do sewing -
we'll use silk again, instead of plastic,
and get it back how it was in the factory."

So they all went back and made enquiries
and put a few dates in their diaries.

*The plan is set, it's all worked out...
What will happen to the poppy factory now?*

Old Egbert took them round the factory
to look again and have a chit-chatty.
They walked around, watching the staff
and talking to them - they had a good laugh.
Sue stood and watched the big conveyors
stamping out the different layers -
how easy and fast they could make a poppy.
Roy was surprised at the quality.
The man who made wreaths was sat by the front door
Chucking the finished ones on the floor,
he was talking to Bob but looking at Sally,
when he saw her it made him happy.
Bob looked around and saw her there
sitting on a black wooden chair,
he looks back to where they were threading the stems
and suddenly shouts, "I can see the Thames!
See for yourself Sally, just down there....
How long have those iron windows been here?
Double glazing we ought to use -
keeps everyone warm without spoiling the views."

Sue wandered through rooms: to her surprise
they were making poppies as fast as her eyes
could see - she came over asking questions
and paying them a lot of attention.
It was nice to see them on their stools
making poppies with special tools.
They said if they were going to be directors
their first thought was to renew the detectors
and cameras and all the other alarms
that make life easy if you're without legs or arms.
Then it needed a coat of paint,
they voted to give it a feminine tint,
that would look really ace.
"We could have a bit of

music in this place...."
"Come on!" says Bob -
he thinks he's the leader,
"Look you've missed a
spot over there.
Don't just lay around
doing nothing,
get on your feet and help
with the painting."
They soon complete their
factory dream,
most of the walls are
painted cream.
The factory is now
looking O.K.,
ready to start
back at work
the next day.

Roy is standing at a
wreath-maker's bench,
when something is stuck -
he gives it a wrench.
There's a bang. Everyone
turns to stare.
There are flowers and bits of wire everywhere.
Suddenly he remembers when he was a clown
a trick like that would bring the house down.
"Invent new cool poppies, brilliant idea,"
he says to himself - the others can't hear.
"I've just had a break-through!" he shouts down the hall,
"Novelty poppies, they'd be really cool!"
And soon he's up to his old tricks again,
making squirty poppies and soaking the men,
designing new poppies that make you look foolish,
exploding wreaths for the particularly stupid,
Jack-in-the-Box ones for little toddlers
and special old-fashioned ones for veterans and codgers.

"They'll be great!" says Roy, "they'll sell for sure,
we'll get more dosh for them who fought in the war!"
But Sue is nervous: "Won't they be harmful?"
"Don't worry," says Bob, "they'll just frighten the rascals."

The very next morning Her Majesty the Queen
received a large parcel. "Oh good, the wreaths have been
delivered." She opens the box - BOOM BOOM!
There are pieces of palace all over the room.
"Help! I think I have lost an eye!"
Her minders rush in. "It's the I.R.A.
Cover the exits as soon as possible,
we must get Her Majesty straight to hospital!"
Her solicitor can barely hear as she yells....
"When we find who's responsible we'll sue them hell!"
Now you know why you can only see
one side of her face on the stamp, thanks to Roy.
Reporters came from every direction
and bombarded Roy, Bob, Sue and Dirk with questions.
"You are responsible for the queen wounding an eye...."
"But you don't understand," Sue screamed, "it was Roy."

But the damage is done, things are all going wrong,
The Sun's headline calls it "The Poppy Factory Pong".
People all over have started a boycott,
they won't buy the poppies. "We're left with the lot,"
groans Sue, "and in addition
the general public are starting a petition -
and if that's not all, the Royal Palace
is suing us for injury with malice.
By the time we've finished with all the lawyers
there'll be no money left to be employers."

That same night, Roy had a dream
about Major Howson and his poppy theme,
and at that moment a ghost appeared:
it was Major Howson - he had a beard.

"Wrap me up in my tarpaulin jacket,"
said his shaky voice. There was a racket
of things vibrating - it haunted Roy,
he imagined he was a little boy,
he used to have dreams every night
and then remember them
in the light.

"You have ruined the workers' lives,"
said Howson, who was supposed to have died.
When he heard the Major, Roy suddenly saw
poppies should just be made for the victims of war.
"So wake up now and tell your chums
it'll go alright, I'll push you along...."
He moves across the landing and flicks the light on
while recalling the words of Major Howson.
He jumped down the stairs and got ready for work,
he just couldn't wait to tell Bob, Sue and Dirk....

*Sue was complaining about the mess -
she couldn't even sit down at her desk.
Bob and Dirk were weeping loudly -
no more mansions, or papping car horns proudly,
the factory was down the drain
like a spider washed away by rain.
"I had a dream, Major Howson appeared!"
"Don't be silly," says Sue, "he's been dead for years."
"I suppose you're right, I'm just being silly....."
"No you're not - there might be something in it,
but how can we sell them when everyone's quit?*

*So many poppies and very few buyers,
the public think we're cheats and liars.
Besides, Asda wanted to expand,
they've made an offer for the land.
The diggers are coming to demolish the lot
and turn it into a vacant plot.....
W-W-What's that moving over there?"*

*"Oh my god, it's haunted here!
Let's get out before they come....."
And off they shot, they were done and gone.*

*The factory was never razed to the ground
because the rumour got around
that it was haunted, and all the workmen
dropped their things and turned and ran.
It stayed that way for nearly a decade
and all that time no poppies were made,
until one day Howson's grandson stepped in
and helped sort the trouble with Roy and the Queen.
"Now how can we get this show back on the track?
The public want their poppies back."*

*Roy says: "There's no money left to make 'em,
every single penny has been taken...."
But out of nowhere Egbert appears:
"I've got a stash saved under the stairs."*

"Where, Egbert, you cunning old fool?"
"Over here, beneath my stool
there's a trap-door to a secret cellar -
you didn't know that, did you young fella?"
He twisted a rusty silver key
into a lock, and suddenly
they went down a staircase which was really old
and turned on the light - there were bold
and colourful red poppies everywhere.

Years ago he had hidden them there
just as a little safety precaution
in case of enemy aircraft action,
and there they were, all fine and silky.
Egbert Withers had saved the factory.

They got all the workers sorted out,
they didn't have to get rid of nowt
except themselves - it was time to go...

Roy now works in a cabaret show
somewhere up north. Bob and his mum
went back to live in their flat in Brum.
But it wasn't just Egbert who
stashed things away -
Dirk had enough cash
for a little cafe
which he runs with
Sue and Kirk and Sally
on a tropical beach in
Hawaii.
And even though it's
hot and sweaty...
they never forget to
wear a poppy.

THE END

Q. What's it like being a writer?

A. What's it like being a reader? It's not like anything, you just get on and do it.

Q. Where do you get your ideas from?

A. The poppy factory was a nice one - just when you're ready to give up, you see or hear something completely irrelevant and maybe in desperation you grab it. I like ideas like that, you don't 'get' them, they kind of get you. Think of it this way: you know what it's like when someone chucks a snowball at you and you try and catch it to chuck back because there's no decent snow where you are. It's pointless - it only bursts in your face, or you end up catching the one with doggy-do in. The sensible thing would be to duck. But it's more fun to catch.

Q. How long does it take to write a book?

A. The Poppy Factory Takeover took from about October to the following July, one lesson out of every three, take off holidays and exams. I would say about twenty-five to thirty lessons, plus sifting through the lines after each lesson, plus the trip, reading up all the material they gave us at the Poppy Factory, and Charlotte Sztybel's time for typing, losing it and retyping. About sixty hours - the time it would take to fly round the world.

Q. Do you like writing?

A. I've always thought it would be brilliant to write a sit-com with someone else - shut yourself in a room, have a laugh, and come out a couple of hours later with a belter of an idea like Men Behaving Badly three-quarters written. I eventually got together with a bloke who wrote some very funny football stuff for the Kiddy Harriers fanzine, and we did a few episodes of a non-league football sit-com. But when it came down to it, we did most of the writing separately and just compared notes from time to time over a pint, so it wasn't all that different really.

Q. How do you get a book published?

A. If you're into writing poetry, you have to keep sending stuff off to the small poetry magazines, and various competitions - if you get lucky you eventually build up a bit of a c.v. and get noticed, or might be able to draw attention to yourself. Forms for most competitions can be found in libraries if you check regularly. All sorts of useful addresses can be found in the poetry section of the Writers' & Artists' Yearbook which is in most reference libraries. You are unlikely to be any good unless you read poetry as well as writing it. The Poetry Book Society would be a good starting place if you want to get genned up quickly (0208 870 8403). Also, if there are any literature festivals near you, go to the poetry readings, buy the books and get the poets to sign them. Get yourself hooked.

Q. Who is your favourite author?

A. David Hart. 'Border Country' for the most fascinating book about writing poetry you will find, and 'setting the poem to words' for the poems. Don't you dread it when a really good friend comes up and asks you to read something they've spent ages writing, what do you tell them if it's crap? I felt like that with 'setting the poem to words' - I didn't know David's poems very well and dreaded not liking the book. But thank god they're brilliant, very off-beat and deep. He would never call himself a children's poet, but here's one I've read in a couple of schools:

With Nansen

*When I was ten I went in search of the north pole
   with Nansen.
From the New Siberian Islands where we'd left the
   Fram locked
in ice we walked into white light. Nourished by
   broken biscuits*

and Wagon Wheels and spied on by nosy seals and
 furtive foxes
we hacked through homework with picks and
 looked forward
to football on Saturday, hoping for floods and sunshine
 to dry out

the boggy field. On the first Sunday in the month
 we paraded
the colours into church and sang plaintive and
 patriotic hymns,
and when we first tried to kill a whale hurling our
 spears after

several days in wait we finished up feeling stupid
 and cold,
exhausted and longing for some steamed chocolate
 pudding
and seconds in the playground through the kitchen
 window,

    then a bear protecting her cubs growled at us,
    then we tried to send a telepathic message
    back to Mr Thomas to say we were doing our best,
    then we played marbles in the tracks of lemmings,
    then we lit a fire and baked potatoes in its embers,
    then we bet each other toffees we couldn't turn
    somersaults on a moving ice-flow,
    then we buried a grass-snake under snow and moss
    and over its poor head placed a twig cross,
    then I dreamed I met the abominable snowman
    and was pleased to wake to the sound of gulls,
    then I made snow-castles with my bucket and spade,
    then Nansen received a telegram from the King
    brought by a strong and courageous pigeon,
    then we reached 86° 14' and after the flag was planted
    we wintered there in Franz Joseph Land,

*and when me and Nansen got home again from
   our expedition,
in front of the whole school assembly we received
   our book token,
and after shaking hands warmly we went our
   separate ways.*

© David Hart

CHAPTER 8

The subjective mind

In schools, the arts subjects go undefended. Just so we know where we are, I'm talking about English/creative writing as well as music, dance, drama, art. In football terms, those subjects form the Conference (the division outside the main leagues): they usually take place in rooms stuck around the margins of the school, or in rooms that have to be given up when exams are on - at other times people walk through to get to somewhere else in the building. Creative writing gets protection by being part of English - but that's because English departments make sure the school knows they are about grammar and Shakespeare, and only do poncey writing now and again so the kids can experience what it must have felt like to be Tennyson.

Arts subjects are set at the bottom of options columns, and the boffs are discouraged from choosing them. They cause problems with the timetable because of theatre trips, concerts and performances. They are patronised by core subjects (Premier Div.) and other academic subjects such as geog., history, business studies, law (Divs. 1 and 2).

Arts teachers justify themselves in terms of giving children confidence, using their imagination, working through social situations, learning to appreciate beauty, coming to terms with their feelings. What cobblers. If you want to get confidence or work through social situations go to a youth club. Why should it take bites out of the timetable? And what about the people who have confidence, can manage social situations, and are in touch with their feelings already?

No wonder arts education gets shoved aside. Art is about precision as much as science or maths is about precision - they are both after perfect precision, and never find it: they are always pushing the frontiers. But art is about the subjective mind, about the fact that the mind is fed by blood and joined to the nervous system. The subjective mind is a core subject, it's at the core of the human body, where the soul is.

It is also about prejudice, love and hate, anger, boredom, humour, obsession, heroism, paranoia, devotion, suicide and all other unstable forms of expression. It's worth getting to know and it's a dangerous thing not to know.

Academic subjects train you to leave your subjective mind out of it and look at life objectively - trust only what you can see and measure, never trust a hunch. Good - the objective is a good discipline, it puts men into space. But if you can only function with the objective mind you're doomed to become a jobsworth, a pen-pusher, clip-board merchant, obedient, over-regulated, and without flair. We all know people who have a huge store of knowledge at their disposal, but still have the mind of a pea: an undeveloped mind, inexperienced, unknowing in the wider sense - i.e. unknowing of the blood and nerve systems that make it human - too soft to know how to use its baggage of learning.

Right. I'm going to try and nail this point, so if you're not into theory, skip.

I want to look at what top people in the core subjects really think about the subjective mind. I am raiding Arthur Koestler's 'The Act of Creation' for this section. There are other books which deal with the interplay of the objective/subjective mind that I've come across: Peter Abbs' 'Root and Blossom', for example, if I remember rightly - but Koestler is the bible. Most of what I am using comes from part two, which sets down the thoughts of scientists, mathematicians, philosophers on the nature of their discoveries and their work.

There are three areas I am interested in:

1. Knowing your mind.

Working with the subjective mind involves the process of coming to know your own mind - of coming to trust your own thoughts and judgements even when you can't fully understand them. It involves self-belief.

The Earl of Shaftesbury put it this way: *'One would think there was nothing easier for us, than to know our own minds... But our thoughts have generally such an obscure implicit language, that it is the hardest thing in the world to make them speak out distinctly.'*

If you ever get to the point of scientific discovery you are likely to be influenced more by intuition rather than direct reason, and if you are unpractised in dealing with intuition, if you mistrust it, you will suppress it before it can offer its insights:

'One phenomenon is certain and I can vouch for its absolute certainty: the sudden and immediate appearance of a solution at the very moment of sudden awakening. On being very abruptly awakened by an external noise, a solution long searched for appeared to me at once without the slightest instance of reflection on my part - the fact was remarkable enough to have struck me unforgettably - and in a quite different direction from any of those which I had previously tried to follow.' (Jacques Hadamard)

'As a sudden flash of light, the enigma was solved... For my part I am unable to name the nature of the thread which connected what I previously knew with that which made my success possible.' (Karl Friedrich Gauss)

(Gauss again): *'I have had my solutions for a long time, but I do not yet know how I am to arrive at them.'*

These are people who have learned to be at ease with their subjective mind; they are prepared to listen to its first, nonlogical signals, though these may conflict with the accepted rules and understandings. I have often thought that the creative mind is a rule-breaker, that is one of the reasons why creativity is mistrusted - but by exercising the creative mind, by keeping it toned-up, fit, in condition, it becomes skilful at free-wheeling without crashing into orthodoxy: it learns how to conduct itself.

'Those who refuse to go beyond fact rarely get as far as fact; and anyone who has studied the history of science knows that almost every step therein has been made by... the invention of a hypothesis which, though verifiable, often had little foundation to start with...' (T.H. Huxley)

'Most so-called 'intuitive' discoveries are... associations suddenly made in the unconscious mind.' (Otto Loewi)

Discovery, the unearthing of new knowledge, is a product of the interplay between the conscious and the subliminal mind. The arts chaperone the subliminal, they interact with unknown areas of existence and, finally, give them meaning - by finally, I mean that the process of engaging the unconscious is indirect, it is not rational or analytical, it is a process of coupling, a process of play:

'The words or the language, as they are written or spoken, do not seem to play any role in my mechanism of thought. The physical entities which seem to serve as elements in thought are certain signs and more or less clear images which can be 'voluntarily' reproduced and combined...

Taken from a psychological viewpoint, this combinatory play seems to be the essential feature in productive thought - before there is any connection with logical construction in words or other kinds of signs which can be communicated to others.

The above-mentioned elements are, in any case, of visual and some of muscular type. Conventional words or other signs have to be sought for laboriously only in a secondary stage, when the mentioned associative play is sufficiently established and can be reproduced at will.

According to what has been said, the play with the mentioned elements is aimed to be analogous to certain logical connections one is searching for.' (Einstein)

I have no reading to support this, but my feeling is that the less concrete art-forms such as music and dance engage the unconscious, or the spirit, at the most primary level, and the more concrete ones like writing and painting bring it to the surface, to the point where we can recognise it and I suppose know it rationally. When I put it like that I feel a little uneasy - the metaphor I am using loosely is that of hooking a fish - but I suppose that is what human progress and civilisation is about: we take the wild element of ourselves, colonise it, study it, and at last come to know it utterly. And English is the last stage of that play at the shoreline of self and spirit - it gives expression, feels for the words, feels for meanings.

This is why precision is so central to artistic expression - without it we catch the wild things and turn them into dancing bears. We engage the inner self in a slovenly domineering way, neutering it, and encouraging those who mistrust it to see it as cheap entertainment, and patronise it.

I will finish with this statement from Nietzsche:

'Consciousness is the last and latest development of the organic, and is consequently the most unfinished and the least powerful of these developments. Every extension of knowledge arises from making conscious the unconsciousness. The great basic activity is unconscious. For it is narrow, this room of human consciousness.'

The rationalist will say, yes, but scholarship is about discipline, you can't have kids wallowing around with all kinds of notions and prejudices not making any kind of distinction between them - it's indulgent, permissive, makes our job harder, etcetera.

At the same time, they know culture is important in life and has to be given house room - so arts subjects are pressured to see themselves as the organ-grinder's monkey, their job is basically to keep the artwork on the walls changed, provide the music and poems for open evenings. We have to show them that this is a big mistake.

If I could put all this more simply, I would say that art is precisely about wallowing around in notions and prejudices. I always do it. If the Aztecs had taken some of their prejudices a bit more seriously they'd still be around. What you don't do is build a philosophy of life on a prejudice without wallowing around in it first.

2. Metaphor.

We come to new fields of discovery through comparison, parallel, analogy, what Einstein called 'associative play'. Koestler says, 'analogy, in logic, means a process of "reasoning from parallel causes"': in English terms, we are talking about metaphor.

This is Henri Poincare, putting mathematical discovery in terms of combinations of ideas which are conducted by the unconscious or subliminal self:

'Figure the future elements of our combinations as something like the hooked atoms of Epicurus. During the complete repose of the mind, these atoms are motionless, they are, so to speak, hooked to the wall. During a period of apparent rest and unconscious work, certain of them are detached from the wall and put in motion. They flash in every direction through the space... as would, for example, a swarm of gnats, or if you prefer a more learned comparison, like the molecules of gas in the kinematic theory of gases. Then their mutual impacts may produce new combinations.'

Francis Galton:

'When I am engaged in trying to think anything out, the process of doing so appears to me to be this: the ideas that lie at any moment within my full consciousness seem to attract of their own accord the most appropriate out of a number of other ideas that are lying close at hand, but imperfectly within the range of my consciousness. There seems to be a presence-chamber in my mind where full consciousness holds court, and where two or three ideas are at the same time in audience, and an ante-chamber full of more or less allied ideas, which is situated just beyond the ken of consciousness. Out of this ante-chamber the ideas most nearly allied to those in the presence-chamber appear to be summoned in a mechanically logical way, and to have their turn of audience.'

These passages not only emphasise the importance of metaphor - harmonising combinations of images to clarify thought - but reading them, you can't help noticing the fact that they rely totally on metaphor themselves to make sense. They are logical thoughts and expositions, but they are only possible through metaphor.

The metaphors (more often similes, i.e., distanced by the word 'like') we piece together logically are usually dull and only marginally appropriate; intuitive metaphor is often only clear, sometimes startlingly so, after it has been spoken: 'I never think - my thoughts think for me' - Lamartine. By developing the subjective mind, we learn to trust the metaphors it gives up, not dismiss them.

For me, there is nothing to touch the poet's trust of metaphor - when you are at one with metaphor, it reveals more and more of its foliage. But we have to remember we are not just dealing with nice turns of phrase here, we're dealing with the primary unit of human progress:

'The winding progress of any branch of experimental science is made up essentially by a relatively small number of original inquiries, which may be widely separated, followed,

as a rule, by a very large number of routine inquiries. The most important feature of original experimental thinking is the discovery of overlap and agreement where formerly only isolation and difference were recognised... An original mind, never wholly contained in any one conventionally enclosed field of interest... seizes upon the possibility that there may be some unsuspected overlap, takes the risk whether there is or not, and gives the old subject matter a new look. Routine starts again...' (Frederick Bartlett)

3. Beauty.

What has beauty got to do with learning or intelligence? Ah, yes, of course, environment: you get more from the pupils if they work in a nice atmosphere - couple of repro Matisses on the walls, landscaped area in the corner of the playground, that sort of thing.

Nothing is more marginalised, no urge is fed more indigestible scraps than the human urge to see and recognise beauty.

This a quote from Keats I was made to learn in the sixth-form when at school. I always hated it:

*"Beauty is truth, truth beauty," - that is all
Ye know on earth, and all ye need to know.*

But its meaning came home to me when I was thinking, not casually but deeply, out of despair, by what absolute criteria - not just a religious one - we could judge right or wrong, good or bad. And I believe the ultimate answer to that is that we can only learn to trust our human instinct - not go with our first whim, but through a process of on-going engagement with the subjective mind - we can learn to know and trust, if you like, chaos. We learn to accept the inexplicable beauty of life itself. Beauty and truth connect in the word 'integrity', which has to do with being integral to the whole that a thing exists in, so it harmonises and has grace. And that is ultimately what guides explorers in all fields of learning and all disciplines.

'Every scientific discovery gives rise, in the connoisseur, to the experience of beauty, because the solution of the problem creates harmony out of dissonance; and vice versa, the experience of beauty can occur only if the intellect endorses the validity of the operation - whatever its nature - designed to elicit the experience. A mathematical theorem by Poincare, and a virgin by Botticelli, do not betray any similarity between motivations or aspirations of their respective creators; the first seemed to aim at 'truth', the second at 'beauty'.* But it was Poincare who wrote that what guided him in his unconscious gropings towards the 'happy combinations' which yield new discoveries was "the feeling of mathematical beauty, of the harmony of number, of forms, of geometric elegance. This is a true aesthetic feeling that all mathematicians know." The greatest among mathematicians and scientists, from Kempler to Einstein, made similar confessions. "Beauty is the first test; there is no permanent place in the world for ugly mathematics", wrote G.H. Hardy in his classic, 'A Mathematician's Apology'. Jacques Hadamard drew the final conclusion: "The sense of beauty as a 'drive' for discovery in our mathematical field, seems to be almost the only one."*   (Koestler)

[* I have altered the sequence in this sentence because I think there is a printer's error - it's from p329 'The Act of Creation' Penguin Arkana, 1989.]

'Schrodinger got his equation by pure thought, looking for some beautiful generalisation... and not by keeping close to the experimental developments of the subject... I think there is a moral to this story, namely that it is more important to have beauty in one's equations than to have them fit experiment... It seems that if one is working from the point *of view of getting beauty in one's equations, and if one has really a sound insight, one is on a sure line of progress.'* (Paul Dirac)

* * * * *

I have exaggerated the prejudice against arts in education, of course. Many non-arts teachers defend the arts more strongly than the people who teach them, and practise them as well. But when curriculum time and capitation money are dished out, it's subjective subjects that get the small share.

You know how academic teachers sometimes patronise the arts by encouraging them? It's good for you to go to the theatre and read poetry, makes you a more rounded person (helps you get through interviews). Maybe arts teachers could reverse this and say, children, you must work hard at your maths/physics as well you know, learn to love rational thought, take it into yourself, integrate it, otherwise you'll never be a fully rounded artist. You'll go through life writing slop.

I will finish this section by saying that, surprisingly, I have always found English a very difficult subject to teach. For example, I've noticed that whatever you do, pupils often make the same mistakes in year ten that they were making in year seven. Don't you ever teach them to spell, exasperated colleagues would say (although they often couldn't spell themselves - have a look at this letter of congratulation that was sent round the staffroom by a head I once worked with: *'Dear Collegues, For the entire week of Ofsted and the numerous weeks of preparation before that I have been filled with admiration at your talent and your tireless energies. The feedback we have been given is of a Christian learning community who's values are lived out. The children without exception rose to support us magnificently. That support is borne of love and respect for the Staff who dedicate so much to their students. Well done!'* I make that three clangers in eight lines) - do you actually make them learn spellings? I'd say, yes: they do well in the test, then spell carelessly in their writing, as before - or they just do badly in the test. They'd say, do you actually teach punctuation and grammar? I'd say, yes, regularly: they do the examples well, and then carry on writing carelessly, as before - or, they continually get the examples wrong even when the point is reiterated. They erect a resistance.

They'd say, do you read round the class with them? I'd say, yes, I have regular lessons of individual and class reading: in class reading lessons I get pupils to read out loud, on a voluntary basis. They'd say, shouldn't you make them do it? I'd say, that makes the experience so excruciating for the reader and listener it's counter-productive. They'd say, shouldn't you be teaching instead of doing reading lessons.

My view is that English is almost impossible to teach because it's afraid to admit it's an arts subject, in case it loses status to the other subjects. It claims to be an academic subject, but that's not how other teachers see it. They see it as a 'tool' subject, i.e., training you up in the tool skills of reading and writing (but not very well) so you can get on and do their subjects more effectively; maybe with a bit of culture chucked in. So English obliges by constantly setting exercises designed to 'refresh' the kids' memories on basic tool skills over and over again - the kids are sick to the eyeballs with it before they've left infants.

If English departments had the same consideration as science departments - i.e., the equivalent of lab assistants, their own photocopier (a decent one) and capitation money that takes into account they are producing things, then you could have good pieces typed and photocopied daily and kept in hand for publications. Kids would get used to the idea that their work was being taken seriously and printed rather than set as material for endless correction, grading and binning - kids don't trust grades anyway ('Was it really worth that sir, or are you just trying to encourage me?').

When you write for the real world, proper standards apply. A teacher either goes in and says, right, apostrophe today, who can tell me the rule, good, now do these, finish for homework; or they could say, who proof-read this, you've got the bloody apostrophe wrong, it can't be printed like that - Sir, I don't know how you... - Then sit down and listen.

If you serve lettuce with slugs on, people won't use your café.

* * * * *

Q. What's it like being a writer?

A. It's O.K. as long as you remember that's who you are. If you forget that, things can get more difficult. Recently, I've spent so much time going round schools telling kids what fun it is to be a writer and giving them witty smart-arsed answers to their questions, that I'm actually quite afraid to get started on my next book, and the vague story-line I've got in my head doesn't interest me. I've let myself get out of shape.

Q. Where do you get your ideas from?

A. Everyone thinks of ideas for how to make money. Ideas aren't hard, they're like fish, you just have to throw out a line and wait for a bit. People are always saying, 'Someone ought to buy that place and turn it into a ──-, they'd make a fortune.' Then maybe it does get bought and turned into whatever and the person says, 'There, I told you - didn't I say it would make the perfect place for a ──-? I told you it would.'

So why didn't they do it instead of waiting for someone else to? I reckon it's because they couldn't be arsed - there's too much work involved, too much hassle, too much risk, and anyway, they're not all that bothered about being rich, really. They make good Monopoly players, imagining they could have done it for real if they'd wanted. I think it's roughly the same with books. Most authors have had the experience of people coming up to them and saying, 'I could write a book if I wasn't so busy all the time.' Ah well, tough. If you're so bloody busy you'll never know.

Q. How long does it take to write a book?

A. As long as you want. A story is a huge great never-ending sausage, you have to choose where you're going to chop it to make a beginning, and where you want to chop for the end. There's no set place. Even if the main character dies, the story doesn't end - it carries on without him. And it existed before he was born, he just wasn't in it, that's all. So you can make it as long or short as you want, depending where you chop it. But don't get carried away: William Golding chopped the beginning and end of a story out of the four minutes it takes a man to drown - it's still a couple of hundred pages long, though.

Q. Do you like writing?

A. When I was working in a school the big thing was, whether you made a good 'team player' - i.e, do you mind people above you taking credit for what you do and covering for them when there's a cock-up. I used to think, O.K., I'm a team player, now show me the team - because the people who made most fuss about team players were invariably out for themselves. When I write, if I mess up it's my fault and if something goes well it's my credit, and I like it that way.

Q. How do you get a book published?

A. Just out of curiosity, I put my computer on sleep just now and went down to count all my rejection letters. It was quite a long sleep: I have four hundred and twenty-two.

Ignore the rejection slips, they don't matter - unless you get one that says something particular about your writing. If they were bothered to write a personal reply, you can't be that bad. Read it carefully and ask yourself if there's anything it says that can help you alter your approach. I think of publishers' replies like sperm, it only needs one in a million to get through, and you've got a little baby.

Q. Who is your favourite writer?

A. I love Ursula Le Guin's 'Earthsea' trilogy. I came across it when I had to split up three year-nine boys who were fighting over a copy (I thought, must be a decent book, so I took it off them and read it myself). She added a fourth book, 'Tehanu' about twenty years later, I think partly to raise the female profile, but I didn't get round to that one; I'm talking about the original 'Wizard of Earthsea', 'Tombs of Atuan', 'Farthest Shore'. An amazing read.

CHAPTER 9

Magazines

The printed word has always had a kind of magic for me, I could happily work in a printer's or even a small reprographics room for the rest of my life. It turns me on. I will do anything to get my hands on a copier when the need arises - it's almost above morality, there's a kind of imperative when I have to get something printed off, and I'll stop at nothing to do so.

The reprographics ladies where I worked used to spot me from distance and go on alert. 'Come on, what are you up to now?' was their typical greeting. Once, feeling they had my measure, one of them crowed to the room, 'We know all your little tricks, don't we - you can't fool us..'; I smiled, acknowledged their supremacy graciously, and continued with the foreigner I was working on. When I left, they gave me a silver-plated tankard with the inscription 'DELBOY' on.

On one occasion, a particularly fussy deputy-head instructed them to lock away the tube of ink from the Reisograph (cheap, ink-based copier - low quality) at the end of each school day because she suspected it was being used for personal copying. Not by me, dear, I like my stuff to be sharp. This incensed the staff, because most of them did copying in their own time, and hence were forced to use a more expensive machine. One day I was there as the tube was being repositioned for the day, and heard one of them say it was running out and would probably need replacing before long. So I waited a couple of minutes, then set something up on it for printing, opened the side panel and called out that the ink was finished. They replaced it and chucked the old tube without checking, which I later retrieved and swapped over with the new one. As I say, I wasn't keen on the machine myself, I just lent the new ink-tube out to colleagues.

※   ※   ※   ※   ※

Nothing beats selling your writing. If you give something away it gets treated with contempt, but when your mates put their hands in their pockets, you know you've got a goer.

I think I'm going to do a little 'how to run a school mag' spot here - I've done enough of the things. I'll number each point:

1. Money gives options, it gives energy, but you have to keep recycling it, and the readers have to see where it's going. In mags I've run, a lot of it went on competitions - many very simple (e.g., 'Spot Cedric Seal' - a minute cartoon seal that we used to lose somewhere among the text and pictures), some more skill-based. We would always give a prize, however poor the return was, and if there were no entries at all, we'd do a roll-over. We would always announce the winner and all other entrants, correct or incorrect, so kids knew they weren't wasting their time. And we always ran a little ladder up the side showing whatever money surplus there was, and a short explanation of what was coming in and going out. Parting with money is a serious business, people like to be kept informed.

2. Frequency. For a mag to go well, it has to come out frequently, and at the same time of the month, or whatever. Otherwise you set something up in one issue, and by the time you come to follow through the readers have lost interest. You need regularity, and above all, you need to get it out. You can't get away with blaming the photocopier, exams or anything else - it has to come out. Once a month is the minimum frequency - once a term leaves too big a gap and it goes cold.

You need a mail-box - a solid thing with a slot and a padlock, in a central place. You have a routine for opening it, and you throw nothing away, not even the gum-wrappers. Have a prominent column in each issue just responding to everything that has been received, the wrappers, even the unprintable notes. Deal with them in an upbeat way; convey that opening the box is fun.

Incidentally, I always had sellers out at exactly the same time - beginning of morning break. None were sold or even displayed before then. If you stagger the selling in any way, people will read each others' rather than buy it. You get sellers in place, hit people in one concentrated burst before they spend their money on tuck, then stop. If you have kids trailing round all day it looks bad; if anyone wants one after the initial blast, they'll find you. Charge a simple amount, or you lose sales fiddling with change; and don't let anyone owe for a copy, it's a pain - tell them to borrow off a friend.

3. The chat-column. Regular columns are good - if you can find two or three people who can be relied on to do a regular column, either some kind of dry commentry on school life, or maybe someone has a particularly interesting out-of-school existence. For example, when the Gulf War was on, we had more than one pupil with a close relative out there; we also had a boot-boy at Kidderminster Harriers; another's father ran a boxing gym in Birmingham which had some big-time users, including a British heavyweight champ named Gordon Ferris; another's father rigged up the sound systems at events such as the Eurovision Song Contest and Live Aid. Someone always knows someone, and if you get a good two-way thing going with the readers, they'll always come and tell you.

My longest surviving chat-columnists were both piss-takers who had a way with words: one called himself 'Mr X', and tended towards lunacy, but clever with it; the other was called 'Biactol Boys', more of a team effort, commenting on school life, but one writer:

THE BIACTOL BOYS

Well, I'm back again, on my own as per usual, and I haven't got a clue what to type about. Have any of you noticed Mr 'Shoulders' Wilson lately? My pal Shoulders always seems to get beaten up over the weekend. At first it was bruises, then black eyes, then it was stitches! And what has he got to show for all his efforts? Yes, his Vauxhall Chevette. Shoulders Wilson participates in blood sports, i.e., RUGBY. But why did I call it a blood sport? Well, it seems that it's his blood that is being smeared on the rugby posts every weekend. Today is Monday, and I've noticed Shoulders is wielding some nasty cuts around the mouth. Already he has tons and tons of butterfly stitches to keep his blood in, but he still continues to play the sport.... I am slowly getting worried about the quantity of blood left in his body. Yes, I know the body is capable of making its own blood, but he is losing more than the body can produce. I think he should give up rugby for lent and try something more dainty like ballet. Or, how about becoming a librarian for four weeks.

Do you find librarians get on your nerves? You ask them for one book and they give you about seventy, and in that seventy you can't find the one you asked for. A couple of weeks ago I visited my local library looking for a book on quantum mechanics. Don't ask me why, I'm not too sure myself, I think I'd been eating too many E-numbers. Well anyway, I approached this woman who looked the librarian type (tons of make-up, huge goggle-like glasses and massive earrings that clashed with the make-up) and I asked her. She said, "Sorry, you'll have to go over to the information desk where the head librarian will assist." So I walked over to this desk where this librarian was hanging out. After forty minutes she finished filing her nails and pushing back the cuticles and said, "Yes, can I help?" So I explained, and she sat down at the computer and started typing, explaining how the computer worked. "Yes, here we are, there are two hundred and thirteen books on quantum mechanics in our district. Unfortunately we only have one in, and it was last printed in 1943. Can I interest you in a cookery course by Delia Smith, it is along the same lines as quantum mechanics."

P.S. We want bodyguards, please send C.V. including a photo to us by putting it in the 'Ad-Lib' box, or giving it to Lovell. We have already turned down Mr Wilson as he is too gentle and has a Chevette with a dodgy Graphic Equaliser. Well, see ya, hope to hear from you!

Paul Scully (originally anonymous)

* * * * *

I'm not making any claims for pieces like this, but they're fun and facile, and readers look forward to them - I suppose it makes a change from wall after wall covered in sensible pieces of work. As the teacher running the thing, they involved me in the occasional head-ache and I sometimes had to tell them to tone the gossip down, but at least that kind of head-ache involves a real product - it's a head-ache worth having occasionally.

4. Get out. I'm not sure I'd do it now, but I remember when the riots first happened in places like Brixton, Toxteth and Handsworth; Handsworth being only fifteen or so miles (and light years) from the school where I worked, I had three regular mag writers ring home and get permission to go to the Soho Road with me that same day, and report on it. It seemed important. The mag was ready for printing, so the whole thing had to be rejigged at the last minute:

THE RIOTS: THE VICTIMS TALK.

By Brian Hicks, Niall Ryan & Mark Donovan

Because of the effect the inner city riots are having on our country, 'Ad-Lib' went to Handsworth, Birmingham, to report on the situation and interview the residents. In order to include this late report the contents have been slightly rearranged, and articles about Miss Roach, Italy, Papua New Guinea, and a poem, will appear in the next issue...

Handsworth looked a pretty run-down place. Most of the shops are boarded up, and some of the shops that are not boarded up have smashed windows. To show the shops are open they have signs like 'WE ARE OPEN' and 'BUSINESS AS USUAL' on the boards. Even Woolworth's was boarded up, and the pubs and the library.

The place was pretty crowded though and people were just going on with their shopping in the normal way. There are immigrants from different races, not just one race, like Asians, West Indians and Africans. A lot of the shops had non-English names like Patel, Singh, etc.

We parked the car and started up Soho Road. We saw this shop which looked ready for demolition because the windows were all boarded up with corrugated iron. We went in and started to interview the shopkeeper. He was a European. He said the rioters should be brought into line and the troops should be brought onto the streets. He was in favour of water cannon, C.S. gas and rubber bullets. He said the riots were caused by outsiders.

Then we went into an Asian shop. The man behind the counter described the night of Friday July 10th, 1981.

He was there at the riot. He said that 200 - 300 youths, black and white, came into one end of Soho Road. First they started looting at that end. The trader was lucky, because his shop was at the other end. He also said that the riot started at 10.15 pm and the police did not come until 11.00. He said he had nothing against the police though - they were good in his area. He said the riot could have been organised.

The shopkeeper said the cause of the riots was not racist but copycat - it was just a copycat thing, when youths see other unemployed youths they just copy them, looting the shops. To stop the riots he said that the parents should be responsible for their children under 16. He also said that he disapproves of plastic bullets because they can kill, but he is in favour of water cannon because they might be useful if a petrol-bomb was thrown in a shop. He thought the media, especially television, dramatised things too much and deliberately made them seem exciting. He also said that not enough money had been spent on the area; housing and education were poor. As we were going, a middle-aged white man popped his head in the shop and told him to get boarded up - "Tonight's going to be the night". But they were both quite cheerful about it.

Then we interviewed two men selling communist newspapers in the street. One of them said the riots were caused by unemployment. He said there were 8,000 unemployed youths in Handsworth. He said the youth had no future, no money and nowhere to go, so they started a riot. He said that the police were racist and beat people up.

Then we interviewed a West Indian in a shop. He said that the riot was a waste of time - just one big loot. He said there were no clubs for them to go to, or any other places. He said that the riots would die down.

The last person we interviewed was a police officer in Handsworth Police Station. In Handsworth the police have been using "community policing" to bring them and the public closer. They drop in on shopkeepers and ask questions and talk with them, they talk to children in schools, community leaders, etc. They also organise football matches, canoeing, etc.

A policewoman said that the television is to blame. She said that when the kids see all that rioting on television they think it is good fun and copy it. A policeman who was listening said that there's a lad about to get three months for his part in the rioting, even though it was his first offence, so it wasn't much fun for him. He thought that was a stiff *sentence, because three months in prison is hard, they are in cells 22 hours a day. But he thought they should be given work to do as well. He said it was outsiders who caused the riots.*

When we asked if the police harassed people or beat them up he said that there is a small minority of bad eggs in the police force; these were exaggerated by the youths involved. On the night of the major riot he said that the police tried to keep a low profile so as not to make things worse, but they lost out - by the time they decided to get reinforcements in a lot of damage had been done.

On the way out of Handsworth we must have seen 20 - 25 police officers in Soho Road itself as a rumour was going round that there was to be some more trouble that night, a week after the main riot.

*　　*　　*　　*　　*

That was a one-off. But having some money in a kitty means that you can give a little support to anyone who offers to do an out-of-school item for you. For example, someone tells you they are going to a major gig at the N.E.C., you give them a couple of quid towards their train fare if they're willing to cover it. It's only a gesture but it shows them their offer is valued, and I can't see anything wrong in it. It gives you a lively paper.

When they get to know you are enthusiastic about anything like that, they will eventually start writing things up without being asked.

5. Good, bad and in-between writing. This is important. Years ago I took over a magazine of good writings by children: it was only bought by the contributors' families and a few loyal friends, plus the odd kid in the lower years who had been conned into thinking the teacher might look on

them favourably if they bought one. I'm not against printing good writings, I've printed enough myself, it's just that they can be quite off-putting when all collected together in an anthology with its tasteful lino-cuts, that doesn't really satisfy anyone except perhaps the head, who can show it off.

Not all good work is suitable for a magazine covering an age-range of maybe seven years. As I said, lot of good work is sold to kids but really meant to impress their parents. That's dishonest. If you want to impress parents, fine, find a more honest way of doing it. Some kids' poetry, for example, can be very finely crafted but quite difficult, and maybe referenced on something from a specific lesson; or you may get a beautiful piece of prolonged prose which is at the same time quite dense and tricky to read - they can be showcased somewhere else.

Equally, not all popular writing is low-grade; we ran a 'Romance' page for a while. Tricky subject - romance is responsible for about as much bad writing as football - but try this:

'What?' I exclaimed. Had I misheard?

'I said we're finished.'

'Oh...'

He left me standing there, outside my house, dumbfounded.

'Boow,' I groaned.

We'd just had an argument - a petty one at that. I opened the gate and dragged my feet along the path. It made a grinding noise with the loose stones. I searched for my key amongst the scrumpled up sweet wrappers and love letters in my pocket.

Love letters.

Chris used to send me them in French. It was the only lesson he could, because Miss Dean never noticed. I used to find them everywhere, in the desk, on the floor. Once he'd folded it up into a paper aeroplane and shot it across the room. It never reached me, it only got as far as Lee.

All the memories came flooding back. I pulled one out of my pocket and carefully opened it, not to rip it.

'Je t'aime.'

I read it over and over again, staring at it. It formed a blur in my mind.

'Je t'aime, Je t'aime, Je t'aime,' I yelled.

The door opened.

'Helen, dear, what's the matter?'

I awoke from my nightmare, or was it a dream?

'Nothing mom, I'd rather not talk about it, OK?'

'Where's Chris?'

'I said, I'd rather not talk about it.' *My voice raised.*

I ran upstairs, ready to grab the tissue box, and pounced at my bed like a lion grabbing its prey. With my head buried deep into my pillow, fists clenched so tight my nails dug into my palm, I cried. I couldn't bear the thought of no Chris anymore. No-one to snuggle up to in the cold. No-one to hold tight to when a scary film was on at the cinema. No Chris anymore, I had to face it.

The next few days at school were torment. Seeing him around and not being able to talk to him. My world had ended. Seeing other couples hand in hand made me feel jealous of the love they had, and kept, for each other. I needed him. I needed his love.

The lesson came that I dreaded - French. I glanced over at his hardworking face. Those eyes - the last time I looked in those eyes was....

Stop! Stop! Face it. I've got to face it. I can't go on like this anymore. Stop thinking of him. Stop dreaming of him. If I carry on the way I am, my dreams will turn to nightmares.

'Helen? Did you hear me Helen? What did I just say?'

'Sorry Miss, I wasn't paying attention.' *I shrunk into my seat.*

'Yes, well. Pay attention - next time it will be lines.'

'Yes Miss.'

All I needed, how embarassing. I could feel his eyes focused on me. I looked down at my work and pretended to write. I wondered what he was doing.

Just then, a little slip of paper, on the floor caught my eye. I picked it up and opened it.

'Sorry,' *I read,* 'please forgive me, and meet me for a hamburger tonight.'

I looked over at him, and he looked over at me. We smiled at each other. I had him back, I couldn't believe it.

'Helen,' *Miss Dean said sharply.* 'That will be one hundred lines - I must pay attention in class.'

*   *   *   *   *

I like that kind of English - it's light, reader-aware, reactive, on its toes, but it's still good English - it's been well put together. But it does have to be watched carefully, because it can tip over into banality very easily. Worst culprits: fake astrology columns, fake problem pages - don't even think about it, they're always hopeless. But I did happily print this, on a hobbies page:

PARLONYMOTIS - THE STUDY OF WORMS.

By Andrea Mills

My hobby is parlonymotis - the study of worms. This is a widely interesting subject. I am in the Parlonymotis Club, which is known throughout the world for its discoveries of many worms which were unknown before. There are 4,000 species of worms - my favourite out of these is the South African Ridgeworm which was discovered two years ago by Alfred Barnabus, the chairman of the board of the P.W.U.L. (the Protection for Worms United League). This worm has two humpbacked ridges which it uses to move along. It is thirty millimetres in diameter, and has a snouted nose which enables it to breathe in flies, which are its main diet of food. It has a store of poison in its tail which kills all enemies who try to eat it - example: South African Moeha cows and also the Seehopen tribe, who eat the worms for vitamins A, B and C.

Another of my favourite worms is the Corneus, or the Sandworm as it is better known. This lives on beaches in Rome, Ireland and Wales. It lives on small shellfish which it catches by the sticky coating on its body.

Worms shed their skins every month and are the most hygenic animals living. They reproduce by a female worm known as the hen laying eggs which are then fertilized by male worms better known as cocks. The worms hatch in about 2 - 3 weeks by eating through the shell of the egg. Worms are fully grown when a week old. They are now a fast dying out species.

The address for joining P.W.U.L. is:
P.W.U.L., 114 Cleethorpe Cres., Tyresborough, LONDON NW5 6SL.

The address for joining the Parlonymotis Club is:

Alfred Barnabus, Parlonymotis Club, Cranesfield, OXFORD OX2 66Y.

© Andrea Mills - 1 April.

*   *   *   *   *

We were lucky with our copier, which reproduced photos brilliantly, and I would constantly have kids come up to me saying, 'Here sir, put this one in, but don't tell Kirsty I gave it to you...' - that can be fun, particularly if staff are prepared to let the odd shot of themselves arse over head on a ski-trip or something go in. I would also reproduce local news cuttings involving the kids, staff, ex-pupils, future pupils (going by feeder schools), and families. This was popular in the school I was in, which fed in from a number of quite separate districts around, so the articles had often not been seen beforehand by many of the kids.

I had a dilemma with ex-pupils who featured in the local press for misdeeds rather than good deeds. My view was that something of this nature should go in: *'Ad-Lib announces the regrettable news that former pupil Willard Poppingly, who will be remembered for holding the senior boys javelin record for two years, received a three-month custodial sentence at Worcester Crown Court last week in connection with a house-breaking offence. We extend our good wishes to Willard and family, and hope that he will be able to find an honest living on his release.'*

I was never quite sure of my ground over this, and didn't actually do it (leaving aside the fact that I would have been prevented from doing it anyway), but did think about it quite often - I mean schools are always quick to flag up the uni successes, aren't they?

6. 'Guidance.' This raises the whole question of censorship, or 'guidance', as a head might call it. Unfortunately I can't offer any suitable suggestions for avoiding it. Flack can come from the most unlikely directions: I can remember four clear-cut incidents that got me in hot water over a period of ten years or so, a fair set of figures in my opinion, but it might be worth relating them.

Two can be construed very loosely as alluding to sex. In one issue I had been given, quite separately, two photos of pupils from their infant days - one in her swimming costume making an exaggerated beach-belle pose while on holiday, the other of a girl in the bath with her Mister Man sponge, taken when she was three. They both knew the photos were going in - I made up a Page 3 format with the following caption: *'Naughty Nicola (17-16-17) enjoys English lessons and water sports, and hopes to go on to a career in leisure! No wonder Mr Strong is smiling!!'*; *'Bathing Beauty Suzanne modelling the new summer uniform (toe-nail varnish optional).'*

I got a letter from the head, generally flattering, except for the sting in the tail: 'The only thing I would have removed would be the page 3 photos - in my view poor taste parodying the worst newspaper ever printed... If you wish to discuss the above please see me.'

I didn't, but not surprisingly the discussion took place, and I was asked to submit the proofs for approval before printing - which on that occasion, I can't remember how, I managed to resist.

In another issue, a teacher was interviewed. One of the questions was, 'What would you like to have with you if you were stuck on a desert island?'; the reply was: 'If she were on a desert island she would take a man, soap, make-up, and a spare pair of knickers.'

I always gave staff proofs of their interviews to check, but this got overlooked in the frenzy of Christmas productions, and she came to me at the last minute: 'Have they really put that in - I didn't mean them to...'. So I collected up a dozen pupils, a dozen new pots of Tippex, sat them down in the library and it was carefully deleted from every copy. It didn't seem worth the fuss in my view, particularly as her answer to another question, 'If she had one day left she would go out and commit a sin and then go to confession', didn't concern her - but we deleted the bit she wanted.

The deletion gave rise to another rollicking (on the grounds that it must have been covering up something untoward, therefore my judgement was suspect in the first place) and demand for proofs to be submitted first.

The third piece I remember giving offence concerned the inclusion of news cuttings on two ex-pupils. In one, the girl, a model student, had simply been pictured at a carnival or something; the other had made it to the regional finals of a cookery competition. What I had done wrong was, obliquely, to have given publicity to 'rival' schools which these pupils had chosen in preference to ours - even though in one case the child had left in her first year at our school: that is, six years previously.

The last occasion involved a cartoon which commented lightly on a one-way system which had been adopted to ease the flow of pupils around the school. It was rigorously enforced, causing some daft situations, such as pupils being allowed out of their class to use a nearby toilet being directed right round the school first. The cartoon portrayed a child going from one lesson to a lesson next door; he is yelled at for disregarding the one-way system, so he turns back, out, round the mobiles, past the caretaker's house, over the hill, down the dale, and eventually makes it to his lesson, where he is yelled at by the same teacher for being late. Quite funny.

The upshot of these occasional scrapes was that I was eventually instructed to present proofs for approval before printing. I would not do that on the grounds that if the school wanted a formal 'voice' there were staff more senior than me better positioned to provide it, and so, after ten years, I stopped running the mag.

I have no advice or wisdom on this whatever. Schools fear the slightest aspersion on their name, and people feel uncomfortable generally with risk-takers. There is always potential risk in writing, and if you take that away you are simply a scribe. But who needs the aggro? You just have to be lucky with your school I suppose.

7. Interviews. School mag interviews are the pits. Find a newish or semi-popular teacher (all the popular ones having been done several times), sit them at a table in their lunch-hour and plod through your list of questions in sequence ('Who's your best friend on the staff; what football team do you support; where do you go on holiday...') regardless of the answers. Staff often give facetious answers, but the kids write them down religiously anyway. It's awful.

If I had my time again I would put a twelve-month moratorium on teacher interviews, on interviews conducted in static conditions in the person's own time, and possibly on general question lists (as opposed to questions specific to that particular person).

Go and find someone different - there are plenty of interesting people about. Also, an interview doesn't have to be done and dusted in half an hour, you can always go back after you've had a look at what you've got. People can often be interviewed whilst they're involved in their work, with maybe a sit-down session afterwards.

Pupil interviewers love sit-down interviews because they're easier for scribbling answers, but why do that? You can't respond to an answer if you are writing it down; and in addition, the subject realises that the whole thing's a struggle and limits replies to single sentences. It becomes an exercise in getting the interviewer off the hook: the interviewer becomes the subject.

The way round this is for the teacher to keep a couple of dictaphones on the ready, and be prepared to lend them out. Have some practice sessions in the classroom - step in at times and ask the rest of the class if the interviewers are on track. Are they finding out what we want to know? Did they let open-ended answers go, or did they chase them up? An example: 'When was your most embarrassing moment?' The subject pauses, laughs to himself, says no, thinks of something else, gives a vague answer: 'Er, it involved a party one Christmas, a game of Twister, and quite a lot of drink...'

This interview actually took place in a school I did a writer's day at: the teacher was good enough to let himself be used as a practice subject. The interviewer began to phrase the next question. I stopped the interview. 'Forget the answer for a minute - how did Mr Soandso react to the question. Write two or three sentences just describing his reaction.' They all did this. Some were read out, causing amusement. 'If we included that it would give a better picture of Mr Soandso than just writing his answer, agreed? O.K. - is there anything else we want to know in connection with that answer?' Big reaction - 'Yeah, WHAT HAPPENED?' Teacher clams up. 'He feels as if he's the accused in court now, he's not going to tell..' 'He doesn't have to if he doesn't want' (a minority view...). 'No, but maybe he half does want, because he brought it up in the first place. Now, are there any questions we could ask that might not put him under so much pressure?'

* * * * *

Kids seem to get overwhelmed when interviewing an adult, even though you have no problem playing them up and answering back all week. The thing to do is find willing subjects to practise on and get away from school - even going for a walk round the block is better than being cornered in an empty classroom.

Having said all that, one pair of interviewers did seem to manage better than most - they worked out a routine of throwing odd-ball questions, but in a charming fashion, and noting the reactions ('very puzzled expression'; 'takes long sip of tea...'); they also included ums and ahs, and so on. It was effective, though a bit hit and miss. Here are the questions from one interview:

1. *Full name*
2. *Date of birth*

3. What would you change your name to?
4. What is the worst name you've ever heard?
5. What fruit do you identify with?
6. Do you think Ivan Lendl looks like a baked bean?
7. How many geese could you fit into your back garden?
8. What's the most useless thing you possess?
9. Have you ever forgotten your wife's birthday?
10. Most embarrassing moment?
11. Does your car reflect your personality?
12. Were you a swot?
13. Favourite joke?
14. What author are you sick of?
15. What's your claim to fame?
16. What music do you dislike?
17. What reforms would you bring to the education system?
18. What are your ambitions?
19. What was your childhood ambition?
20. Who was your childhood hero?
21. What was your first job?
22. Are you an impulse buyer?
23. Have you any phobias?
24. Do you believe flowers scream when you pick them?

Quite effective - it certainly sorts those who don't want to play ball from those who do. But it is still only one type of interview, suitable for people like teachers that you know already, and there has to be a place for other types.

8. The finish. The thing has to be finished off and presented absolutely right. You can't have mistakes, mistakes aren't cute, they're a pain in the arse. The philosophy behind them is, it doesn't matter, we're only kids. No chance.

I also managed to get kids to lay out and photocopy to the same standard. None of this, we're only kids, we don't know how to adjust the copier. They had to do it right, and they had to leave the copier and the copier room immaculate. It was only possible to do this well out of school time, you can't have staff queueing up behind kids to use their own facilities. So I arrived at the following system: at that time some of us on the staff had organised ourselves and a few friends into a football team which played in the local leagues (Hagley Academicals: my daughter used to look out for Hamilton on Final Score and say things like, ooh look dad, you got a draw). On alternate Sundays (she didn't twig) we'd play our home games on the school pitch.

I made an arrangement with the caretaker that I would come in an hour or so early with the production kids, two or three of them, and we would set up the copier and start running the thing off. With luck it would be going smoothly by the time the other players arrived and I would join them. At half-time I would go back in and check. If there was a problem I'd try and sort it and they'd sub me if I didn't make it out for the start of the second-half, thus saving them the embarrassment of taking me off later.

It was a good system, obviously relying on a lot of consideration from people and a lot of luck. The kids got proficient on the copier, and never ever buggered it up for example by trying to poke out a piece of jammed paper with a scissor blade like someone I know. I was talking to the maintenance bloke once and he said the worst jam he'd had to deal with was at Birmingham Uni, where someone had tried putting a T-shirt through. Ha! Superb.

* * * * *

There was a massive time-investment in all this. I did it because I was hooked - I'm sure I was meant to be a journalist - and because I found the alternative way of teaching English intolerably bleak, felt like I was a pianist teaching chopsticks all day.

Here's a piece to finish with: G.C.S.E. oral assignment - the authors delivered it with sublime timing, dressed in khaki shorts, binoculars, with pens, ordinance survey maps and bird-identification charts poking out of their pockets. I scrounged their notes and printed them up:

BIRD WATCHING

(Simon - already in hide; Andrew - comes into hide)

S - *Morning Andrew*
A - *Gosh, you're here already*

(Andrew sits and looks through binoculars. Simon goes on talking.)

S - *Yes, I was up with the...*
A - *Lark*
S - *Quite*
A - *There's quite a few birds here today*
S - *Yes there are*
A - *You know, I was watching the news the other night*
S - *Were you?*
A - *Yes. I saw that Branson chap, came down in the Atlantic didn't he? You know I thought he was going to...*
S - *Goosander*
A - *Exactly. But he was picked up by the R.A.F. wasn't he?*
S - *Yes... And then there's all that Iran-gate stuff, isn't there?*
A - *Oh yes. That Oliver North, I think he's telling fibs.*
S - *Do you...*
A - *Yes. I mean, if he thinks anyone would...*
S - *Swallow*
A - *that story, he's got to be*
S - *Raven*
A - *mad. I agree. He's*
S - *Robin*
A - *all that money off the state. I mean, what can he expect?*

S - *Still, it's all been cleared up now.*

(Silence for a few seconds as they look for more birds)

A - *You know her from number 32?*
S - *Eider duck*
A - *I don't know her name, but I overheard two ladies talking and they said she's going to have all her teeth taken out.*
S - *Bullfinch*
A - *No, honestly*
S - *What?*
A - *Sorry. Anyway they said she would have to have false teeth but she said she wouldn't...*
S - *Avocet*
A - *That's right.*

(Silence for a few seconds as they look for more birds)

S - *You know, the wife was late getting up the other morning.*
A - *Was she?*
S - *Yes. She went to catch her bus but she almost missed it.*
A - *Did she?*
S - *Yes, she had to*
A - *Thrush*
S - *That's right. It's a good job she's*
A - *Swift*
S - *or she'd have missed it, exactly. And then when she finally got onto it she couldn't tell the driver where she wanted to go, she was*
A - *Puffin*
S - *so much, that's it. But it all turned out well in the end.*

(Few seconds silence as they look for birds)

A - *Hey! Look over there...*
S - *What is it?*
A - *I can't quite see. I think it's a...*

S - *Lesser spotted crested warbler*
A - *No...*
S - *Black throated diver*
A - *No...*
S - *Green backed bulla bulla*
A - *No...*
S - *Well what then?*
A - *Number seven bus. Come on, it's time to go.*

Andrew Orme

* * * * *

Q. What's it like being a writer?

A. A struggle.

Q. Where do you get your ideas from?

A. It helps to be really nosey. I would like to have been a journalist, policeman, lawyer or psychotherapist because they get to know people's secrets. But I've picked up a few being a teacher. I used to open kids' books from the back first and read all their messages before marking their work. I was also good at listening to private conversations. If you turn away and stare hard at a poster for a while they forget you're there.

Q. How long does it take to write a book?

A. Actually, I'm surprised how little you get done in a day. I'd say my average is two to three thousand words, which is about six to ten sides of A4, handwritten, and I've seen kids do that much in a two and a half hour exam. My record was about eight and a half thousand, (twenty-five sides) but I was extremely fired up.

Q. Do you like writing?

A. Yes, but not letters or cheques.

Q. How do you get a book published?

A. I used to think that eventually one of my pupils would get a job as a publisher's editor (thanks to my unstinting encouragement and inspiration) and then contact me to see if I could possibly supply them with a script for publication. But it hasn't happened yet.

Q. Who is your favourite author?

A. Jane Gardam. She has the most delicate, observant touch. 'Bilgewater' is brilliant, so is 'A Long Way from Verona'. 'The Hollow Land' is a collection of beautiful quiet connected short stories - another book that I liberated from a hostile environment and will never give back.

CHAPTER 10

Prose Pieces

I'd like to say in this section that the examples of good writing are the result of stimulating, on-the-ball lesson ideas, but the truth is they often sprang up from the dullest lessons. You can't keep the human spirit down when it's got something to say.

This is a year-10 autobiography:

Terror is a silver monster, rotating faster than the eye can blink.

- It's that dream again, the one where I wake up frightened, beads of sweat glistening on my hot face. Sometimes I scream, but no-one hears, or someone hears and pretends not to. Now I am calm again, eyes heavy, brain tired, and drifting slowly into a sea of black, warm and black, quiet and black. Then, whirr, click, coming closer, nearer, the giant metal blades spinning, cutting, tearing. 'Wake up,' I will myself, 'it's only a dream,' but my mind does not respond, my eyes will not or cannot open.

Now, it's all quiet and dark again. I am lifting my heavy eyelids. Everything is silent. A chink in the curtain allows light to spill into the room - it's morning. Downstairs someone has turned the radio on - I have to get up, now!

* * * * *

I am nine, and I lie awake at night. Sometimes I will read, by the finger of light that slips between the shadows to my bed. Sometimes I will simply think - about nice things. But always, underneath, I know this is a pretence - a postponement. For, as soon as the light on the landing is clicked off and darkness soaks into the surroundings, I am alone, and very open. I can feel the icy coldness around me, as the night creatures edge closer towards me. I huddle under the blanket so that they can't get me. I think. I am trying to think happy thoughts. But, the dark is too pressing. Now I am thinking about death. I have never known anyone who has died - just what happens after the last trace of light flickers from your face? I am imagining what it is like to be nothing, have nothing, feel nothing, to live in a world of nothingness.

My eyes are wet now - I have frightened myself. It helps to cry. I want to go next door, to hug my mum, to make her reassure me. But I can't. I'm not wanted. She's in there with him. He doesn't care, he just looks at me like I'm hassle. Nobody understands.

* * * * *

I am six now, my parents are divorced. This means that they do not live together - my dad lives in Bridgnorth. When my dad is here, with us, my mum shouts at him; when he is gone, she cries. Sometimes at night I can hear my mum sobbing into her pillow, lying on the bed that my mum and my dad bought together. My dad gets upset too - but he doesn't cry like my mum. Even so, I can still tell. After he has gone back to his new house, my mum says nasty things about him, and calls him a bastard. She says that he was off with other women, but I don't believe her. She says that if we ever left her then we'd find her 'dead in a gutter'. When I go to bed I worry about dad, all on his own.

* * * * *

Now I am seven, and my parents are still divorced. I go to Sutton Park Primary School and my best friend is called

Kerry. My big brother, Peter, is a year older than me - he is in the next class up. At school today we did numbers, and I was the first to finish up to number ten! At playtime, Kerry and I played 'Roundabout Land'. To play this, you have to put your arms out, and spin around until you feel sick. When we stopped playing, I felt really sick.

My mum has got a new boyfriend - he is called John. He is about the third boyfriend she has had since she got divorced from my dad - my dad hasn't got a girlfriend yet! I don't like John, because he smells of oil, and has got rough fingers.

We go to see my dad every weekend. I think that it is funny when my dad changes my baby brother's nappy - but he's getting better at it now. Jamie's two now!

* * * * *

I was eight years old last August. My dad's got a girlfriend now, she's called Sheila Hughes. When she told me her name, I thought she said 'Shiela Shoes', so that's what I call her. She's very good at drawing - she drew me a rabbit at the weekend!

My mum's got a new boyfriend as well. He's called Pete and he looks like he has just walked out of a loony bin. The boyfriends that she has had so far are as follows: Bill, John, John, Dave, and now, Pete. Pete wears thick glasses that make him look mentally unstable! Peter (my brother) and I have nicknamed him 'Beanpole'.

I want to live with my dad.

* * * * *

I am ten and I attend St John's C. of E. Middle School. Already I have obtained a dislike for organised education of any sort.

The alarm bell rings - loud and raucous, jerking me from my drowsy cloud of sleep. I sit up instantaneously, as I throw my arm out to turn off the noise. In doing this I forget that I'm in a bunk and bounce my head off the ceiling - it has got to be a Monday.

I get to school and realise I have brought the wrong books - this is a typical day at school. As I stumble into my lesson I find a chair and sit down, ready to return to my slumber. 'And what exactly did you do last lesson?' a booming voice enquires. I look up to see at least eight foot of solid teacher.

There is nothing more I dread than being asked questions by teachers. If a teacher even looks at me, I feel they can read my mind, see through to my soul.

'And what exactly did you do last lesson then?' the voice repeats. I can feel my face turning red, my body going hot, sweat pouring out of my forehead. As I stammer my answer, I hate myself, for giving him the satisfaction of seeing me flustered. I keep my head turned to the desk. I can feel a thousand eyes burning into the back of my skull.

Over the other side of the room the same question is being asked. A cheeky retort greets the question. How I envy that person - I wish I could be so confident.

My mother is still going out with Beanpole - I think it's a record!

I still want to live with dad.

*   *   *   *   *

I am still ten, but now I am living with dad. There is not a lot of difference, except that dad doesn't shout at us, and the house is a lot neater. Peter is also living with us, but mum would not let Jamie come. I feel sorry for him, all alone with her and 'Beanpole'.

Now I am upstairs. I have brushed my teeth and washed my face. I am climbing into bed. I think about Jamie. He is five now. I miss him. There is a picture at the bottom of the bed. In the semi-darkness, the features form into Jamie's. As I turn over, I can feel a lump form in the back of my throat. But I am not going to cry. Here, in the dark, it is easier to think about things. I think about what Jamie could be doing. Now, I am thinking, 'What if something happened to Jamie?' I am crying silently - why? I feel so miserable, all alone in a big dark room. My cheeks sting where the hot tears spill onto them. One runs onto my lip and I lick it off - it is comforting. The salty tears are drying on my face, and my thoughts are becoming blurred. Now I am slowly slipping into dark... black... sleep.

*　*　*　*　*

I am eleven and I am waiting in a car. The car park is lit by the dull orange glow from the street lamps. The sky is grey. The hospital is a dark silhouette against the silvery sky. It is time to go in now. I am walking up the grey slabpath to the hospital. Now I am sitting on a grey plastic chair. Now I am walking through two grey doors. A lift is opening. A nurse walks out of the lift. A tiny, wrinkled, pink baby lies in her arms. 'This is your new sister, Sarah Louisa,' says my dad. Dad told us about the baby last September - it is February now. Sheila and he aren't married, but I don't mind. My mum minds though.

*　*　*　*　*

As my eyes open, lifting the veil of sleep, I can sense that there is something different about today - the air is alive with excitement. I can feel a heaviness pushing down on my toes. The darkness has not yet dispersed, so I am feeling around the bottom of my bed for my stocking. I have found it. I hold the delicious lumpiness in my hands for a while. Now I am emptying it onto the bed - it is Christmas.

* * * * *

I am twelve, still living with my dad, and still missing Jamie. I am in my last year of my middle school - I'm a prefect now. The alarm rings, and I am getting up. I walk downstairs and open the back door. I am cold, but it is worth it. I am walking onto the frosty grass, smelling the air. The morning is full of the smell of sugarbeet, how I love that sweet, earthy smell.

Now I am in the car, being driven to school. I am stepping out of the car, onto the dark grey school drive. This morning the path sparkles, as though it was studded with a million tiny diamonds. Now I am walking up the drive, sliding my shoes along the icy surface. Now I put my hand up to a leaf. It is cold to the touch, and sticks to my fingers with icy fastness.

I no longer have such an aversion to school, in fact I find it quite bearable. I have also discovered that teachers might be human after all.

* * * * *

I am thirteen and living with my mum. She has moved to a house near the Merry Hill Centre and Peter and I decided to give it another try - I don't know why. I suppose it's because I missed Jamie, and felt like a change.

Now it's my first day at school - my new school - 'Thorns'. Even the name sounds hard. It is a big school. As I am walking towards it, the massive building looms above me. I feel nervous, and I need the toilet. I am walking into the classroom, and scanning it for a friendly face. Now, in the corner, I can see a familiar gaze, Kerry. She is smiling, welcoming me.

It is breaktime now. I am confused. Surrounded by a group of pupils. There are questions that I can't hear, comments, muffled. Cries and shouts all rising together in a cacophonous whirl of sound. Now I can see a pair of smiling eyes, and a boy's voice saying, 'You've got frog eyes' and laughing. Now a pert pretty girl is imitating my accent. 'One comes from Kidderminster,' she is saying in an over-posh voice. I can feel tears beginning to prick the back of my eyes. I am turning, now, running. Away from the noise, the people, the strange Black Country accents. They are behind now. I can stop.

* * * * *

I am fourteen now, and I'm living with my dad again. We have a dog now, called 'Wags' - he resembles a pot-bellied pig because all he does is sleep and eat.

All that I want out of life really, is to be happy and, if happiness for me is living in a cardboard box (or a wheelie bin!) and being free, then that's what I'm going to do. On the other hand, if happiness is what the advert says then maybe I'll take up cigar-smoking.

Julie Fowler

* * * * *

It's pointless commenting really. We all get these crystal clear, wonderful pieces from time to time - grading them is a sin, but we get round it, no lasting damage is done. Obviously the girl writing that autobiography would find it hard not to be absolutely focussed, and I would guess that was how she came to make the choice of that perfectly right, existentialist style and the episodic, slightly jumbled arrangement. I'm not sure I can say that a teacher 'brings about' good writing; possibly, 'provides a backdrop of acceptance' and maybe, 'gives proper accord' to what is written. When going round schools I often write with the groups I am taking, and my ideas are clearly no better than theirs - it's just, I tell them, that I give more weight to my ideas than they do. And maybe a teacher who gives the proper weight to pupils' writing and is alert to their intentions can make a difference to what they write... Although - what about the good pieces that turn up in exam situations?

I'm sitting on it.

This is a year-ten, from the title 'Out of this World':

The driver slammed the brakes of his car down with a screech, but it was too late. The body of the girl flung itself pathetically at his windscreen, and slid off the bonnet of the car onto the road. A shocked on-looker telephoned for an ambulance.....

* * * * *

Being dead wasn't actually as painful as Claire had imagined it to be. Of course, actually dying wasn't wonderful. No-one could say that being knocked down by a Ford Fiesta was a 'fun' thing to do. However, now it was over, and she had recovered from the shock of seeing herself dead, it really wasn't so bad.

Claire walked through the door, which had suddenly appeared in front of her, into a room rather like a reception area of a large hotel. Several people sat on the leather chairs reading magazines, one man sat by the fish tank, tapping at the glass, trying vainly and aimlessly to make contact with a totally oblivious fish.

A young lady sitting behind a typewriter smiled, and in a rather sickly-sweet voice said:

"Hello, which service do you require, Heaven, limbo or Hell?" The latter word was somewhat hushed.

"Er, do you mean me?" stuttered Claire.

"Yes, which service, Heaven, limbo or Hell?"

"Well, I'd like to go to heaven, if that's alright."

"We're nearly full but if you'd care to wait over there one of our personnel will assist you. 'Bye, have a nice day."

Slightly bewildered at the last comment Claire did as she was instructed, and was greeted by a prim looking lady, in a blue pinafore and white blouse.

"Hello dear, let's start with your name."

"Claire Jefferson."

"Fine, now complete this sentence: 'I want to stay in heaven because ....' in no more than thirty-six words."

This was incredible, it was like some sort of farcical competition. Claire thought for a moment.

"Because, it's a welcome alternative to earth."

"Yes...I like that one. It's for the slogan you see, we need some sort of catchy phrase for the advertisement."

"Advertisement! You're advertising heaven!"

"Yes, we're starting a promotion campaign on earth: you see the 'other place' is taking all the trade; I think it's the amusement arcade that does it."

"You mean more people are choosing Hell in preference to Heaven?"

"Yes, but do try not to refer to 'the other place' by its name, it distresses the other residents so."

"Can't God do something?"

"God! Gracious, no, we got rid of him years ago."

"Got rid, of God!" shouted Claire.

"Well actually, he resigned. There were, and still are, so many people who think they can do his job that he didn't think it was worth it anymore, so, he and his family and the saints and apostles and a few of the elder residents here, left."

"Where did they go?"

"Heaven is a vast place; they went out to the wasteland to contemplate solving the earth's problems."

"But who runs heaven, looks after earth? What about all the people who pray to them, are they ignored, what happens?"

"Computers, it's all done with computers."

"Oh."

"Now, come this way, we'll find you a mansion to live in for the rest of eternity."

Suddenly the whole scene changed. Looking across the green fields she could see a large white house, it was beautiful. Before she could even imagine what it was like she found herself in its hallway. The house was like a Roman temple: large marble pillars supported the high ceiling. The house was filled with Ming vases and art nouveau fruit bowls; it had a feeling of luxury and wealth.

"It's situated in four acres of land; it has two tennis courts, the kitchen is filled with all mod-cons - not that you'll feel hungry anyway, - there's also a sauna with a jacuzzi, you have an indoor and outdoor swimming pool, a gymnasium, the list is endless."

"It sounds wonderful, it looks wonderful. Is there a catch?"

"No, no catch." At that the woman vanished.

Claire sat down in the comfy peach coloured sofa and table. Thin, wispy clouds started to emerge through the floorboards and up popped a rather hideous looking middle aged man wearing a T-shirt, Bermuda shorts, beach shoes and a baseball cap. He looked like an American tourist.

"Hello." His voice had an effeminate drawl.

"Hello," replied Claire. "Are you a neighbour?"

"You could say that," replied the man.

"It's beautiful here, isn't it?"

"You could say that, but it's no different to the other place you know."

"Who are you?"

"I am the devil, in one of my manifest forms."

"Oh, really?" Claire was surprised at her calmness.

"You'll hate it here ducky, really you will."

"Why? It seems lovely, yes, it is lovely," she reassured herself.

"Boredom dear, utter boredom, it drives them all to me in the end."

"Why, if it's no different to Hell?"

"At least in Hell you can be miserable - here you're meant to be happy."

"I'd rather be bored and here than bored and in Hell."

"It isn't the masochists' paradise it's made out to be."

Claire was quite amused at him using the word 'paradise' while referring to Hell.

"It's a fraud then, it isn't like I expected it would be."

"It never is like anyone expects it to be; we like to keep the element of shock - there's nothing like it to make people miserable; coupled with boredom, well it's perfect utter Hell."

"It sounds dreadful."

"It's no different from here, after you've had your fiftieth swim of the day and beat the machine at tennis there is nothing left for you to do. There aren't any neighbours, no friends to have a laugh with. I'll see you again."

"I doubt it."

"Never doubt anything. Believe me you'll see me sooner than you think." At that he vanished.

People had a habit of vanishing here; Claire wondered if one day she would be able to do the same thing. She didn't know whether to believe the devil - but if what he said was really true then it would be like Hell for her.

All those people who lead good, honest lives hoping to reap their rewards in Heaven, only to find when they got here that God had resigned, Heaven was being run by estate agents, prayers were being monitored by computers, and Heaven was the same as Hell anyway, so they might as well have been wicked. How awful, all the illusions shattered - even the devil didn't come up to expectations.

Oh well, she had the rest of eternity to find out whether it was all true. She wondered how long eternity was; probably a very long time. Maybe she would phone the devil and ask to try Hell for a ... trial period.

Daniella Woodfield

I have often given kids an open-ended title like this, and before writing, forced them to throw down half a dozen ideas in the space of a minute - no thinking, just freewheel; then again, quickly, another half-dozen; then, thirty seconds, another three. You'd think it wasn't possible, but it is - you have to be very definite, make them do it, do it yourself as well. And then ask them to rate their ideas, one to fifteen (or however many they've done). Where are the best ones - in the first group they wrote down, the second, the third? The answer is - anywhere: there is no pattern. But doing this, and going over it with a group, is a good way to tease out the possibilities of a subject. I have never collected any of these lists in, but to give an example, here is a list picked randomly from a few of my own I've kept:

Journey

1. *Growing up, personal dvt.*
2. *Train journey, desc..*
3. *Late night, London undergrnd.*
4. *Walking in freezing weather*
5. *Working as bus conductor*
6. *Australia*
7. *In ambulance*
8. *Career*
9. *Plot of a book, journey of the plot*
10. *Going into the millennium*
11. *Space shuttle*
12. *Pub crawl*
13. *Submarine crew*
14. *Safari*

(Didn't manage fifteen.) The kids I was working with had all those ideas covered, between them, and many others. It is also interesting to use a random choice of ideas when the lists are done, get them to write on whichever comes up first, regardless of preference. Again, it is important to do it yourself, with them. My reason for this is that I feel there is too much control in writing, kids (people) brush and comb their ideas and get them ready for church - you need ideas to spring out at you and catch you unawares. Invariably, when I do this exercise, there will be a clutch of kids who have surprised themselves with what they have written, doing it this way, and who can't wait for the chance to continue.

But in Daniella's case the title was just one of several offered with little preparation apart from my usual warning to avoid cliché. As I said before, I would always make copies of good writing and have them available for anyone to read, and I think you can see the influence, two or three years later on, in this:

GIRL IN A COMA

I slumped back into the passenger seat and closed my eyes. I let the sun gently caress my face as I was lulled into a sense of calmness. My mind began to slip away from the commotions of the past week, and think of the future. Slowly I fell into a deep slumber.

I thought I must have been dreaming when I heard the screech of brakes and the car careering towards us, but I was to learn that I hadn't been.

When I woke up I could feel a dull heavy throb in my head. There was a monotonous thump against my skull. It was dark around me, but I would see a tiny prick of light flickering and wavering above my head. I tried to raise my arm to snatch at the light, but soon realised there seemed to be no function in my arms or legs.

From the bottom of my stomach I could feel the feeling of isolation creeping up my tingling body. Where was I? Why couldn't I hear or see anyone? Most of all I was scared, scared at the prospect of what was going on.

"Hello," I cried out, but there was no sound coming from my mouth. Why was it I could hear myself, but no voice broke the darkness around me. I realised there was no use

trying to work it out now, I was feeling tired, my whole body was tired. I once again closed my eyes.

"Will she live through it, when will she come around, do you think she can hear us?" All of a sudden I could hear a mixture of muffled sounds rising and falling in pitch, echoing all around my limp body. I could feel something cool and starched lying over me. I couldn't as yet see what it was because I couldn't see past the darkness.

The sounds that I was beginning to hear were becoming more acutely recognisable. They were voices and they were voices I knew, and then quite gently, if not hardly at all, I could make out blurred shapes darting from one side to the other. I continued to try and focus on these shapes. They slowly began to take form, I could make out human shapes, people all around me. Then these faces and shapes became my relations, my mother, my brother. I surveyed the room and it clicked that I was lying on the white starched sheets of a hospital bed. The walls were clean and bright and the sun cast shadows around the room, a nurse stood in the corner and a stranger was comforting my mother.

I was so immensely glad to see them. "Mum, Mum you're here." My voice was raspy and hoarse, it sounded odd. My mother seemed to make no apparent response to my call. "Mother for God's sake listen to me." By now I was crying at the top of my voice.

"How long will she be like this?" my mother's voice was shaky and her eyes were brimming with tears. What did she mean "How long will she be like this?" What was wrong with me, why did it seem as though everyone was doing their utmost to ignore me.

In desperation I tried to beat my fists down onto the bed, but no matter how much I tried I couldn't call up the power to move them. My limbs just lay there helpless and pale on the bed. I could feel my body begin to sweat and shake and suddenly I was engulfed in total panic.

* * * * *

I was no longer lying silently in my own world apart from the others, I was screaming, screaming at them and me. By now they were filing one by one out of the room leaving me dejected and lifeless, alone and confused. I tried to call after them to stay, but knew that my attempts were all in vain. There was something drastically wrong with the situation I was in, but I just couldn't grasp at the whole thing. Lying there I watched the passing of time, the sun rise and fall and still I felt completely isolated.

They came again. One by one they sat beside me, held my hand and tried to find something in my face that would give them a glimmer of hope. They would talk to me and yes I would answer, but they couldn't hear my replies. Sometimes I would cry to myself in frustration not only for me but for them. How awful it must be for them knowing that my mind and organs were active but were trapped inside my body that wouldn't work. I understand now how it must be for physically handicapped people being trapped inside a useless body.

It was like life imprisonment inside a prison with absolutely no visitors allowed. I'd heard about other people like me, yes by now I'd realised I was in a coma. It was frightening knowing that I could be like this for months even years. Not being able to grow up like others of my age, not being able to tell my family how much I love and would miss them when they were gone, but I also knew that I could come round at any time and everything else would have been just like a bad dream.

A day wouldn't go past without someone coming to see me, to stimulate my body back into use, and how I would try, with no avail, to grasp at something, to tell them I was still there. It was frustrating, annoying and tiring to know how close I was to them, but also so far away from them at the same time.

I will never know how long I was there, for day after day passing me by. Then one day it was over. I could see the light of the early morning sun streaming into my room onto my skin. I could hear the tip-toeing of footsteps on the vinyl outside my door.

It was opened by a fresh-faced doctor who strode over to my bed. Inside I smiled at him, if only he could see. Then he turned to the machine that had been my permanent companion. What was he doing. No, he wouldn't, he couldn't, didn't he realise that I was a human being, alive. Yes, I was still alive, why couldn't he just wait, just a while longer. I screamed at him to stop.

"No, don't do it, please no!" My voice reached a crescendo, but it was too late. With the flick of a switch I faded from reality into a memory.

Sofia Pope

* * * * *

It's a lovely experience to see that kind of piece developing from what's gone before - the continuation of an idea rather than theft of it - assuming it was influenced by that piece, which I'm not sure of.

I've a feeling the next title came off an exam paper:

LONELINESS

The boy sat in the classroom, and watched a fly crawl slowly up the wall.

'Did you see the match last night?'

He turned to look at his friend. Short of stature and big of mouth seemed to sum up Tom. John looked back at the fly.

A cool breeze drifted through the room, and a deathly silence fell. John's concentration on the fly vanished as something nicked at his mind. Where was the talking of his friends? Where was the droning of the teacher? He turned his head to find himself in an empty classroom. Where was Tom? Everyone had gone! He quickly stood up and ran to the door. It was locked. He tried barging it with his shoulder, but only succeeded in bruising himself. He ran to the window. It too was locked. John was in a room, trapped, and he was alone.

* * * * *

John sat down at his desk, and started thinking. How had the people in the room gone out without him noticing? And why had they locked him in? To take his mind off things he reached for his bag to get some work out. His bag was gone! Then he thought. Tom must have taken it.

'When I get my hands on you, Tom, your life won't be worth anything.' Then he realised. It was pointless talking. There was no-one to listen to him, bar the fly. He looked back at the place where the fly had been. It was gone. John looked around the room, but there was no fly.

He walked over to a book-case and looked at all the titles to see if there was one worth reading, while he was waiting to be let out. Yes, they would be back soon. This was probably one of the teacher's hilarious jokes. 'Well, ha ha, I can take a joke,' he thought aloud.

The bookcase did not contain much of interest - two dictionaries, a thesaurus, and a selection of other books. Then one caught his eye. It was Robinson Crusoe, by Daniel Defoe. Well, it would be interesting to read about somebody with the same plight as himself.

Slowly he turned the pages and read. After about what seemed an hour and a half he was a quarter of the way through the book, and his eyes were tired, so he put it down.

He was now getting worried as to the whereabouts of his 'friends'. Had they forgotten about him? He walked up to the door and tried it again. No. It was still locked. 'Let me out!' he shouted.

* * * * *

John opened his eyes. He must have fallen asleep while he had been crying, he thought to himself. He stood up and stretched his aching limbs. For a third time he tried the door, to no avail. He was seriously worried now. No, not worried. Frightened. Outside it was beginning to get dark. He must get out. The door was a literal 'no-go' area, and he was fifteen metres up. Certainly enough to do himself some serious damage if he broke the window and jumped out.

He sat at his desk and carried on reading his book.

Two hours later, he turned the last page and put the book down. He had not been able to concentrate properly and had only read half the pages. He had to have a conversation or something to stop him from going mad.

'Hello, my name's John. What's yours?' he said in his normal voice.

'John. Isn't that a coincidence,' he said in a slightly higher voice.

'Fancy us both being in this situation at once.'

'Oh, not really. You see, the reason you're alone is that you're unliked.'

'Shut up. That's a lie!' his normal voice said.

'Yeah? That's why you're on your tod locked in this room. You have no real friends.'

'Shut up. Shut up. Shut up,' John shouted, covering up his ears. The second voice vanished. For the second time that day he cried.

* * * * *

John's eyes were sore from crying when he noticed something on the wall. It looked like a small black dot, but it moved. He got up to walk over to it. And he heard the slight buzz and realised it was the fly. He was really happy. He had been so lonely, the sight of the fly was actually comforting. He was so happy he stepped back and almost tripped over his bag. How had it got there? He had been sure it was not in the room before. The thought of this made John's head hurt. He sat down.

'... And Sylvia Plath seems to focus on natural strength.'

The voice rang through his head until it reached his brain. He jumped up. Everyone in his class looked at him. Where had they come from? How had they come back in?

'Sit down you idiot!' Tom said.

John looked at Tom in bewilderment and sat down.

* * * * *

A fly crawled up the wall. And amidst the droning of the teacher, and the talk of football, John sat. Although he was in a room full of people, he was alone. His subconscious had shown him this, which was the nearest to any sense he could make of it.

* * * * *

Tom focussed on a cloud through the window. He looked at his neighbour, John.

'What an idiot!' he thought.

Just then a cool breeze drifted through the room.

Iain Price.

* * * * *

Some pieces you sense are written out of a need, and in those circumstances people seldom need much more than the invitation to write, and a bit of peace and quiet. I remember Anne Fine talking to a large audience of teachers and educationalists who earnestly questioned her on the role of the teacher in providing the right stimulus, encouraging drafting, etcetera, and I think she got a bit pissed off with all this. 'Who was the most memorable English teacher you had at school, how did s/he specifically foster your writing talent...?' The same question rephrased for the umpteenth time: she took a long breath and said, her most memorable writing teacher was an old boy who drank heavily and didn't like children; he would come in on a Monday morning with a faint boozy bloom on him, fetch out his paper, and tell the kids to get on and write without a peep till break-time. It was the most blissful experience of her school life; and for good measure, she added that the thought of a teacher making her go back and redraft a piece of her own writing repelled her - she'd rather be made to drink a bucket of cold sick.

With apologies to Anne Fine for mounting and framing a throw-away answer, but it does help to reverse situations sometimes and see from the successful pupil's position what an insult it is to solicit credit where it is not always due.

I wish I could figure out precisely what makes a good teacher. I wonder if a good teacher is not so much a wizard as basically someone who is not a bad teacher - who responds at least adequately to pupils and situations and furthers his subject in a competent way? I believe that concept exists in child psychology - is it Melanie Klein? - the concept of 'good enough' parenting, the child will develop within the normal channels, with its share of talents, as long as its parenting is not so random or hostile as to actively damage its development.

I don't know. I'm still sitting on it.

Here's another one on the subject of aloneness, which seems to have a certain purchase with teenagers:

FIRST FLIGHT.

It was one of the darkest nights of the year. Cloud cover dispelled the starlight, leaving only the cold, heartless glare of the naked lightbulb. The grimy white plastic face of the clock read half-past twelve, though sleep was hard to find. Staring through a small gap between the heavy curtains, Jim fixed his eyes on the colourless world beneath the artificial orange street-lamp. The world pressed in on his heart, wishing for the freedom to walk through sprawling suburban streets, without the tether of fear that pulled him back.

He closed the heavy velvet curtains, stood up from his armchair, and walked slowly to the kitchen. The light flicked into life as he brushed the switch, revealing the small but homely kitchen. He put the kettle on, watching the steam billowing to the roof.

He switched on the radio, and tried to find a station still broadcasting. He found the news, and he listened as he made his coffee. Nothing of any real importance to him was said, and he wondered how many people took any notice of the useless drawl emitting from the radio. He switched it off.

Picking up the newspaper, he walked to the small, tidy living room. He sat down, drinking his coffee, and glancing uninterested at the multitude of headlines. Only fifteen days to Christmas, he was reliably informed by the blackened print. God, what a farce. People waited excitedly for months for one day of hypocrisy and drunkenness, while some suffered alone.

Despite the coffee, he dozed into unconsciousness, and slept till morning.

He woke with a start, glancing around. The doorbell rang with a piercing tone, and he slowly went to answer it. Upon opening, he was met by the cheery face of Mr Stubbins, from the society.

'Morning!' beamed Mr Stubbins, walking into the room.

'Hi.'

'Have you progressed at all, with your phobia?'

'To an extent.' An uneasy silence raised his pulse.

'Look, you've got to work at this. There is no other way.'

'I know, but... It's just a trial, that's all.'

Mr Stubbins sat down, and clasped his hands.

'I want to try an outing. I'll stay with you, so there's no way you can get into trouble. If you want to come back here, just say the word.'

A long silence.

'I'll try it, but I can't guarantee anything.'

'That's all I wanted to hear.' Mr Stubbins stood up sedately, walking to the door.

'Get your coat, there's a frost on the ground.'

Jim picked up his jacket from the back of a chair and put it on, bracing himself as he did so. He walked to the door.

'We won't go far.' Mr Stubbins led the way, Jim staying close.

'How are you feeling?' said Mr Stubbins, considerately.

'Nervous.'

'Just keep close, there's nothing to be nervous about.'

They walked to the top of the first flight of concrete stairs. Beyond that, he saw the dirty gravel of the car park stretching out before him.

Slowly, his blood pulsing, he moved down a step.

'Keep going.'

He froze. The tether was pulling him back, and his heart pounded. He held back the panic.

'I've got to go back.'

'Sure?'

'Yes - now.'

They turned, and paced back up, Jim continually quelling the desire to bolt to the door and lock himself in. He made it to the door, and calmly closed it.

'I'm sorry.'

'It's O.K. - at least you got that far.'

They both sat down with their thoughts, resting in silence.

'Look, I can't see you next week.'

Jim eyed him, quizzically.

'I have to see my sister - she's in a bit of trouble at the moment. I'd appreciate it if you could just try looking out the door now and again.'

'Will that help?'

'Any exposure can help. Agrophobia is caused by non-exposure.'

'I'll try.'

'Anyway, I'm sorry you couldn't make it down the stairs, but I have to go. I'll give you a ring sometime to arrange a proper session.'

He left, saying goodbye as he walked through the door. Jim was alone.

The days passed, and Jim tried to face the thought of the first flight. He didn't open the door for three days. He was alone.

Two days were left till Christmas, and he felt hopeless. The snow rested on the windowsill, bathing the room in a white light. He walked to the door, and clasped the handle. 'There's nothing to be afraid of,' he thought. The door slid open, and he walked to the stairs. Don't panic. His blood raced, he felt himself losing control. He took one step. Keep going. Don't lose control. He made it down another step, and another. He reached the bottom. He looked out, seeing the blanket of snow. He ran for the flat.

He opened the door, and stopped in the doorway. He'd done it. He went in the house, content.

He felt a hope in his heart. The first flight had been covered, the first step taken. Perhaps it wasn't such a bleak winter, after all.

Dominic James-Moore

*   *   *   *   *

Another from the title, 'Out of this World':

I was walking on Saturday, in a place called Netyn. It is a little town on the coast of Wales. I was going down a steep road towards the sea. It was a cold day, and I had my fishing rod with me. I walked as far as the road went, which went into the sea for launching boats. I went up to the sea wall and climbed up to the top. I sat there watching the gulls going round in circles and flying about.

I jumped off the wall and went down to the sea. I cast as far as I could, and sat there holding my rod. I reeled in and found my hook to have gone. I pulled it in and looked at the line. Nothing wrong. I wondered how it could have happened and walked round to the life-boat slipway and put another hook on. I found a mackeral and cut it up on the wall, and put it on my hook. Then I walked round and stared out to sea.

There was no noise, and the sea was perfectly still. I felt strange and wanted to sit there for a long time. I looked down and saw a face peering at me. I looked again and saw lots of heads. They were seals. Grey seals. I did not want to disturb them, so I kept quiet. It was getting dark and I felt hungry.

I walked back up to the sea wall and went into a shop. I bought some sandwiches and sat down and ate them. A gull hopped up and I saw something shiny in its mouth. It was my spinner, and the gull left it at my feet. I picked it up and looked at where the gull had gone.

I walked down the road again. It was eight-thirty, and nobody had got to the beach yet. I remembered once I had been at Sussex, Brighton. I had seen a bottle and I had picked it up. I had thrown it into the sea. Then I had waded in and picked it up and thrown it further out to sea. This time, I could not get it. I went to the sand and sat down.

I was in a jungle with a group of other soldiers and I was firing. Firing at a plane. Every time I fired, my shoulder hurt and I was nearly deafened. I loaded and I fired. I could not see the plane. I waited and saw it coming straight at me. I fired and got an answer O.K. - a burst of bullets whizzing over my head. I ducked and shouted to my friends. They were nowhere to be seen. I ran everywhere to see if they were there, behind that rock, under that big branch. At last I *found them. But not how I had expected. They were lying on the floor, blood oozing out of their wounds. Being a soldier was a stupid thing. The fighter had missed me, but had got my friends.*

That evening I made a big fire, and dug a deep hole. I buried my friends where we all used to sit... and wait for the planes to shoot them down. Then I saw a plane, I ran and shouted, waved, because now my friends were dead, I was marooned. Then I saw that it was the enemy's plane. I shot and shot, and hit the tail. Then I remembered how sad I had been when my friends died. I stopped firing and watched the plane fly away. I had spared a man's life and felt proud.

I felt a pain in my stomach. I was dying.

Then I was back on the beach.

Alex Klaar

*   *   *   *   *

And one from Julie, who did the autobiography:

ALONE.

Sometimes it is better to be alone and think and sometimes it is better to be with people. Alone you can sit and think and ponder and wonder. Peace, no rowdy noise, no pressure on you to talk, to move, to make a sound. Some people can't stand to be alone - they feel lost, unwanted, bored. Sometimes I feel like that too - I need noise, chatter, company, and even though I am alone, I want somebody to come and be alone with me - but it's impossible for more than one person to be alone, together. Very rarely, once in a blue moon, two people will sit together, both lost, both deeply involved in their own thoughts, and they will feel alone - but never truly alone.

Paula was alone. She sat thinking on the top of the roof. It was the school roof - out of bounds during the day, but at night it was open, free, a permitted place. The cool wind rustled her jacket and blew her long dark hair into a tangled mess. For what must have been the twentieth time that night, Paula allowed her head to fall back and she stared up at the stars, entranced by their lively brightness against the night sky. Then one of the bright specs slowly began to move - a shooting star! Paula closed her eyes and wished - wished that nothing ever had to change, that she could stay here forever and never have to venture back into reality.

'Oy - you!' Her dream shattered. Slowly, peeling her eyes away from the sky, she looked down. A small group of people were standing below her. She had not heard their arrival and the announcement of it had shocked her. Paula turned her head and stood up. She slowly made her way over to the iron stairs and silently walked down to the bottom. The group was there to greet her.

' 'Allo darlin'.' Paula turned to look at a tall youth. His skinhead reflected the moon, and an ear-ring protruded from his nose. Two girls ventured to the front of the group. They both wore heavy make-up and were scantily clad in short skirts and low tops.

'Can't you speak?' spat one of them, her bright lips curling into a sneer.

Ignoring them, Paula casually walked between the two of them and began to start home. However, the two girls were not happy to let her do this.

As Paula walked, she could hear her heart beating so loud that the footsteps of the two girls were sounded out. Unconsciously, she began to walk faster, up the alley, down the lamp-lit street, in and out of the soft pods of light cast by the street-lamps. Now, Paula could feel bodies close to her, and before even she had a chance to turn around, she found herself pushed up against a wall.

Silence, deep silence. Two pairs of sharp eyes staring into two pods of soft dark brown.

'We'm goina learn you to talk when you'm talked to...' - A sharp voice cut into the silence.

Paula felt a ball of rock fire into her stomach. She bent down to meet a knee flying up to her face. Then she was down, crouched on the floor shielding her face from the white trainers. It went on forever.

Then it stopped. Two pairs of feet echoed down a quiet street, leaving red-eyed, tear-stained Paula as we found her, truly alone.

Julie Fowler

✽   ✽   ✽   ✽   ✽

Bullying gets a lot of air-play in schools, and it's a phenomenon I find really interesting. I don't really mean that: I mean, outside the race-related, drug-related and basically criminal forms of bullying that intrude on school life now, there is a sense in which bullying has to do with the management of power, with hierarchy and pecking order. Personally, I never came high in pecking orders, but I was careful to stay in with the groups who did, even if it meant standing by while some other poor sod got it.

I used to occasionally give kids a chain-writing exercise, in which they would write a paragraph or two on anything they had on their mind, no restrictions, and as they finished I would go round passing their books on to other pupils, who would respond to the passage and continue it in some way. Sometimes this would run for a whole lesson, and they would have contributions from several classmates before their own books came back to them. I emphasised that they are a guest in other people's books, so they should wipe their feet and observe the courtesies. It goes well if the class has a good dynamic. The question of bullying came up in one of the books - this was a year eleven group:

'——- is a mixed school. There are many different types of people in the school, and it doesn't often work very well. In every year there have been people who are different in some way, and they are the ones who get ridiculed. Now, this happens at every school, but from my experience, the teachers here don't take enough notice of it, so it carries on in a milder way. The teachers think that they have stamped it out, but it always goes on, so the teachers have achieved nothing.'

'If we're talking about bullying here, teachers haven't got a clue, you seriously need to learn to stand up for yourself no matter how big your opponent.'

'With bullying you cannot win. If you tell the teachers nothing is done and if you beat the crap out of the bully you get done. You can't win.'

'You're all over-reacting. This school is brill, you have your closest and bestest friends and then there's those you can't stand, and you end up fighting, that doesn't make it bullying.'

A short, inconclusive debate, pity. All hierarchies are cemented by bullying - you only have to look at the police and the forces - and schools, possibly reinforced by their age structure, are classic hierarchies. There is constant power-related attrition involving kids, management, outside bodies, parents, teachers.

So I would say in that sense, bullying is a form of constant regulation, making people conform to the group and observe its conventions and pecking orders - it preserves stability. Not being a person who conforms very easily... in fact I have a compulsion to undermine hierarchies, formal and informal, so I'm not speaking up for this, merely saying it helps to know where things come from before you start trying to dismantle them. For example, it seems to me that any school wanting to make serious inroads into bullying needs to look closely at how it manages and regulates its own power structures in the first place. The prefect system might be a good place to start.

At the end of a longish spell of supply teaching some time ago I took my leave of a class which had given me a rough ride (cover teachers being the lowest of the low in the pecking order), but who I had eventually got to know and like teaching. Me: 'Well, it's been nice working with you, even though you were difficult to begin with - but I accept that, I know kids like to have their bit of fun...' Boy at the back: 'We has to gip you sir, to see if yu'm worvy..'

Here is a light piece that deals with school pecking order:

A COMPREHENSIVE GUIDE TO SURVIVAL FOR FIRST-YEAR STUDENTS

Introduction

So, you've finally made it to the 'big school'. It's been a long trek, but there's no respite, you've got to start all over again - but now you're on the bottom rung.

It is important to have some idea of how to work your way up to the top, as you were last year, at your primary school. This guide, if followed correctly, should allow you to survive the day-to-day traumas encountered by your average first-year pupil.

Chapter 1: The First Day

The first day of high school life can be either extremely exciting or daunting for a new pupil. Whichever it is for you, you should not allow your emotions to show too much. If you appear petrified, you will be labelled as a 'puff', especially if you are a boy. If you appear excited, then you shall be seen as either a swot, who can't wait to get down to work, or a mad-man who has a strange affinity for school.

The best front to put on is of a calm, quiet student. This is essential for your first few days, otherwise you will be noticed, which could have its serious consequences.

Chapter 2: Transport

When travelling to school, it is usual to catch a bus. This large mobile object comes in a variety of colours and sizes but has a main purpose of transporting pupils to and from school.

There are a few important points to remember when travelling on the school bus:

1.) It is imperative that first-year students sit at the front of the bus, preferably downstairs. The back of the bus is reserved for members of the upper school who do not take kindly to 'little people' stealing their seats.

This seating arrangement is also beneficial as the top deck of the bus is reserved for smokers at all times.

2.) Do not shout or scream in an irritating fashion on the bus. Due to their immense workload, the prospect of travelling to school is not as exciting for members of the upper school, therefore any irritation during the journey may result in the exploding of short-tempered pupils.

3.) It is not necessary to wait at the bus-stop at 6.00a.m., as this shows an enthusiasm laughed at by the upper school.

4.) Do not stand on the stairs of the bus. Due to the size of some of the upper school pupils, it may be possible for them to trip up on a 4ft 6 pupil standing on the stairs. Should this happen, you are well advised to hide your bag as you are in dire trouble.

5.) Do not smoke on the bus. This is a desperately important rule for all pupils to adhere to, up until the fourth year. Pupils who attempt to smoke and consequently cough their lungs apart will receive no sympathy from the onlooking upper-school members, who will merely laugh you into the floor.

6.) Do not be too eager to get to school. It has been known for pupils, in the past, to stand up as soon as the bus leaves the bus garage in readiness to get off. This is another example of tell-tale enthusiasm which will be noticed.

7.) Above all, when passing the coaches from the middle school, do not sink to their immature depths and begin to flick the 'v-sign' violently. This in no way enhances your standing as a hard-man, merely as a prat.

If you travel, on the other hand, with your parents, in a car or similar vehicle, do not allow your mother to kiss you in public - even mothers straightening ties can be an embarrassment. Also ensure that your mother does not return to school in the middle of the morning with the sandwich box that you left in the kitchen at 8.30a.m.

Chapter 3: Uniform

It is, of course, important to make a good impression in your early days, though it is more important to make a good impression with the present pupils than with the teachers. In the light of this, uniform should be smart but not immaculate.

Remember boys, no Farah or Trutex trousers, they went out with the dinosaurs, and girls, knee-length skirts are regulation with the staff, but a disaster with everyone else.

The school tie shall be worn backwards, with the thin end prominent and the other end tucked inside the shirt. The knot on your tie should be as small and quiet as possible.

195

Blazers are an extremely sore point. They should be incinerated or 'accidentally' left on the bus at the earliest juncture. The longer you keep your blazer, the less credible you become.

Trainers are not essential, but if you are going to wear them make sure that they are not: Adidas 'Kick', Hi-Tec 'Squash', Dunlop 'Green Flash' or any style of Nicks, Gola and Go-Sport.

Two final points on uniform:

Girls should never wear knee-length socks - no matter how cold or what your mother says, this is an absolute no-no. Also, no matter how tempting it is for you boys in Kidderminster, no drainpipe trousers or slip-on shoes are allowed.

Chapter 4: Uniform in Games Lessons

Just a short note to make sure that you don't look silly in games lessons. The standard rugby top is O.K. if you have it baggy, and try not to wear it for too long. What is not acceptable is the wearing of skin-tight white T-shirts and shorts. The aforementioned trainers are also not advisable.

Chapter 5: The Teaching Staff

This section is not particularly long but nevertheless very important. It has taken a great deal of time and experience to meet the match of many teachers; sometimes it is impossible.

For those new-comers who have not yet broken the five-foot barrier, there is the added problem of being 'engulfed' by the large teacher.

Names will not be named in this section in case this guide gets into the hands of a member of staff, therefore you must decide yourself which teachers you can play-up and which teachers you should not. Look at a teacher's classroom manner. Do they seem in control of the lesson? Are their lessons usually held in silence? Have they a widespread and interesting array of essay titles?

A tell-tale sign of an unstable member of staff is one who threatens to send you to a more senior member of staff. It is possible to play this teacher up.

It is advisable to make notes on teachers in all lessons and from your notes calculate who you can mess about and to what extent.

Chapter 6: Break-Time Conduct

Break-time is a blessing for members of the upper school, who need to get rid of some tension. A good way of doing this is by 'borrowing' the football of a first-year pupil in order to play for themselves. It is unwise to attempt to retrieve the ball as this will result in an untimely tackle by the elder pupils. Do not even threaten to report these people to 'the Boss' as this will result in the football ending the day underneath the 4.51 to Worcester Foregate Street.

Do not dare to 'take on' the upper school at a game, as this will mean a lesson in kicking people.

Chapter 7: Tricks and Traps

On account of the considerable sense of humour owned by many members of the upper school, they may find it irresistible to play a trick here and there on the younger, more gullible members of the school. A few pieces of information which should ensure you are not tricked are supplied here:

1.) The building across the road is not an extension of the new block, it is in fact a different school. Do not be fooled by this.

2.) It is not necessary to walk four times around the playing field to reach the geography mobiles, but due to the level of interest of geography lessons this may be advisable. This is another common trap by fifth or sixth formers.

Chapter 8: The Toilets

When entering the toilets at school, it is advisable to develop a rather heavy cold or sever all sensory cells in the nose, as to avoid the various pungent odours. Also, make sure that you never need to 'defecate' in the school toilets as the seats are more often than not decorated with bodily fluids and the toilet roll is more suited to smoothing down wood in the C.D.T. rooms.

* * * * *

Finally, do not cheek the members of the upper school, particularly the prefects. You will live to regret this if you do, and will be thrown back down the ladder to survival.

Follow the rules carefully in this guide, and you may succeed in your aim to reach the summer holidays, and eventually to the end of your school career.

Good luck.

Tony McCooey

[Written in Jan 1990 by the way, for students of school fashion.]

* * * * *

'Guide' essays became popular for a while, after that one did the rounds.

This is an unusual piece from a fifth-year (year eleven) - she has made a mistake with the name of the daughter:

THE YOUNGER GENERATION.

Clara Willis was sitting peacefully on the pale green carpet, in the sitting-room playing with her dolls. Beside her were a pile of dolls' clothes, a miniature plastic horse and a glass of orange squash. She was humming an unrecognisable tune to herself at the same time as diminishing a plate of chocolate biscuits, balanced precariously on top of her curled up left leg. She would have been a perfectly normal six-year old girl, if it wasn't for the fact that the sitting-room she was in was part of the house belonging to her married fifty-two year-old daughter. Mrs. Willis was seventy-eight years old.

Meanwhile in the kitchen, Mrs Doreen Willis was trying desperately to fight an urge to throw a plate at her husband Tom:

"My mother is not senile! She's just going through a difficult stage at the moment."

"Yeah, she's at a difficult age - being five years old when you're really seventy-eight, can lead to a few minor problems I suppose!" Tom replied sarcastically. Doreen picked up a plate; it was her best china; she quickly put it back on the table.

"You know she can't help it. I wish you'd be more sympathetic. She only started going like this after Bill died. She met him when she was ten years old; she only had her early childhood without him, therefore she only knows that kind of life without him being there. That's why she's like this. It's logical, really."

"Of course it is." Tom stared at her.

"You don't believe me, do you?"

"No. Anyway, why did we have to get stuck with her?"

"She's my mother. She hasn't anywhere else to go. Would you want her roaming the streets?"

"As long as it isn't my street, yes!"

Doreen picked up the plate again. "For the good of your health, Tom, I sincerely hope you didn't mean that last comment -"

※　　※　　※　　※　　※

Clara had become fed up with playing with her dolls. She walked into the hall and discovered the game of seeing how many stairs you can jump down at once, before you got scared: a game that children must have been playing ever since stairs were invented. Clara easily jumped off the first stair. She decided to be more ambitious and try the second stair.

"Doreen, please put that plate down."

"I will not."

"Oh, don't you start going senile as well."

"My mother is not senile!" She put the plate down, nevertheless.

"O.K. then, she's mad! I don't feel safe living in the same house as her - I dread going into a different room in case she's sitting there, playing with those stupid dolls of hers: I can't stand it any longer!"

"But where could she go?"

"Take her to an old people's home. Tell her it's a children's home, she might go then! They'll give her a nice big room and she can play with her dolls on her own, for the rest of her life. Then, maybe I can walk round my own house without being the slightest bit frightened. Is that too much to ask for?"

"Yes! As long as I have a moderately sized house and good health, no parent of mine is going into an old people's home."

"That means we have a choice: either we go and live in a shed or you jump out of the window and break your leg!"

Clara jumped fairly easily off the second stair and crawled up onto the third.

"Are you trying to be funny?"

"I thought you liked funny people. You seem to be sticking up for your stupid mother enough. She's as funny as they come!"

Doreen picked up the plate. She glared at Tom.

"Put that plate down."

"I will not."

"Put it down."

"All right I will!" Doreen let go of the plate. It smashed on the floor.

Clara jumped off the next stair. She landed in a heap on the floor. She lay motionless, staring up at the ceiling with expressionless eyes. A small patch of carpet turned colour from pale orange to deep red.

"That's the best china! Why did you do that? You are getting senile!"

"So it's OK to abuse my mother but not the china!"

"I've never abused your mother in my life!"

"You want her locked away!"

"No I don't, I want her in an old people's home."

"For as long as she lives, my mother is not going in an old people's home!"

Doreen was the type of person who always told the truth.

Helen Price

* * * * *

Q. What's it like being a writer?

A. I imagine it must be quite pleasant to be a famous writer, because you can have the reputation but still keep your privacy unlike T.V. personalities for example, who get pestered for autographs in the street. People don't recognise authors. The other thing is you can still be just as good when you're old, whereas a lot of people reach a peak in their jobs quite young and it must be hard going downhill after that.

Q. Where do you get your ideas from?

A. What I want to know is how you get rid of bad ideas. Sometimes you get one and it seems to hang around like a smell affecting everything else you think of; you fling the windows open but it won't go.

Q. How long does it take to write a book?

A. It's hard sometimes to remember that a reader will get through your story in a fraction of the time it took you to write it. I've often had pupils come to me saying their story's going nowhere and they're fed up with writing it. When you go through it you realise they've got bogged down in a passage where nothing much is happening, and they're afraid the reader will be bored stiff. As soon as they see it through the reader's eyes, they can tell it will only take a few minutes to read, and it's not messing up the story, it's probably helping it. So when the going gets tough, remember, it might take a long time to write but that's not going to be a problem for the reader.

Q. Do you like writing?

A. I like writing longhand better than the computer. In 'And Smith Must Score...' the main character says, *'If I've got words to write, or drawings, or calculations, I like to feel the pen at the end of my arm. I don't want something with its own mind, I want it to be my mind and my arm alone, and my pen doing what my mind and my arm tell it to. And if I go wrong I like to cross out. I don't believe in deleting. I like to look at my mistakes and say, "That's where I went wrong, and that's where I crossed it out in a rip, and that's how I put it right." I like to doodle, too. When I'm thinking. You tell me how to doodle with a word-processor.*' I didn't have to get into character before writing that...

Q. How do you get a book published?

A. When I started writing this book I had one novel published, and one self-published. Now I've got six of mine self-published, including this one, and have published one by another author, Steve Bowkett. It's brilliant watching the covers come together and turning a mass of bits of paper into a book, you can't beat it. But you have to put a lot of time and money on the line to market them, as I mentioned before, otherwise you'll just have a garage full of unsellable stuff and a crippling overdraft. The trick is - do you really know if your stories are any good, or do you just hope they are? If you don't know, you'd better make sure you find out because if you get it wrong you're not a self-publisher at all, you're a vanity publisher and you're going to lose a lot of money.

Q. Who is your favourite author?

A. I would like to mention a Canadian author whose books had an incredible impact on me when I was a boy. His name is Ernest Thompson Seton. The two titles I remember were 'Ruggylug' - which I've lost - and 'Animal Heroes' which I still have. This is what the fly-page says:

'ANIMAL HEROES
Being the Histories of a CAT, a DOG, a PIGEON, a LYNX, TWO WOLVES & a REINDEER
and in Elucidation of the same over 200 DRAWINGS
By ERNEST THOMPSON SETON,
Author of Wild Animals I Have Known, BIOGRAPHY of a Grizzly, TWO Little Savages etc. NATURALIST to Govt of MANITOBA'

Written exactly like that, about a hundred years ago. I remember them as wonderful sad stories of animal life in the wild, and would love to hear from anyone who knows anything about them (especially if they have a copy of 'Raggylug' going spare...).

[I have just found out there is a 'Best of Ernest Thompson Seton' (details at back) ed. Richard Adams - of course, I can see the influence now...]

CHAPTER 11

Horror

A vast amount of what young people write is sensational, in-your-face blood, gore, punch-ups, shoot-ups, along with the weird and wild alien figures, transmogrifying monsters, parricides, fratricdes and all the rest. Unfortunately, I have no sympathy at all with the genre(s), and this makes it difficult for me be objective when looking at that kind of writing.

It's not because I find the pieces bleak and nihilistic, there is usually too much relish about them for that, they just appear to be so lazy. Whatever you write, your story operates in a fictional landscape of some kind, and this needs to be coherent, and the rules by which events are controlled have to evolve somehow - or, if they don't exist, it might be helpful to make the odd acknowledgement to the reader when offering your version of chaos.

Alternatively, we could be at one of those fault-lines that cuts off one generation from another for a decade or so and I've simply lost touch. I remember the disbelief of the generation before mine when we had our first Beatle haircuts... Ah, well - here are a couple which I enjoyed. I wouldn't exactly call them hard-core, though:

THE DAY THE BIRDS DIED

"BLAAAARK! Bluk Bluk Bluk."

The noise came from behind the tree he leant against. Chris gritted his teeth as he prepared for the verbal onslaught. The familiar school uniform emerged from behind the tree.

"Pack it in, will you!" he whined, but John Cambell continued with his impression of a chicken. He strutted clumsily around Chris with his body bent from the waist,

hands close to his chest waving his elbows and his ponytail bobbed obediently as his head sharply turned in different directions. The music of laughter from his friends persuaded him to carry on.

"AAAAH, what's the matter? Is the chicken not very happy?" Paul Hargreaves sneered, noticing Chris's obvious discomfort. Chris threw him a venom glance, he hated him, he was the front man for the four hard-knocks. He hated them all - Billy White, John Cambell, Paul Hargreaves and Stevie Clark who returned Chris's glare with ferocity, and to carry more weight shoved him hard, landing Chris heavily on his back gasping as the air shot out of his lungs. He grunted as he quickly recovered from the shock, he heaved himself up and noticed Christie Stewart watching a fair distance away, shaded under an alcove of trees. Billy White followed his eye and spotted Christie. "Get lost, bitch," he yelled, and Chris watched as she hesitated, then turned her back and ran.

"Bastards," he hissed, his anger now overcoming his fear of what they'd do to him.

"What was that?" Stevie glared at him. "You callin' us bastards?" He was the tallest of the four, sporting long shoulder-length, blond hair with a distinctive nose that looked remarkably like a rose-thorn. He was a vicious fighter, as Chris had observed previously in a fight between him and Andrew Carter. Three blows had floored him causing a badly broken nose, bruised throat and a fractured jaw. The results had Andrew Carter taking four weeks' rest off school and Stevie Clark two weeks suspension.

"Are you ignorin' me, chicken...? I said, ARE YOU?" Stevie's infamous temper was being fuelled by the delay as Chris failed to reply. Boiling point was reached as Stevie brought his fist crashing down hard on his face. The impact split Chris's lower lip sending blood cascading onto his shirt; he stumbled to the floor as Stevie followed through, the momentum curling his hand into a phoenix fist and ramming it into Chris's gut.

The injury blows acted as a signal to the rest of the lads as they advanced on the crumpled sixteen year old, kicking, punching and stomping. Chris felt a pain in his arm, another on his chest, and cried out as an excruciating sharp pain in the small of his back struck him. He guessed it was probably a toe-poking kick or stick of some sort. His guess was confirmed as a thick beech branch crashed onto his shoulder. He tasted the familiar salty taste of his crimson life fluid in his mouth and yelled out in agony as he was repeatedly kicked and stomped on the head. His head. It hurt. It hurt bad. It hurt real bad. His head. He heard shouts from a distance away, then he heard nothing.

He emerged from unconsciousness with his head singing and he didn't like the music. It felt like a vice was clamped tight around his temples, and someone was sadistically turning the screw. The familiar stench of disinfectant rose into his nose like an unwelcome finger. He was lying down, and as he swung his legs off the couch his head sang louder and he groaned, massaging his bruised temples. Most of his body ached, he tried to stand up and succeeded until his leg muscles gave way and almost collapsed as a spell of dizziness hit him.

The door opened and a woman followed it, he recognised her as the school nurse. A very much needed member of staff in this school, whose main jobs were curing eyes that had been caused by 'banging into a door', stomachs that were caused by 'eating the wrong food', and bloody noses induced by 'atmospheric pressure changes'. She was no fool though.

"What are you doing young man? Get back, you've had it rough." He obeyed and watched her as she poured him a glass of water. She was small, about 5 feet 3, and she wore a shiny head of chestnut brown hair that was cut to a style that he thought was called a bob. The flesh on her face was pretty and, as he was presently admiring, she had very shapely legs.

She handed him the glass of water and he looked briefly at her eyes that were sparkling chips of sapphire. She smiled reassuringly at him, causing her cheekbones to rise, creating a prettier face. He smiled back and lay down. "Don't you worry now. Paul Hargreaves and his group will be dealt with. Your father will be coming to pick you up any minute now." She treated him to a kindly smile. He returned the smile, treating himself to an appraising glance of her ample breasts.

*   *   *   *   *

Christie had come over to talk to Chris. She didn't know what she'd say to him but she was sure he wouldn't turn her away. She waited outside in the approaching darkness working up courage to knock on the front door. She saw someone enter the kitchen, from the window that was nearest her she could see a dark figure near to the fridge at the far end of the room. It was Chris. She watched in silence as he opened the fridge door and took out a large piece of raw steak, the blood dripping from it as he removed it from the metal tray. He lifted the steak with one hand, looked at it for a moment, then tore off a chunk with his teeth. He chewed with difficulty, blood dripping from his chin. Chris grinned in satisfaction as he indulged his gluttony. Dark rusty stains smeared his cheeks and some of the red liquid dripped from his fingers. When he opened his mouth a piece fell to the floor and quickly he picked it up and rammed it back in.

Christie turned away and fled from his house revolted.

Chris stuffed the remainder of the meat into his mouth then carefully licked every last drop of blood from his fingers.... Something was wrong. Something was most definitely wrong. He had seen the doctor last week and been treated for concussion, he had taken his pills to ease the pain. Ever since his lamping in the woods he possessed a constant urgency for raw meat. His head ached. Chris put his hands to the back of his head, the palms of his hands massaging his temples as if to try and cease the slow throbbing pain. Which, surprisingly, it did, but the pain returned and it returned with malevolence. It felt as though there was an invisible hand inside his brain and it was scratching the inside of his head. He realised who had done this to him and the more he thought about it the more he despised the group who did it. His fury built up, he reached for the garage keys hung up on the wall. He would get revenge, he was not the bird, they were. They were chickens, and they were his delicacy now.

He unlocked the door and grabbed hold of the nearest implement and tested its weight. It made his heart race, although its colour was fading to the orange of rust it was still in good shape. He looked at the sledgehammer and held it with affection like a mother would hold its child. Taking up a screwdriver as he left the garage he grinned and thought of the song the chickens would sing. The song will taste sweet. He was sure of it.

(Author unknown)

*   *   *   *   *

That was fifth-year (year 11) work; the next two pieces are by fourth years:

THE STRAIT-JACKET OF CLOCK AND CALENDAR

What is time?

This was the question which had baffled scientists, philosophers and other great thinkers throughout the ages. Now, thanks to the sheer brilliance of our own scientists, we have the facilities to finally answer the question.

A group of super-fit, ultra-intelligent agents were ordered to travel back in time. I drew the short straw.

But first I must explain myself: I have no real name, simply a code number, G678. I only need a name on a mission, so why not use a fake? As air scientists approached their goal, the Institution decided that, with GIB-7's clear expertise in genetic engineering, our "Genies" should create humans suitable to join the time corps, and strong enough to withstand the unknown rigours of time travel. In short, I am a prototype model which is disposable.

Now, one thing I have forgotten to tell you is the era of my existence: I apologise, for I never needed to say it before; I am from the Realm of GIB-7, and I was made during the reign of the Seventh Institutionalist (that is, 2523).

I had to pass countless physical and mental, stamina, and agility tests before I was pronounced fit for my mission. My equipment includes drugs which would make me linguistically and socially fluent wherever I went; weapons so efficient and inconspicuous that they could easily be mistaken by the untrained eye as extravagant clothing accessories, and, most important of all, a brain-tracker which could pinpoint my whereabouts in the event of my inability to return.

On the day of my departure, I experienced the most peculiar feeling. Incredible tremors ran through my whole body, my stomach turned into an enormous knot of twisted, cramped, agonising muscle, and I nearly passed out. Then I found myself in the middle of a large hut, which smelt strongly of sweat, sleep and dirt. Someone blocked the doorway. I swallowed a pill.

"Why, what are you doing here, stranger?"

It was a young man, not so much curious as violent. "Well, speak stranger, or I'll let my staff ask the questions." From inside his tunic he brought an evil-looking cudgel;suddenly I felt the urge to speak.

"I was walking along, and suddenly felt a sickness come over me. No one was in here so I slept."

"You cannot have slept. My wife was in here but a short while ago and she mentioned no stranger."

Talking would obviously get me nowhere. I took an inch of gold braid from my dungarees and reeled over, sticking it to his boots as I did so. Then I concentrated, as he fell to the floor. Taking two buttons from my shirt cuffs, I placed them between my thumbs and either side of his head; I was able to drain, duplicate, and replace his thoughts, then I stripped him and dressed myself in his clothes. Using his knowledge of life in 1392, I made my way towards the local wisewoman and asked her how to return to my time.

"Ye Gods, 'tis a mad, possessed worker. Out of here, I tell you."

Then I sat down and tried to think things logically. If I was here from the future, I know what has happened in history, and so if I try and change the course of history, I can't be here, so I must go back to where I started from.

I made a decision: to go to London and try and kill the King.

I got to London, though paying my way was hard enough. I had to use my mental skills wagering my money and my physical skills in wrestling bouts and the like, but, before what was called Christmas, I reached the capital. Never before had I seen a place such as London: poverty and riches, beauty and disease, so close together. I came to the King's court, where I was made a member of his entertaining staff.

I spent a long time with the King, and became a firm favourite of his, before I was allowed to perform to him alone. This was my chance, and I stabbed him with his own sword. Then I felt myself slide clumsily away down the helterskelter of time. My theory had worked:

"The Morphail Effect states that you cannot live as a paradox, so whenever you change something you should leave alone, you become totally alienated to that era and are ejected out."

So, you cannot change what has been. Other experiments showed that what will be, will be. There is no escaping the straitjacket of clock and calendar.

Philip Howell

* * * * *

This one is a bit formulaic, but well delivered:

THE LAST TIME

I can remember the last time I did. Even though it was so long ago it doesn't seem vague in my mind at all.

When I think of the last time, I think of the worst time I've ever had in my life. God forbid if it happened again. I don't think I could cope. Jeez man, I don't know how I did or even if I did.

I can remember what I thought that day. I was so angry, so upset, so flustered that I felt I was going to burst. I've been filled with hate since that day. It's changed my whole life thinking about it. I don't know whether or not I'd do it again. My dad says we shouldn't regret things because we just keep wishing to change the past and eventually it'll screw up your mind. Then again, thinking about it sometimes from the look in his eyes when he sees me I think he regrets it too.

For goodness sake. This sounds so morbid doesn't it. Well why don't I tell you what happened. I can't tell you from the beginning because you need to know what happened before that to understand. Well, here goes...

It is about a friendship. A friendship between a friend, Amy, and myself. We had a close friendship, like sisters. I used to tell her everything, she knew all my secrets. We went everywhere together, and once we went to the cinema in town together. Mum and dad didn't mind having her around all the time, she was like family. My mum always reminded me though, that Amy had her own family. I said I knew that but I always used to wish she lived in my house.

I can remember when I lost my favourite necklace and Amy appeared out of nowhere in my back garden holding it.

Amy could always make me laugh, the way she jumped and ran about. She was wonderful.

We were always happy together until dad lost his job. Then things started getting tense. To make things worse for my parents but not for me, Amy's family went away. They asked us to take care of Amy. They said they would come back for her. They never did, or never got the chance to either.

Amy and me saw each other not only every day but nearly every hour of the day, twenty-four hours a day.

Things got worse and worse. My whole family were always moody and bad tempered. I didn't know what to do, even Amy seemed drawn back.

On April the 20th. That's the day it happened, I can remember that day exactly. Amy hadn't been well so mum said she couldn't go out. If she had've come to school I could have saved her I suppose.

Fate, I guess!

When I got back from school I was in a good mood. Why, I don't know. I went inside the house. I remember this bit well because we have four steps on the front of my house which lead up the porch to the front door. I jumped up them in one leap. The first time ever. I can remember feeling so proud! I stood at the top looking down on the garden and feeling as if I'd just climbed Mount Everest.

213

I went through the door with a big smile on my face, only to see my parents in the living room. My mother was crying and my dad was soothing her. I could hear them talking.

'Dave,' my mum sobbed, 'she'll be so upset, she'll never forgive us.'

'Jane, stop it. She will. Anyway, you know how hard up for cash we are. For once we'll have a proper meal which doesn't taste like flea-ridden carpet doused in gravy.'

'Oh, but don't you think she'll... Oh, hi baby. Did you have a good day at school?'

Bummer, mum's spotted me.

Then I remember replying to her, 'Yeah, great it was - what's wrong and where's Amy?'

'Nothing's the matter dear. Your mum is just upset about a programme on T.V. Now that you're home let's have dinner. Amy has... just gone out for some fresh air, she'll be back later.'

After my dad had said it he stood up and made his way to the kitchen with my mum. I went in after them and sat down. My mum sat down whilst my dad pulled out a backing tray from the oven with three plates on it. It was meat and gravy with tiny new potatoes. Yuk, I hate potatoes.

That's all I thought. I wasn't at all suspicious, just filled with distaste over the fact that I had to eat potatoes.

I tasted the meat and couldn't quite place what it was. Beef? Nah... Pork? Nah... Chicken? No way, and not turkey either. Wrong colour. Lamb? Maybe.

'Dad, is this lamb?' I asked.

My mum burst into tears and screamed at my dad: 'We have to tell her, Dave.'

Now I was getting angry that I didn't know what was going on.

'Tell me what?' I asked.

'Honey,' my dad said in a gentle voice. The same voice he used when he tried to get my pocket money off me. 'Today Amy had an accident. She broke her leg running. Mother and I decided it best to put her out of her misery.'

'I want to see her now!'

'Dear,' my mum said, 'I need to get you new shoes for school. I can't afford food.'

The comment was self-explanatory. I'd just eaten my best friend, I thought. I ran upstairs sobbing into my bedroom and locked the door. All I could think was the colour of her fur and the way everyone said she was the cutest rabbit ever.

That was the last time I saw her.

Lauren Scheuermann

* * * * *

It can be quite effective to take the position of a younger or less literate person when writing, if it's not overdone. Stunning examples such as Russell Hoban's 'Ridley Walker' and Hugh Scott, 'Why Weeps the Brogan', come to mind.

It was coming up to G.C.S.E. one year, or G.C.E., or 16+, or whatever was on the menu that year, and I gave a class a pep-talk about the language paper, saying that they should be careful to pick an open-ended title for the essay writing question, rather than something like 'A Day in the Country' or 'The Fairground', which would channel them into a dull, adjectival style that might be competent but was unlikely to catch the examiner's eye.

One girl, I noticed, was listening to me, but with her arms folded, one shoulder forward and her head well back - a kind of defiant posture. I didn't say anything. Next day she handed me this:

THE FAIRGROUND

It was a beautiful day and I was really happy. I was going to take my bike but Daddy told me not to because I had lost the key to the padlock and he didn't want me to get my bike stolen, so he told me to walk and he would buy another padlock soon. He gave me my pocket money and I ran off.

It took me quite a long time to get to the fair and I wished I had my bike. I had wanted to go to the fair at night when the lights would seem even brighter, the music louder, and the atmosphere more exciting, but Daddy said he was too busy to take me so I had to go on my own in the daytime. Nevertheless, I was still quite excited - it wasn't every day the fair came. As I got closer I could hear the loud, raucous music, the shouting, and screams of exhilaration. I ran the rest of the way, unable to contain myself.

When I actually got to the fair, I didn't know what to do first. I had eighty pence - you thought I only had thirty didn't you? Well, I'd told nanny about the fair and she'd given me fifty pence. I decided to buy a candyfloss first; after all you can't go to the fair and not have any candyfloss can you? After that I wandered round. I fancied a go on the shooting gallery but I was too small, so I hung around watching other people for a while. Next I wandered along to the coconut shy, but I don't like coconut very much so I gave that a miss. Finally I came to the big wheel. I must have stood for about half an hour just watching: it seemed to reach dazzling heights. I considered having a go; it seemed a bit scary, but I dared myself to go on. I paid the lady and I got in a seat with a big girl and then we were off. My tummy was feeling really funny and the big girl kept screaming. Once I looked down and the people looked like coloured blobs; I didn't look down again because I felt really dizzy. When I got off my legs felt like jelly and I couldn't speak or think properly.

I was feeling a bit shaky when this man came up to me and asked if I wanted a drink because he said I looked a bit green. I accepted the drink he offered and then he told me to go and sit down until I felt better. Of course there was nowhere to sit, being a fairground, so he said I could sit in his car. He opened the door of a red car and told me he'd be back in a minute. I got in the car and lay down. He came back smiling and asked if I wanted to go home. I said yes please, and I was just getting out of the car when he said he'd take me home, and I said no thank you, but he pushed me in anyway and rushed around to the front seat and quickly drove off.

I started screaming that he was going the wrong way but he said we were taking a short cut and I'd better shut up. I sat back and sulked, looking out of the window with increasing fear because I didn't recognise where we were going. We seemed to go for miles and I started screaming again; I was really frightened by now. Suddenly he stopped the car, got out and got into the back. He hit me round the head and then gagged me and tied me up and threw me on the floor of the car, then he got back in the front and drove off again. I started crying because the ropes hurt my wrists and ankles and the gag hurt my mouth, and I was scared.

Eventually we stopped and he pulled me out of the back seat onto the floor which was cold and damp, even in the summer. I looked around and saw I was in a dark wood. The man took the ropes and gag off and I was going to run away but I was so tired, so very, very tired. Then he took all my clothes off and took a stick and beat me with it and I screamed and screamed and screamed and screamed but nobody ever came to help me; and then everything went black.

I woke up, not in my bedroom, but in a nice, quiet, peaceful place far away from horrible men with sticks and lots of nice people are looking after me and Tiddles our cat is here, the one that got run over. I do miss you though, give my love to Daddy. And Mommy, please don't cry.

Dawn Snookes

*   *   *   *   *

CHAPTER 12

A-Level

The image I had of myself when I went into teaching wasn't to do with the routine regimentation of young people in the herd, it was more to do with the idea of master and apprentice: the wood-turner at a lathe with the youngster, starting a piece off, handing it over, taking it back, pointing out a technique, handing it back, until there is a finished piece that satisfies both of them in different ways. This is what you get with the A-level literature personal study.

Ideally, the student chooses what he or she wants to study, with a bit of guidance from the teacher. Some teachers simply set the texts and give a choice of questions, for example, or give a 'free' choice of text from a pre-selected list. But to go from where the student is at can be a brilliant experience, assuming you can find where they're at of course - but then helping them to find the starting place can be interesting in itself.

With trepidation, I am going to put in what I think is a good, but fairly typical example. It is long and in places a bit confused, and you may decide to skip. But I want it to go in anyway. What exactly am I claiming for it? Not that it or any of them are ground-breaking pieces of literary analysis, but that they show a young person at the cusp - still awkward, but at the point of independent, confident critical thought. And to be someone's guide at that stage is one of the great experiences in life.

This one came about when its author showed an interest in the idea of the anti-hero in literature. I stifled a yawn (not Holden Caulfield again) and prepared myself for a dull one. But around that time the Daily Mirror ran a banner headline describing John Major as a nerd. I'm one of these people who were ambivalent about Major - in one way I thought he was the ultimate wimp, and in another he seemed quite subversive and morally strong. You can't beat a bloody great contradiction to get the juices going, so I said to her, why don't we look at the concept of the nerd? Before diving into books, let's think about people we see as nerds, put our heads together next week and see what common ground we come up with.

I thought of one or two the following week, neither seemed exactly right (whatever that was). There was a drama lesson scheduled with a younger class and I gave them a theme for improvisation in groups; while I was watching them I became acutely aware of a boy who was very small, uncool, with a high voice, totally immersed in the group, animated, earnest, humourless. And yet he was orchestrating the whole thing - cajoling, directing, correcting, fussing - and they were all complying: he would not be denied.

Whatever a nerd is, he was one, and I felt I could make sense of the John Major connection. John Irving's 'A Prayer for Owen Meany' came to mind. We had our meeting, and the whole thing sprang to life:

FOLLOWING THE NERD IN LITERATURE AND LIFE

An exploration of weakness in Lord of the Flies, Coral Island, Blue Remembered Hills and A Prayer for Owen Meany.

I intend to explore some of the themes and weaknesses present in Coral Island, Lord of the Flies, Blue Remembered Hills and A Prayer for Owen Meany, examining how effective I believe them to be.

I feel that both Coral Island and Lord of the Flies are diminished by the fact that females do not play an important role in the novels. Even when a female occurs in Coral Island she is a 'woman in distress' (P.284) and so must be helped. I feel that Blue Remembered Hills deals with the situation in a more equal manner. In this play there are two girls, Angela and Audrey, although they exist in a separate hierarchy to the boys - for example the boys say a cabin 'ent for girls, cabins ent'(P.62). The female characters in Coral Island where they exist tend to be weak and dependent and have no personality. They are characterless. This is clearly seen in Coral Island as Jack perceives Avatea as a 'good cause'(P.261) who needs saving. He wishes to take her to the Christian Island where her lover is chief - 'once there Avatea would be safe'(P.273). Avatea's safety is totally dependent on Jack.

The weakness of the female characters is also demonstrated in Blue Remembered Hills where Angela admits that she 'wanna go home' (P.73) and that 'we been bloody crying and all down in here'(P.75).

I feel that the lack of female characters is important as it emphasises how the nerd in these four novels is always male. In Coral Island it is Peterkin, Lord of the Flies' nerd is Piggy and also Simon, Blue Remembered Hills has Donald and Raymond as its nerds, while A Prayer for Owen Meany's nerd is Owen.

Hierarchy plays a major role in all four novels. It is particularly evident in Coral Island, which presents a very clear hierarchy which is not challenged. It is headed by God and the Missionary - their purpose is to guide the story to a proper conclusion and so they exist on a separate level to the other real characters. The proper conclusion is one through which the author's message may be portrayed. In Ballantyne's case it is to show that English Christians are superior and are able to survive any situation with their pride remaining intact. The novel's message is to show that the English are born survivors who are never in serious danger. The novel is a defence of civilisation against savagery. Jack heads the group due to 'his being older and much stronger and taller than either of us, he was a very clever fellow, and

I *think would have induced people much older than himself to choose him for their leader, especially if they required to be led on a bold enterprise'(P.23). Jack is therefore automatically obeyed, no matter what.*

Ralph places himself next. When speaking to the pirates he says that he is *'made of such stuff as the like of you will never tame.'* Peterkin is considered inferior to Jack and Ralph due to his *'capering and jumping about like a monkey'(P.22)* as well as his *'very unobservant nature and his animal spirits'(P.24).* This links him with animals, which are always lower. They are always spoken of in terms of their use. A prime example of this is the aquarium which Peterkin builds: it was *'stocked with various specimens of anemonies and shellfish, in order to watch more closely'(P.57).* Its purpose is to develop their knowledge, replacing one theory with another: *'we came thus to know that crabs grew in this way'(P.38).* Another example of this is when Peterkin *'wants a pair of shoes'* (P.113), he kills the pig with the toughest hide. He does not consider that it is the grand maternal sow, it is simply one of *'the glorious spoils of a noble hunt'(P.114).*

The other characters are classified according to their colour and style of dress. The darker skinned and less clothed the person the more savage they are, and therefore lower on the hierarchy structure. The hierarchy structure is very important in defining the nerd. The nerd is always placed at the bottom of his hierarchy. This is because the nerd is different to the rest of the hierarchy. The nerd does not conform to what is acceptable. This can be for many reasons, but mainly because of their sensitive nature and physical weakness, and because they don't 'fit in' with the group - they challenge it or undermine it.

It is important to understand that the nerd must be a member of the hierarchy of the immediate group. It is the immediate group that is important, because it is possible for people to be excluded from the hierarchy. This is particularly true in the case of Simon in Lord of the Flies. He is isolated from the hierarchy, he is just ignored, and therefore is not picked on as a nerd for he is not considered worth picking on as he is not in the hierarchy structure. The 'beast' itself, the 'Lord of the Flies', points this out. 'They think you're batty... there isn't anyone to help you. You're not wanted.' (P. 158-159)

This idea is also important when looking at Peterkin in Coral Island. He does not appear to conform to the idea of being a nerd, for although he displays animal behaviour which places him lower down the hierarchy he is not like the other nerds because he is nowhere near the bottom of the hierarchy structure in Coral Island.

It is important to realise, although Peterkin is at the bottom of the immediate group, he is not a nerd. This is because he does not have a sensitive nature, he is as insensitive as the other characters. 'Peterkin walking along the beach towards us with a little pig transfixed on the end of his long spear!'(P.79)

Peterkin is not a nerd because he is not weak. This can be seen by the previous quote - he has the strength and courage to attack and kill. 'Peterkin and I dashed through the bushes towards the prisoners . . . whom Peterkin and I set free.'(P.159-160) 'Peterkin and I flew to the rescue . . . and in less than ten minutes the whole of our opponents where knocked down or taken prisoner, bound hand and foot, extended side by side upon the seashore.'(P.161)

As it can be seen, Peterkin has strength and courage, he is not weak. Peterkin is not a nerd. He is just smaller and younger than the other two characters. 'He was little, quick, funny, decidedly mischievous and about fourteen years old.'(P.7) This is in comparison to Jack's eighteen years. Peterkin is not a nerd, he does not challenge the group like the real nerds do, he always conforms to it. Jack tells him to 'fly through the bush, cut the cords that bind the prisoners *and set them free.'(P. 159) Jack* has commanded this and so Peterkin obeys without question.

Those below Peterkin such as the blacks and the pirates cannot be nerds because they are not in the immediate set. This set consists of Ralph, Jack and Peterkin, so the others do not qualify as nerds. It is, therefore, necessary that the hierarchy be examined to determine how it operates and therefore the role the nerd plays in it.

As a person's position in the hierarchy in Coral Island is lowered they become more animal like. This is represented by the evilness of the native people. The natives' position is indicated by their blackness: they are described as 'as black as coal', (156), with a 'black beard and moustache'.

Along with blackness is the nakedness of the people which puts them in the category of animals: 'a band of naked blacks'(P. 196); 'the lowest orders generally wore no other clothing than a strip of cloth'(P.205).

Associated with the evilness of the blackness and nakedness is the idea of uncontrollable frenzy. This particularly highlights the animal nature of the lower orders in the strict hierarchy.

The natives are described as having 'massive clubs and dashed each other to the ground'(P260-261). All this activity places them at the level of animals and they are constantly described as such: 'more like demons'(P.155), 'wild men and beasts'(P.39), and 'terrible monsters'(p.l56) 'breasting over the swell like hundreds of black seals'(P.212-213).

Peterkin shows signs of animal behaviour in the novel, but not to this extent. Peterkin progresses up the hierarchy as he matures. He is first described as having 'a very unobservant nature' with 'animal spirits'(P.24) while towards the end of the novel he has significantly changed, for he has matured, taking him further up the hierarchy and away from being a nerd. 'Peterkin's manner was now much altered' and 'often *there was a tone of deep seriousness in his manner'(P. 169). This maturity is shown clearly by his making comments about the natives' animal and immature nature. Peterkin does not conform to the idea of the nerd for he does not have a great understanding of human nature, and is not seen as an outcast. Neither does he have the physical disabilities and quietness that the other nerds present. Peterkin is not a nerd, he is merely a young immature boy who matures throughout the novel as he experiences what is seen as others' immaturity and animal behaviour.*

The hierarchy in Lord of the Flies is challenged. It is made more complex by the classifications of hierarchy: physical strength and mental/spiritual strength, which I shall come back to. 'There was the brilliant world of hunting, tactics, fierce exhilaration, skill; and there was the world of longing and baffled common sense.'(P.77)

Ralph is the natural leader who is first selected as chief. Yet Jack challenges Ralph's leadership and forms the hunters. He becomes the top of the hierarchy: 'Jack's uninformed superiority and offhand authority'(P.22). Jack has a military style which is clearly shown by his 'watchmen' at his 'fort' in order to 'challenge' any intruders. Jack's military authority elevates him to a tribal god: 'the Chief has spoken'(P.155).

Roger joins with Jack as he becomes leader. Roger was an apparently quiet boy, but is raised to a higher level of physical hierarchy under Jack's leadership. This is the hierarchy of strength and brutality at which Roger is ruthless. In both Lord of the Flies and Blue Remembered Hills a quieter hierarchy is hinted at and slowly develops, involving a challenge to conventional ideas of strength. This occurs because of the breakdown of civilized nature. Jack is a dictator and because of this Roger feels he is in a situation in which he is free to show his strong tendencies for violence and cruelty. This is because he knows they will not be his responsibility but Jack's. Roger is not a leader himself but helps to make Jack stronger.

Piggy is at the top of the 'world of longing and baffled common sense'(P.77). He is the intellectual, the thinker. He is sensible and mundane - yet it is he who holds together the civilization on the island. When he dies so does the challenge to Jack's hierarchy and any perception of order, for Piggy is the adult figure. The littleuns are at the bottom of the hierarchy as they follow whoever is in charge at the time without considering why they do.

The nerd challenges conventional hierarchy based on strength. It appears that physical incapabilities are part of the role of being labelled a nerd. This can be clearly seen in Lord of the Flies in the case of Piggy 'for he was shorter... and very fat', 'he looked up through thick spectacles'(P.7). He is not allowed to run 'on account of his asthma'(P.9). Ralph describes him as an 'outsider, not only by accent but by fat and ass-mar and specs, and a certain disinclination for manual labour', he was 'a bore' and 'his matter of fact ideas were dull'(P.70). Piggy even admits himself that he has spent a lot of time in bed. 'I bin in bed so much I done some thinking. I know about people. I know about me.'(102)

Piggy is not alone as Simon is also a thinker - but is a mystic. He is not understood, yet it is he who is able to see the message put across by Golding. Simon is not able to be put into the hierarchy as he is so different to the other characters. He simply ignores the hierarchy and goes off on his own. He can't communicate with it, this can be seen by his faints and stuttering. This is clearly illustrated at the beginning of the novel when 'one of the boys flopped on his face in the sand.' The reply to this action is that 'he's always throwing a faint'(P.22). This indicates that his fainting is a regular occurrence, and that he does not merit serious consideration from the group.

Simon is also prone to hallucinations which can be seen when he talks to the pig's head, the 'Lord of the Flies'. 'Simon was inside the mouth. He fell down and lost consciousness.'

This is in contrast to Piggy who needs the hierarchy. This can be clearly seen towards the end of the novel when Ralph wishes to give up. Piggy demonstrates his need for the hierarchy in the way in which he attempts to raise Ralph's spirits. 'You're still chief.'(P. 172)

The idea of the nerd having a physical weakness can be seen throughout the other works. It is particularly evident in A Prayer for Owen Meany, as Owen is painfully short, he was 'a little doll' and 'was the colour of a gravestone... he appeared translucent at times... as though in addition to his extraordinary size there was other evidence that he was born too soon.'(P.14). For Owen to be heard at all he 'had to shout through his nose'(P.15) causing his peculiar voice.

The hierarchy in Lord of the Flies is very different to that of Coral Island, which is far more rigid and one-track. This is very similar to Blue Remembered Hills which has a very clear hierarchy. Although the hierarchy is challenged, unlike in Lord of the Flies, it remains intact. The hierarchy is, like Lord of the Flies, divided into two classes. In this instance it is the superior boy's group, and a separate hierarchy for the girls. Wallace Wilson is at the top of the hierarchy as he is 'cock of the class'(P.45). Peter is ranked as number two, this is partly to do with his father's status in the army: 'Peter's dad has a stripe'(P.43). John is third in the hierarchy structure and Willy is fourth. This also has bearing on Willie's father's status, for he is unfit for the army - branding him a 'loony'(P.43).

Raymond and Donald have weaknesses such as Raymond's stammer, 'they won't let you be a marine if you do stutter'(P.62), and Donald's sense of fear for the mimicking of a duck, 'quack! goo on, flap your wings!'(P.68). This rates them at the bottom of this hierarchy.

Below the boys' hierarchy is the girls'. They are shown to be lower on the hierarchy structure because of the boys' attitude to children. They place children and babies at the bottom of their hierarchy structure as they call them 'sissy', 'cry baby' and 'babby'. Along with them are placed 'loonies'. This is particularly evident in the case of Donald Duck as he is considered by the boys to be a loony and so is consequently placed at the bottom of the boys' hierarchy.

The boys place the girls below themselves, this can be clearly seen by them calling each other girls' names as an insult, e.g., 'Katie'(P.60). They place themselves above the girls because they associate women with the babies, which they are above. The girls associate themselves with babies as Angela has 'a pram ... which holds a chocolate china doll called Dinah'(P.51) with whom they play Mummies and Daddies and they 'play house'(P.62). To this the boys reply that it is 'a sissy game... mummies and bloody buggering daddies'(P.62).

Angela is seen as better as she is prettiest - 'pretty, with ringlet curls and blue ribbons'(P.50) - leaving Audrey as number two, 'plain with cheap owl-like metal framed glasses and short, straight hair'(P.51). Donald Duck finds himself in this separate hierarchy. His weakness is emphasised here as he plays with the girls: 'I be supposed to be the daddy here'(P.51)

The most admired characters are the tough boys, such as Wallace Wilson, even the girls accept that. This can be seen by Angela wanting to marry him: 'we be going to get married. With a ring and all.'(P.59).

There is a struggle within the girls' hierarchy as they try to up their status. Audrey seems to be particularly concerned about it. While they play their Mummies and Daddies game she ups her status by choosing a job (a man's role) - 'the nurse. I wanna be the nurse'(P.52) - whereas initially she was only a sister, then a 'naughty' sister. This is more 'boyish' because it challenges adults. Finally she raises her status to that of a nurse. It can also be seen that they try to reach the boys' level by pretending to have cabins because cabins 'ent *for girls'(P.62). 'We gotta cabin in the trees'(P.6l): in fact they haven't got one, they intend to build a house, but the boys will only become involved if it is a fort.*

Audrey: 'We ant really started. Not yet.'

Peter: 'Not to play house in. We want summat better than that.' Willie: 'Like a fort. With guns and that.' (P.62)

The hierarchy is kept by the use of rules, 'that's a rule, that is'(P.63). The use of rules is also found in Lord of the Flies, but fails to secure the hierarchy:

'You're breaking the rules.'

'Bollocks to the rules!'

The pecking order, as in Lord of the Flies, is challenged, particularly by Audrey who tries to elevate herself to the boys' hierarchy as she is prepared to fight: 'Shall I bash her in for you?'(P.59) The main challenge is by John whose challenge to Peter results in a fight. John wins this and the new order is established.

In a similar style to Blue Remembered Hills is A Prayer for Owen Meany. The hierarchy is very clear, particularly to John, because he is the narrator, and therefore it is clear to the reader. Yet this is not always clear to the characters around them. Owen Meany is special and deserves the highest status, yet due to his physical appearance, 'the smallest person I ever knew; so small that not only did his feet not touch the floor when he sat in his chair - his knees did not extend to the edge of his seat'(P.15), and his 'wrecked voice'(P.13) - due to this he is seen as below everyone else.

Owen's status is both raised and lowered by his speech, for it makes him stand out, but it does not conform to the norm. The reader is constantly reminded of Owen's disability and uniqueness by the capitalising of all his speech. This is a particularly effective literary device as it serves as a constant reminder to the reader of Owen's nerdishness and self-

importance, and refusal to accept the group's placing of him.

By the end of the novel it is clear how much higher Owen is in the hierarchy than the other characters. Although Owen shows how special he is, he believes he is Jesus and has been sent for a purpose which is slowly revealed to him, he does not abuse his position by telling others about it and expecting their respect.

Owen does not expect any special treatment because of his disability and obvious extraordinary knowledge and insight. John's mother and grandmother pay for Owen to participate in social events and also pay for his schooling, although Owen does not expect this to be done for him and strongly objects.

Owen is a particularly unusual nerd because he has the power of God. He is a visionary and has God's help. Owen is always correct and possesses amazing insight into the world's problems, yet despite this he does not lecture others or claim that he is right and others are wrong. Therefore he conforms to the group - he remains within it. Owen has a clear insight into the Vietnam war - 'THERE'S NO END TO THIS, THERE'S NO GOOD WAY TO END THIS'(P.104), 'THAT'S NOT THE KIND OF WAR WE WIN'(P.105) - yet Owen does not expect others to believe in what he says. Owen does the job that he believes he was sent to do: 'GOD HAS TAKEN YOUR MOTHER. MY HANDS WERE THE INSTRUMENT. GOD HAS TAKEN MY HANDS. I AM GOD'S INSTRUMENT.'(P.100) He is determined to stick to his beliefs, a theme common in the nerds that I have studied.

It is interesting to note the person who is narrator. In Coral Island it is Ralph, in A Prayer for Owen Meany it is John Wheelwright - Owen's best friend; Lord of the Flies is observational by the author as is the play Blue Remembered Hills. In all the texts that I have studied none are written from the point of view of the nerd. This is necessary in order for the nerd to be seen in context. The reader would not *benefit from the nerd if they were told from the beginning that the nerd was correct and had the best ideas, because the reader would not be able to see the nerd in his context. It is necessary to see how others react to him.*

It does not seem fit for the nerd to be the storyteller, even in the case of Coral Island where Peterkin does not fully qualify as a nerd. Ralph is able to be objective about Peterkin which could not be portrayed to the reader if Peterkin was narrating.

Lord of the Flies is observed by the author. This works well as Golding is trying to put across a picture which involves the thought processes of all the characters. He is trying to create an image of man as a whole, of evil in society in which the nerd plays an unsuccessful part. It is almost a biblical view.

The religious element of the novel deals with man's inherent evil, or original sin. Simon is chosen to explore the boys' spirituality. He tells Ralph with absolute assurance that they will get back from the island - 'I just think you'll get back alright.'(P.122) The use of italic emphasises his absolute confidence and faith in God. He inhabits a 'dubious religion'(P.64). The fact that Simon uses the term 'you'll' indicates that he knows he won't be returning with the others. This is reminiscent of Owen Meany. Simon, like Owen, has realised that he will die and accepts this, but unlike Owen, Simon only rarely communicates with the group. Whatever represents evil, or potential evil, is confronted by Simon, not in an aggressive way, but in a solitary, searching way.

Blue Remembered Hills, as a play, is observational. The events just occur, there does not need to be a narrator as the thoughts of the characters are portrayed by actions and, more importantly, the spoken word. We learn about the nerds by the comments and actions of the other characters. This is an important part in labelling a nerd, for a nerd is not properly accepted by others of the group.

The nerd does not conform to the hierarchy. He does not fulfil the other characters' expectations. The nerd offers something different to the group but the group do not wish to listen as what is being said spoils their fun, or they are afraid to listen.

In Lord of the Flies the other characters are reluctant to listen to Piggy as they wish to go out, hunt and have fun, while Piggy is more concerned with organisation and ensuring that they are rescued. This idea can also be seen in Blue Remembered Hills as Raymond is concerned with the squirrel, he realises that they have gone too far by killing it: 'we k - kul - killed him'(P.55). He is the only one to make the others accept that they killed Donald Duck, the others agree that they were hiding and were not there, yet Raymond replies 'poor old quack quack'(P.84).

Owen Meany, too, seems not to be accepted because people are afraid of him - particularly by his physical appearance. They do not accept him because what he says either makes sense to them and it spoils their fun so they ignore it, or they are not ready to accept or understand what he says. Owen realises the true meaning behind the nativity scene. He tries to explain it to the people in the town, but they are only concerned with 'kings, angels, shepherds, donkeys, turtle doves, Mary, Joseph, babies, and more!'(P.165) Owen understands the true meaning and asks the Father to 'FORGIVE THEM; FOR THEY KNOW NOT WHAT THEY DO'(P.165).

This does not just occur in Owen's childhood. For when John is trying to find a way out of the Army it is Owen who explains his options and helps him to make a decision, because John is not willing to face up to the reality of the situation. 'DO YOU WANT TO GO TO VIETNAM? DO YOU WANT TO SPEND THE REST OF YOUR LIFE IN CANADA?'(P 524)

Nerds tend to be able to face up to the reality of the situation and put aside the fun for the benefit of the group. This is why they are not accepted and are at the bottom of the hierarchy. The real nerd is misplaced by being put at the bottom of the hierarchy, for Piggy, Owen, and Donald Duck are not the nerds that they are thought to be by the other characters. The author is able to achieve this idea through various literary devices, particularly using the narrator to present the idea that the nerd is in fact right.

I feel it is necessary for the understanding of the nerd to be gradual and this can be achieved by the reactions of the other characters. This enables the reader to see that the nerd offers the best advice through the narrator's realisation. In the case of A Prayer for Owen Meany it is necessary for the reader to put their trust in the nerd as John only understands Owen in retrospect - but the reader is given injections of this throughout the novel. 'God knows, Owen gave me more than he ever took from me - even when you consider that he took my mother.'(P.106)

The idea of the nerd's heroism and understanding being gradually realised can also be seen in Lord of the Flies and Blue Remembered Hills as well as In A Prayer for Owen Meany. In Lord of the Flies Piggy becomes increasingly blind - as his glasses are stolen and smashed, so he becomes increasingly more frightened and ridiculous as the novel proceeds. This gives the impression of his nerdishness being heightened. His heroism at the end of the novel is a complete surprise to the reader, but then the reader realises that Piggy was the sensible one all along, he was a 'true, wise friend'(P.223). His role has been revealed very late in the novel, it had not been noted earlier. This is because the reader too wishes to have fun and enjoy the island. The reader does not accept Piggy because he makes sense and spoils their fun, or because they are not ready to accept and understand what he has to say.

Blue Remembered Hills provides the reader with two nerds, Raymond and Donald. Raymond surprises the audience/reader only in the very last scene when suddenly the others are cowards and he is not.

Angela: 'Hiding in the trees, weren't we?'

John: 'That's right. We didn't see nothing.'

Raymond: 'Poor old quack quack.'(P.84)

Donald surprises the audience/reader by his cunning concerning the jam jars: 'You mean, you took a stack of jars the shop had already brought as empties and - by Gar! You got him to buy 'em off you all over again...!'(P.70) The nerd is portrayed as stupid yet Donald displays great intuition and creativeness - 'I bent no cissy, be I?'(P.69) In the same scene the prisoner of war escapes. The tough characters are afraid but Donald wants him to escape.

Peter: 'One of them bloody Ities have got loose.'

Donald: 'I hope they don't catch him.'

Peter: 'I hopes they do.'(P.72)

Peterkin surprises no-one into an understanding of his nerdishness for he is not a proper nerd. He merely continues to conform to the group's expectations.

The author shows the reader that the nerd is in fact the hero. He makes the nerd great. The author is able to see the character as he really is, in terms of what he has to offer. He is able to realise that society is afraid of the nerds and the only way in which they can suppress their fear is to ridicule. The author tries to bring this across to the reader and this can be seen in three of the texts that I have studied.

The text is a progression of the realisation that the nerd is in fact great. It helps to break the stereotype of the nerd's weakness and insignificance. I have discovered that this progression of realisation and greatness is often shown by the character having the first and last lines of the text. The first line often depicts the nerd as a stupid, dull person who the reader will consider to be a nerd. As the text progresses the reader discovers the true character of the nerd so the last line is stunningly different to the first, as the nerds greatness has been expressed by the author and realised by the reader.

This is illustrated particularly well in the Lord of the Flies. Piggy develops from a 'short, fat boy' to a 'true, wise friend'(P.223).

It can also be seen in A Prayer for Owen Meany. John begins the novel by describing the game which he and his classmates played with Owen. It was their 'game of lifting Owen'(P.15). They would 'pick up Owen Meany and pass him back and forth, overhead'(P.15). This game is reminisced by John at the end of the novel, but it contains insight. 'We believed that Owen weighed nothing at all. We did not realise that there were forces beyond our play. Now I know they were the forces that contributed to our illusion of Owen's weightlessness; they were the forces we didn't have the faith to feel, they were the forces we failed to believe in - and they were also lifting up Owen Meany, taking him out of our hands.'(P.637) The reader is now able to appreciate what Owen stood for and how special he was, he was not a nerd.

Donald Duck also has this development but not to such extent as Owen. The first scene in which Donald Duck is present he is playing Mummies and Daddies with the two girls. The image of a nerd is being created. But Donald Duck's power is shown as, like the other nerds, he is the subject of the last lines: 'Poor old quack quack.'(P.84) The nerd's power is fully conveyed by it occupying the start and finish of the text. The development in character is also shown through this effective literary device.

This technique is not used in Coral Island. Peterkin does not have the first or last line. Neither does he develop so fully as a character, he merely matures. Simon is different again -

his heroism and fearlessness is realised earlier in the novel; he is too Christ-like to survive. He has the power to talk to God (or the devil) so he is symbolic, not real.

I have also noticed that these real nerds are in fact tragic heroes. Again this is not true in the case of Peterkin.

The author uses a very strong literary device to show how the nerd should be appreciated and that often it is not until the nerd is not present that he is really appreciated. The three nerds Piggy, Owen and Donald Duck all face the tragedy of death.

Piggy dies triumphant in the eyes of the reader. His final speech is almost a summary of the message that Golding is trying to put across to the reader. 'Which is better - to be a pack of painted niggers like you are, or to be sensible like Ralph is?.. Which is better - to have rules and agree, or to hunt and kill?.. Which is better - law and rescue, or hunting and breaking things up?'(P.199). Golding shows Piggy's strength but it is not enough for the brutal savages: 'the rock struck Piggy... the conch exploded into a thousand white fragments and ceased to exist. Piggy's arms and legs twitched a bit, like a pig's after it has been killed.'(P.200) This is Golding's message for humanity - for him it is important to listen to the nerd in life, but humanity slaughters him like a pig.

A similar event occurs in Blue Remembered Hills as Donald Duck becomes trapped in the barn. The other children shut him in, unaware of the fire that is raging inside: 'the other six have slammed shut the door, putting the stone back up against it'(P.83); 'Open the door! Please! Please! Open the door! Plea-ea-ea-se!'(P.83). By the time the children realise, it is too late as Donald is 'wholly engulfed in the flames'(P.84).

Donald Duck is unlike Piggy, for he does not give a great speech, but he brings home a message to the other children -

he turns their comedy into a tragedy. Their fun and teasing of him went too far. Donald Duck tried to tell them to stop, but like Piggy he is ignored and is killed by his 'friends'.

Owen Meany's death is arguably the most tragic for he has known for many years when he will die. He has to work out why this will occur, this is achieved by the literary device of dreams. Owen is truly unselfish, he has the knowledge that he must die, yet he does not spend time dwelling in self-pity. He is always prepared to help others and this is how he finally dies in a heroic act, his whole life has been dedicated to saving a group of small children, orphans. He truly is a tragic hero. 'YOU'RE GETTING SMALLER, BUT I CAN STILL SEE YOU! Then he left us; he was gone.'

John Irving uses Owen to show he is not a nerd but is highly talented and special. He, like the other authors, shows the nerd to be great for they are able to see what the nerd has to offer. They try to get the reader to realise that what the nerd offers is valid and correct. The authors use these tragic heroes to break the mystique and stereotype of the nerd. The strengths of the 'tough' characters are shallow and not useful to the group. For example in Coral Island Jack lets the fire go out; in Blue Remembered Hills Peter leads the others to trap Donald Duck in the barn. The nerd has weaknesses too but also sympathy and insight: 'I know about people. I know about me.'(Piggy, P.102) This is a 'feminine' strength which the usually male-dominated group does not like to recognise.

The nerds that I have identified have all been male. Although females do feature in some of these works they are not portrayed as nerds. The male nerd has 'feminine' qualities, such as sympathy and understanding of others. This is seen as a weakness which leads to his rejection from the group. I believe that this shows why there are no female nerds. I feel that this is also reflected in life around us, because those people considered to be nerds are mostly male. They are considered to be a nerd because of their female characteristics and qualities.

In these three texts, Lord of the Flies, Blue Remembered Hills and A Prayer for Owen Meany, the nerd is triumphant. He is understood by the author and made great. This leads me to consider if the author is maybe a nerd, or has the function of the nerd, in both the sensitive and heroic sense.

What is a Nerd?
Bottom of hierarchy set.
Physically weak.
Offers something that the group is afraid of or does not want.
Tragic hero.
Male.
Sensible, quiet.
Does not conform to the rest of the hierarchy.

Katy Cluley

*   *   *   *   *

Because good sixth-formers are so rewarding to teach, and because they are about to leave schooling completely behind rather than hang on to it as their teachers have done, they are probably the most manipulated group in any school. You don't think you are, you think you've got it completely sussed by the time you leave, but you haven't, not quite.

The young are attracted by power - you're mesmerised by it. No matter what you say, when it comes to the crunch you look out of the classroom window and say to yourselves who has the best car, who gets out of the shit jobs, who doesn't get messed around and have to grovel all the time (like us) - I'm going to be like them. The key to manipulating kids is in the display of power.

Manipulation of sixth-formers - a step-by-step guide:

Disorientate with false marking, this is particularly effective with star-grade G.C.S.E. pupils, knocking the confidence out of them and generating a dependency culture;

improve marking slowly as they conform to your agenda, and greatly just before the exam, showing that your intensive revision lessons are beginning to bear fruit.

If you have an office, maximise it: don't hand out advice on uni choices or go over essays informally, give them a time to come to you in your office; if they have to wait a while for you to finish dealing with someone else, or you take phone-calls during your session with them, they must understand that your time is a gift which you have bestowed on them.

Treat them like first-years initially, make as few concessions as possible, certainly not over work deadlines, though seating arrangements may be formally informalised in the shape of a semi-circle or three-sided square; as they conform, start coming in a few minutes late with trays of coffee and biscuits, creating a seminar atmosphere.

Work with texts you are completely familiar with teaching and can back up with photocopied notes and hand-outs from previous years, ensuring you are never caught off-guard by a question; it is wise to choose 'worthy' texts from the literary canon which can be handed down, baptising the students in the holy water of culture.

Run additional twilight and early-morning sessions, upping the status of your subject against others and generating a kind of 'inner-circle' ethos; if a pupil asks to be excused from a session, convey the impression that the progress of the group as a whole will be affected.

Power dress on the day of the exam, swish into the hall as it is about to start and make a show of checking that everyone is there with pens poised to do you justice; stand at the front just before the signal to start is given and skim through the question paper nodding sagely; stay for the first five minutes, walking up and down the rows beaming, then disappear.

Keep displays of thank-you cards and gifts from grateful pupils as long as is decently possible, giving prominence to those with dedications such as 'Thank-you for pulling me through against all the odds'; 'Thank-you for knowing my limits and helping me to reach them', and similar approved wording.

They never seem to twig.

CHAPTER 13

The Headmaster's Daughter

I had a class, fair, quite fun to work with, who were coming towards the end of year nine, and was told that I would be taking them on for the next two years to their G.C.S.E. exams. The Birmingham Readers & Writers Festival was taking place, and I thought as I was going on with them I might as well take them to a couple of events. One was Berlie Doherty, and a book she spoke about at length was 'Tough Luck', which she had written with the help of kids whilst on an attachment at a Doncaster school.

On the coach back one of mine said, 'You write books, don't you? Why don't you write one with us?'

I have always been very private about what I write, no-one sees it until it is completely finished and I don't even like talking about it before then - but I thought, what the hell, doing things the other way hasn't got you very far. So I decided to give it a bash.

At this point I have taken a break to see what bits and pieces I have kept from that time, and I realise I have everything - every idea, every scrap of paper that was handed in to me. It's actually quite exciting to read it all through again, and trace how the whole thing came together. I'm going to take the risk of reproducing some of it, and when I get to the read-through stage of this book I may cut it out.

In the very first lesson, I started by polling the kids on their preferred subject/genre:

sex/dating 15
crime 7
murder 12
drugs 5
violence 8

> *sport* *6*
> *horror* *12*
> *sci-fi*.. *3*
> *phobias* *5*
> *trauma*... *1*
> *exams/school* *11*

As you can see, about four ideas stood out from the rest, so, as I was game for anything I said I would try to mix sex and dating, horror, murder, and exams and school. I asked about tone:

> *tragic* *3*
> *humorous* *16*
> *realistic* *3*
> *melodramatic*................................ *4*

Ideas for characters - kids:

> *skiver*
> *class prat**
> *rebel*
> *dumb*
> *big-head*
> *boffin**
> *poser**
> *bully*
> *quiet/shy*
> *victim**
> *good-looking**
> *average/normal**
> *trouble-maker*
> *kind*

I don't remember how the voting was done, but the asterisks were the most popular. Adults:

> *senile/dotty**
> *ex-serviceman*
> *drug pusher*

'In my day...'*
strict parent*
unemployed
pub wallah
child beater
professor
trendy/tries to look younger*
grumbler*
tramp
old rebel*
pervert/peeping Tom*
bus driver
workaholic businessman

Teachers:

picks on pupils*
good listener
can't control*
strict
average
religious nut*
nice guy
humourless
wise/been around*
selfish*
over-protective
fanciable
childish*
friend

I gave them the homework of filling out a couple of the characters and putting some ideas together, and I did the homework too. I don't have a list of all the ideas, which remained in their books, but I have a list of the ones that were chosen:

1. The 'Better' - pupil who's always taking bets

2. *The head's daughter - uses dice to make decisions*
3. *The Better & head's daughter get off together*
4. *Multiple ending, using dice to chose*
5. *Headmaster murdered*
6. *Some kids on community service punishment - they see something they shouldn't*
7. *Breaking in & finding something in old head's house*
8. *Old head's wife keeps bees*
9. *Funeral section*

So at this point we had a genre, a style, a few possible characters and plot lines. When I finally got my head round it, I realised I wasn't keen to do murder - for one thing I find the idea of police investigation boring - but I was prepared to bump someone off from natural causes. They went into a huddle, and said, O.K., but it's got to be someone important - we want you to kill the head.

No problem.

So the construction of the plot trundled on in that way. As we got to the detailed stage a lot of the kids lost interest. I didn't feel I could impose a project on them that basically involved a book I was going to write, so I prepared work as normal, and exempted the group who still wanted to continue with the story. They would write up episodes as they imagined them and mull over things with each other, before coming to me to negotiate.

I put in some work over the summer, and so did some of the group. I mulled it over some more and decided to make a start in the October half-term. I got it underway, and from then on it was the early morning stints again. I still have the 'progress chart' I pinned on the classroom wall and used to fill in so they knew how things were going - occasionally I would read a finished passage to them, something else I would never have done previously:

28.10.91	*4,200 words*	*p12*
30.10	*5,200*	*p15*
4.11	*6,300*	*p18*
5.11	*6,600*	*p20*
11.11	*7,300*	*p20*
12.11	*7,800*	*p22*
20.11	*9,000*	*p25*
22.11	*9,900*	*p28*
23.11	*11,300*	*p32*
26.11	*12,300*	*p35*
27.11	*13,100*	*p37*
15.1.92	*14,100*	*p40*
16.1	*15,300*	*p44*
17.1	*16,300*	*p47*
21.1	*17,500*	*p50*
4.2	*18,200*	*p52*
5.2	*18,900*	*p54*
6.2	*20,000*	*p57*
11.2	*21,400*	*p61*
12.2	*23,000*	*p66*
19.2	*23,700*	*p68*
20.2	*24,600*	*p70*
21.2	*25,800*	*p74*
28.2	*39,100*	*p112*

It's interesting to look at that now - I can see my usual morning output was five to twelve hundred words, not bad for three hours maximum, then it looks like I banged the last bit off over the February half-term: about 15,000 words for the week. It was a short book, one of my weaknesses: I don't think I follow ideas through in nearly enough detail - 'lazy' is the word that springs to mind, then I think, no, a person who gets up at four in the morning to write books can't be lazy. Just afraid of where they'll take me, maybe..

Here is a section from the Forge, a disused building where the pupils hang out. Dooley is an old deputy head who thought his career was over, but now the head has died, he's acting-head and one of the main candidates for the job. Paul is the 'better':

CHAPTER 9

You know you're ancient the day you discover that first-years don't know what chalk is. It's true. They've never had the experience of listening to a stick of chalk tap, squeak and scrape its way down a pock-marked greying board while the teacher drones at you over his right shoulder. I miss it, I do. You knew you were in a school when you passed those fans of board-rubber marks on the outside wall of every entrance, and the class clown smeared his hand from the gully of dust and went round smacking the backs of blazers with it. First years these days, they've lost touch with all the traditions, you see them strolling around discussing profiling forms and career options, they think schools are places of learning.

As a matter of fact, that reminds me, next time you hear me going on about dear old sweet old Mr. Dooley, just pinch me will you. He's got the most vicious temper when things go wrong. You go weeks without a hint of it, then suddenly he blows like a volcano, face all fiery red, eyes bulging, usually at some group of boys who've decided to get his rag up. He's fine when the girls keep smiling and the boys keep quiet, and everyone does what they're told, then he can play the old village schoolmaster and fount of wisdom to his heart's content. It works best with first and second years. You don't learn a fat lot, except how to keep him in role for forty minutes and make life easy for yourself.

Rumour has it that in the days of chalk and blackboards he kept a slipper in his desk. When a boy misbehaved (I don't know what he did about girls, made them wash the staff coffee cups probably) when a boy misbehaved he would have him over a chair at the front and slipper him. The special little Dooley version of this was that he had a number chalked, in reverse, on the slipper sole - the number of boys he'd slippered from the start of his career. So when it was your turn, as well as a sore backside you'd have 1008, or whatever it was, branded right way round on the seat of your trousers.

I don't know whether that's true, but I've heard it a couple of times from different people. I've also heard that he didn't used to blow his stack in those days, just calmly changed the number on the shoe while the victim slunk back to his seat, and then carried on with the lesson.

Funny, his old classroom still exists, in fact it's still sometimes used for lessons, like one of those Victorian working museums where you go to watch them making peppermint humbugs and candles. We call it the Forge. It has got a number, but only the new teachers use it. Everyone else calls it the Forge. It's completely detached from everywhere else in the place, over by the netball court - it's got iron window frames, desks that haven't seen the light of day for twenty years - the cuts and carvings go down a couple of inches now - great concertina radiators with a dozen coats of paint on them baking slowly all winter, and of course a blackboard on an easel which you raise and lower by pegs attached to little chains so they don't get lost or pinched. At nights and weekends the door is padlocked.

It was joined on to the rest once, well, joined on to the metalwork room anyway, but that got knocked down for the netball court, they cut plastic sheets in labs now instead - so it stands quietly on its own like a shrine to days gone by. It's a perfect haunt for bullies, snoggers and smokers.

And gamblers. It's one of Paul's little dens, he's won and lost fortunes there. It's the place to go if you want to lay a bet on any event in the school calendar you can think of. He actually sits there, can you believe it, like a lord in residence two or three mornings a week, just collecting in, paying out, laying odds on anything you care to name - house *tournaments, football teams, swimming galas, head boy, head girl, prefects, detentions, suspensions, expulsions, prize winners, runners up, exam placings, classes, sets: you could lay a bet on who's going to get pregnant if you wanted, teacher or pupil, and the sex of the baby; you could bet on a couple of kids having a fight, they often do. He sits there bold as brass, odds chalked up on the board, always changing, always following the ebb and flow of money. All the sixth form know, they're his biggest customers though so it's kept in the family if you know what I mean. It's the biggest open secret in the school.*

Actually, we're not all raving gamblers: most people don't go there to bet, they wouldn't be so daft, they go there just to hang around, to sniff the air and get the feel of things. Everything that happens hits the Forge first. If you bust up with your boyfriend you can find out what your chances of getting back together are before you know yourself. It's that kind of place. It's the place to be. And of course when exams come round that's where you head for the minute you get through the gates. Whole year groups mill round, you can't move for people. It's like the Great Barrier Reef - all the different shoals mingling together, all darting for coral at the sniff of member of staff, re-emerging as soon as the shadow passes. I wouldn't miss it for anything. You don't know you've revised till you've been down the Forge first thing to check your odds.

First thing, I go down to check my odds for English, down the long side of the building, round the back of technology and there it is, just as I was saying, chock-a-block with people from my year group. Paul's doing good business; I can't get in but I can see through the window. He's like one of those Hindu gods with a dozen arms, his hands are everywhere, taking bets, changing the odds, rummaging in the formbook. He never takes a bet without adjusting the odds slightly, it's like the Stock Exchange, and he never gives odds without thumbing through his formbook. Kids would give a lot for a glimpse of that book, it has the lowdown on everything and everyone, and it's bang up to the minute too, he makes entries all the time, if he had the dates of our periods down there it wouldn't completely surprise me.

Actually, I have seen a book as well-used as Paul's formbook, but only one: our milkman's delivery book, that gets a fair bit of stick, he has to keep a massive great elastic band round it to stop the pages springing up in all directions like a bramble bush.

I try and edge in at the door, the trouble is, no-one's going out; when they've made a bet they hang around in case they miss anything. Even the boffins are there, Claudia, trying to get a price for her French, very quietly. 'FIFTEEN TO ONE ON,' Paul shouts, though she's right by him. A great knowing hoot goes up, making her blush like wildfire. 'That's not fair,' she whispers. 'TAKE IT OR LEAVE IT,' he scans the rest for a more interesting punter. 'Fifty p. then please...' 'FIFTY P? THAT MEANS YOU'LL WIN THREE AND A HALF.' 'Oh dear...' The coins blur in her purse. 'I'd better make it a pound.' 'POUND THE FRENCH GIRL, FIFTEEN TO ONE ON, PAY HER IN EUROS,' he barks to his mate, who's also taking them down. The swarm moves this way and that, but never out of the door. I'm still not properly in when the buzzer goes. I give up and head for form.

* * * * *

Afterwards the typescript went round the class, and they wrote all sorts of corrections and comments on it - e.g., 'The way that some words were underlined was <u>slightly annoying</u>. Half the underlined words weren't that important, so this confused me.' 'One minute Adrienne is in Kay's bedroom, next paragraph she's totally changed her life. It's only a while on we twig it's a few months later.' 'We didn't think you *were the type who knew about the words snogging, getting off, or swearing, me and Donna thought you were the innocent type (speaking ways).'*

So that was it. It would have been nice for it to have gone on and been published, but that didn't happen. But it was a good project, I think, a symbiotic thing - good for me, good for them. A nice adventure.

* * * * *

Q. What's it like being an author?

A. Kids pester you to write books for them. This is true, I often get kids coming up to me in schools and telling me to write stories about them, and send them copies when I've finished. The other thing you get all the time is when people tell you something funny, or unusual, then say 'I expect you'll write a book about that now', as if writers just sit there waiting to pounce on the smallest coincidence so they can turn it into a blockbuster. I don't think so.

Q. Where do you get your ideas?

A. The year-ten group lobbed up the ideas for The Headmaster's Daughter, but I figured out how they would fit into a story.

Q. How long does it take to write a book?

A. The Headmaster's Daughter took five months of early mornings, and about four months fiddling with ideas.

Q. Do you like writing?

A. I enjoyed working on this with a group, but was quite bad-tempered during afternoon lessons whilst writing it, because my body-clock was always telling me it was three hours later than it really was.

Q. How do you get a book published?

A. As I said, this one wasn't published - I couldn't get anyone interested. But years later I read a section to a secondary school class whilst on a writers' day and the teacher pounced on it, read it overnight, and said she thought it should be published. I took it home and re-read it and thought, yeh, she's right, it's not that bad. So it's now available through Crazy Horse Press, details at the back.

Q. Who is your favourite author?

A. I think I have covered my favourite authors now, so I will just mention a couple of books relevant to this chapter and the last one. A Prayer for Owen Meany is written by John Irving, who wrote The Cider House Rules, Setting Free the Bears, etc. - he is really funny and unusual, but I didn't include him because he doesn't specifically write for the young. Murder and school is a recipe for bad writing, but Kathleen Peyton did it brilliantly with A Midsummer Night's Death.

CHAPTER 14

Bishops Wood

A few years ago I had a class of second years reading books of their choice, and as the lesson came to a close I asked them to pack away and pay attention to me so I could talk to them for a minute before the buzzer. I would always allow for kids who just wanted to finish the page, but one pupil ignored me altogether and simply continued to read. The next time I glanced at her she had pushed her book away, put her face against the desk and her shoulders were rocking in the way kids do when they are sharing a private joke in class. I had to shout at her before she would look up, and when she did her eyes were puffed and red with tears. She had just finished reading Anne Frank's Diary.

I remember this incident vividly, and offer it as a way into a difficult chapter.

I have often been startled by the pieces young people write recalling the death of a loved one, a grandparent often, or perhaps a pet. This is the acceptable face of death, a recalling, a brief visiting of the past. But the first time I had writing on death as a very present thing came as a shock to me and to Maggie Holmes, who was our poet-in-residence at that time. She had been working with a small group of third years (year nine) and had given them a free session as a way of finishing off a series of structured writing lessons. The pieces that were given in were done so in a scrappy, self-deprecating form, almost defiantly, as if in expectation of criticism.

Maggie was upset when she showed them to me - she had done a lot of writing with the group and felt she had built up a trust with them, and in their final session they seemed to be saying, this is what we think of writing poems.

We pored over them for a while, they seemed very throwaway and difficult to place - but you get a sixth sense about this: there is a kind of writing that seems to be banged off without concern for adult response; in this case it probably wouldn't have been handed in at all if Maggie had been a teacher. It may be gibberish or smut, or it just might be that the subject is taboo and it has been knocked off almost furtively, as if to avoid detection.

Without the adult gaze, young people's writing sometimes becomes more alive, the imagery and syntax are different. A lot of school writing has that special intelligent polish, that awful veneer of falsehood - bullshit - that the practice of real expression is supposed to break down. Do you recall that piece, 'The Spinner' in the first chapter? How spot-on the expression was? He was used to not having his work taken seriously and I guess he wrote in a completely unselfconscious way because he didn't believe it would be read seriously this time, either.

Maggie and I typed the poems out. Several of them were about cancer. I believe terminal cancer was a factor in the lives of three of the families of that year-group, although the boy who wrote the two poems below says he was unaware of that and didn't intend what he had written to be taken seriously. I shouldn't argue, but can't help saying that we don't intend our dreams to be taken seriously, but they may be serious nevertheless. I think they are breath-taking, in form and imagery; I have included a picture that went with them, I'm not sure why:

> *I have known my mom for a long time now,*
> *The first time I saw her we met at a party.*
> *It was love at first sight.*
> *I realised that she was the mother of Ivan when I was six.*
> *But now she has another problem.*
> *Cancer.*

I see cancer as a black goo-like tar
Dribbling down her shoulders.
Her hair goes crisp and brittle
And if a plane goes past it floats away like dandelion
    spores.
I try to catch it in a bucket but I'm too slow.
I help around the house now
And trot around the garden looking at the bears.
Oh my mind is going.
My mom may be going fat now,
I can't remember what she looked like before.

* * * * *

* * * * *

Black clowns remind me of death,
Always smiling
But never happy.
14 clowns in a noddy car
Squirting water
Hating each other.
Several raspberries warn against a pie
Like creeping cancer
In a cage.
The clowns lick each other
Pretending to like each other,
And catch AIDs.
The clowns turn zulu and throw spears at their friend
And they burst her.
She squeaks
And the clowns giggle.
Death makes me quiver,
It's too enormous for our small human minds.

*   *   *   *   *

Then came the accident on the M40 that took away thirteen lives. What do I remember about that time? The overwhelming blanket of flowers, people stepping between and around them in utter silence, only the scents spoke; my son calmly looking at it for the first time and breaking without warning into uncontrollable tears; kids from the school wandering around in threes and fours hugging and holding each other; the group that stood bleak-eyed outside the room of Eleanor, our friend who died, because they had music timetabled there and didn't know where else to go; the pack of counsellors who descended on us in a sudden deluge of care, their spokesman saying they would be with us today, tomorrow, the day after, they would never let us alone. Then afterwards the main foyer, empty except for a graph on a stand telling everyone how much money was coming into the memorial fund, I will always remember that.

A few months afterwards some friends of ours who lost Claire their daughter asked me to form a group where brothers, sisters, friends of the children who had died could express themselves and reflect informally - where they could work with art, drama, music, writing, and be completely themselves. It wasn't something I was confident to do, so I passed it off. But they were determined, determined but slow, the way things are in bereavement, it immobilises.

What changed everything was that we found a wonderful place to meet in, a circular environment centre built in woodland: Bishops Wood. Bishops Wood, with its chime bars, running water, hides, feathers, fossils, nests, shells, candles, bowls and bells, housed us and held us for two years.

How little we did and how much. West Midlands Arts and Children in Need gave us funds with which we brought in occasional arts people and therapists - but always practising artists. Our wise people, how important they were. My gut feeling is if you really want to create a writing ambience it's not a writer you need as much as simply a wise person, someone who can help the you go into your private places. Ours were the poet David Hart, who came as a friend and remained with us throughout, and Lisa Watts, our storyteller, with her cushions and ringing Tibetan bowls, who gathered things in for us. We passed the time painting, modelling, dancing, fiddling and thumping, writing, talking, talking, talking. We were there for those who died, there in the miserable, wretched times and there to sing their memory. If it became dreary and disjointed Bishops Wood was always holding us, giving itself to us. Our wisest participant.

In all that time I doubt if I offered two or three ideas to help with writing, it seemed that to do more would be to make a 'subject' out of what had happened. Once I suggested that they might focus on the season, because where we were was very much cradled by the seasons: to keep whoever they were thinking of in mind but not to deliberately write about them unless they felt compelled to, and not to try and 'interpret' the season in a symbolic way, simply to respond to it.

Another time, early on, I noticed that a lot of what was being written was confined by religious teachings, the poems tended to focus on heavenly outcomes. My instinct was that there was a block caused by the dilemma of betraying the friends they had lost on one hand or their religious beliefs on the other - there seemed to be a conflict. I read Dannie Abse's poem The Water Diviner*, which concerns the fear of losing his creativity, and pointed out that to be prepared to let go of your religion, and trust that it will find you again is a surer sign of faith than to hang on tightly for fear of losing it. I'm not religious, but that's how it strikes me. I believe that freed some of the writing that followed - or maybe they were just ready to move on.

*[The last stanza reads:

Repeated desert, recurring drought,
sometimes hearing water trickle,
sometimes not, I, by doubting first,
believe; believing, doubt.]

David I remember doing some sessions on the circles and cycles in life, and on journeys and boats. It was good to have symbolism to dodge in and out of. But I think what was overwhelmingly important was the natural grouping of people behaving naturally in a natural place and accepting the natural expression of others. No-one claimed seniority in grief. What was expressed by a five-year-old was worth the same as what was expressed by a sixty-five-year-old.

I would like to offer a sample of the pieces from that time - not all came from Bishops Wood. Steve and Liz Fitzgerald, whose idea the group was, now run a bereavement group entitled Bramble's Trust, and it is their intention to bring out a comprehensive publication of the Bishops Wood writings. If you would like to get in touch with them, send an s.a.e. to the address at the back.

FRESH FLOWERS

Fresh flowers on my birthday, your birthday
They remind me of the day you left me
When people sent flowers
To give a message of sympathy
To find a way of helping,
An effort to understand.
But no-one could understand
The pain, desolation, confusion,
Unimaginable grief and sorrow.

The perfume of fresh flowers
Followed me everywhere,
Hundreds of bouquets
From around the country:
Red roses,
Purple irises,
White lilies,
Yellow daffodils.

Now I take flowers to your grave,
The only way I can show I still care.
I put flowers on your grave
On your birthday, my birthday.
There are many other flowers,
A symbol of those who loved you.
I will never smell fresh flowers
Without thinking of you
And the day you left.

Christmas time mistletoe and wine?
The old is past, there's a new beginning?
Christmas is a time to celebrate
To have a laugh with our friends
And exchange our love.
But Christmas is not the same
Because just that one person missing
Breaks my link of love.
I want to share Christmas with you
And the past to come back to me.
There will be no new beginning,
Life will go on, because it has to;
But for me, without you life will be dull.
I see no light in the darkness
To fulfil my wish to mend my broken heart.
This Christmas is the same as last,
Full of tears because of the happy times.
They have not gone, but you have,
In body not in mind.
I will try to celebrate this Christmas,
And I'll try to carry on
But to me there seems no point
Now that you have gone.

I want to scream and shout at you to make you understand, but of course I can't because you're a teacher and I'm only a pupil. How dare you look at me like that when I ask to be excused from your lesson to go and see a counsellor. Your look tells me that you don't believe I'm upset, you think I'm just trying to skive your lesson. I probably do look unconvincing because I have learnt how to hide my grief from those I know will be unsympathetic. What you don't understand is that even if I stay in your lesson I will learn nothing because my mind is constantly occupied with problems that I cannot deal with. It is not just you, but many others who react like you, that are holding me back. For you make me feel that I am different from everybody else and I should not be behaving this way. You are adding to my problems by making me think I am the only person who has ever needed more than the 'acceptable' couple of weeks to grieve. Of course this 'acceptable' period is expected by those who do not experience tragedy firsthand. Those who do not endure great loss cannot know what a complicated and long thing the 'grieving process' is. How dare you have an opinion about what I should do when you have absolutely no idea what I'm going through - they weren't your friends, you didn't grow up with them. Although I'm sure you suffered from their loss you do not know how deep the emotions from this run. I am not asking that you try to understand completely because you cannot, but just let us do what we have to do. For you must realise that only we know what we need to do to help ourselves.

* * * * *

ONE FOR EVERY THOUGHT OF YOU

If I were to collect a leaf from the woods,
One for every thought of you,
There wouldn't be a green tree left in this world
Their branches as bare as my life.

If I were to write a word on a page,
One for every thought of you,
There wouldn't be a word that hadn't been said
Yet my feelings would remain unexpressed.

If I were to draw a line on a canvas,
One for every thought of you,
There wouldn't be a picture that hadn't been drawn
Yet none as beautiful as you.

If I were to sing a note in a song,
One for every thought of you,
There wouldn't be a song that hadn't been sung,
Yet none as sweet as your voice.

If I were to cry a tear from my eye,
One for every thought of you,
There wouldn't be a tear that hadn't been shed
Yet my mourning for you would continue.

THE SCREAM FROM WITHIN

It starts slowly,
In the pit of my stomach,
Making me feel sick inside.
It builds up into a fire
That burns away at me
And then spreads upwards into my throat,
Choking me so I have to fight to breathe.
My heart beats faster and faster,
Louder and louder,
Until its pulse resounds in my head.
It fills my head until I can hear nothing else.
I open my mouth to scream the loudest, longest
Scream from within -
But nothing comes out.

I have a picture of that Monday after,
Walking Charlene's class through
The lanes, subdued. I wasn't their teacher;
We could not be in the scene we walked in,
Nor the other, the terrible, we could not
Make that our place either. And so
We walked through. They hung on to
The company of each other, talked
As they caught up, and when they
Walked on I played the role of
Looking over them, without looking over.
It was a sensation of coming away from
A spin, but still spinning, lost in the spin.

Now, two years later, the same group
Walking the same lane in the sun,
Subdued, but part this time of the surroundings,
In present time. A horn blows from behind
Woods, a huntsman probably miles away practising.
But no - he appears in full hunting trim
Halved by a leafless hedge placed as if
To hide the puppeteer's hand. Others follow,
Hounds yowl, spill over styles panting
At scattered scents among the year's last sugar-beet tops -
Voles, badgers, cats perhaps, the damp winter fields
Mid-brown and muddy - eeling under and up
In their single sleek pack like an anteater's tongue.

I could watch this scene play itself over
And over in thin afternoon sun convincing myself
That what happened before hadn't happened at all,
They are here, we are one, there was no interim,
Only now we have learnt the worth of each other.
But it won't do. My words slide cluelessly over, under -
They are safe, the dear ones they snort after,
Away, gone forever into the weave of things,
First to take their long turn in death
While we the living stay to witness the
Sad silly splendour of our own lives.

LAST NIGHT

Last night I had a dream about you,
That you were here right by my side.
You were laughing at me as if nothing had changed,
As if you never went away at all.

Last night you came to me in my sleep,
At first your image was so hazy,
But then I heard your voice come through,
As if you never went away at all.

Last night you were standing by me,
You were talking about the old times,
About all the things we did before,
As if you never went away at all.

Last night I remember you coming,
And laughing at me as I slept.
How I wish that you were here again,
As if you never went away at all.

TRAPPED

Trapped in the dying season.
Trapped by the grey mornings
That bring darkness to my heart.
Trapped by the evenings
That draw quickly in engulfing everything.

Trapped in the dying season.
Trapped by the thoughts in my head
They mean everything but nothing.
Trapped by the feelings in my heart
They cloud my days.

Trapped in the dying season.
Trapped in frosts that kill the flowers
And cover the green creation.
Trapped in cold north winds
That numb my soul.

Trapped in the dying season.
Trapped in the season you died too
Leaving suddenly without a goodbye.
Trapped in the pain of last autumn
When my world was shattered.

* * * * *

Writings from a passage of time that will never work its way fully into the past.

* * * * *

Truth is water, it can't be held. As soon as you trap it, it becomes nothing. So what relationship with life is possible through writing, or can it only ever be a packaging of what is cheap and false? I wish I could resolve that in my mind. It seems to me, though, one can pass through life dead in spirit, and possibly the arts help keep us in tune with the rhythms of life, keep us in touch with our losses, and the thread of human spirit...

I would like to finish this chapter with two pieces. The first is a poem I love by the Bromsgrove poet Molly Holden, who continued writing through the illness that ended her life in 1981.

After The Requested Cremation

A steady north-north-west wind preferably,
though an east wind would do as second-best,
and so my bones' smoke and innocent ashes
would carry into Wessex or the west.

I'd like my dust to be deposited
in the dry ditches, among the fine grass of home,
on hills I've walked, in furrows I've watched making
in Wiltshire's chalk-bright loam.

If not that then Wolverhampton's chimneys
might send me Severnward; that would do instead.
Those rose-red farms, those orchards, have all been precious.
I'd like to fertilize them when I'm dead.

Make no mistake though, it'll not come to choosing.
There'll be a west wind in the week I go.
Or else my southern dust will fall on hated highways
and be for ever swirling to and fro.

Well, as I'll never know, it doesn't matter.
I'm not, in truth, romantic about death.
Only I'd like the right wind to be blowing
that takes the place of breath.

* * * * *

The young write endlessly about killing without ever touching on death, but after the accident that seemed to change for a time, and it became strongly present in some of their fictions. The following piece was sent to me by a year-twelve pupil who kept in touch after I left.

AMY BROWN

Mom's white top is bloody. Her sneakers make no sound
  on the white tiles.
She says dad is dead.
Red and white look so pretty.
I don't know what's going on.
My nose bleeds. It hits the floor.
More red and white, more pretty.
Dad's dead? I ask but no words come out.
I can't speak. I'll stay forever a silent person.
I can't take this.
Emily's crying and Nick is sad.
My nose-blood hits the floor just before my head.

* * * * *

I'm lying under my purple cover. I see a mask at the window and my voice comes back.

AAAAgh.

That feels so good that I keep on screaming. Now mom and Nick and Em are here. Where's dad? I think.

Amy, I think, they can't hear your thoughts. So I scream it.

Where's dad? Mom starts to cry. Yeah, I remember, dad's dead. I scream more. I can't help it.

Em hits me and I shake and sob. I try to talk, and discover that I can.

I kiss mom, Nick and Em and shake all night.

* * * * *

I want to make a noise as big and scary as a gun noise.

The blue plates might work. When they fall, they clatter like metal and silver and chimes and music, not like steel and black and death and a big pop.

Stupid blue plates. They all die. When there's more, they're louder.

* * * * *

Ugly-bugly lady. She smells of cigarettes and shampoo. Her name is Wanda, and her favourite word is share.

Mom shares. Em shares. Nick kind of shares. They look at me. They're so gullible - what do I have to share? NOTHING. I didn't kill anybody.

Wanda says share. I say fuck you. Nick's eyebrows disappear into his big hair. Em's eyebrows pop out of her eye-sockets. Mum starts to cough.

Wanda smiles. Patronising whore. She knows nothing. I leave and go back to my home.

* * * * *

One night, we talk. I cry a bit and Nick cuddles me and I like to be cuddled and loved.
I miss dad, I tell mom.
She agrees.
So does Emily.
So does Nick.
We are all united in our missing dad-ness.

Cushla Brennan.

CHAPTER 15

Friendship

Kids attach a great deal more weight to friendships than we do, in my experience, and I believe that's our loss. Have a look at these comments, for example, from leavers' yearbooks:

I decided to write this piece about my friends because things are always easier to write than to say. I think it was probably just after the accident, in year nine, that I started to appreciate how lucky I am to have the friends that I have. There are some people I just don't get along with, but there always are, but the friends that I do have I really don't deserve. They are simply the greatest people you could ever wish to know. I think the reason why we all get on so well is because we are all so different. I always think to myself, 'You're so lucky', and I am, because I don't deserve their friendship. They are amazingly nice to me and I'm sure that I will never again in my entire life meet such wonderful people. So thank-you for your friendship and thanks for making my life less stressful.

* * * * *

Whilst in the last two years of this school, I have realised how precious friends are. I can remember how I used to take them for granted, but now reality has set in, they are the most important things to me, and I don't know what I'll do without them.

* * * * *

I have got a main group of friends who are really special. So now I know never to take them for granted, and that you must always appreciate them.

* * * * *

When I think of the priceless times that staffroom friends over and over turned dross into gold my eyes well up in gratitude. Occasionally I recall an incident or conversation so vividly I find myself laughing as if I were there again. There is only one more step to becoming one of those sad gits that walks down the street in passionate conversation with a room full of people, absolutely blind to the stares of by-passers and the roar of traffic.

But this is not something that has happened only since I left - I made a conscious decision a few years ago that my friends, and I include those among the kids I taught, were worth more appreciation than I was giving them. People leave after decades of service and pleasurable company and we chip in and buy them a present before waving them off; people die, and we drop everything to get to the funeral and pay our respects. This is all upside down, we always wait until the good times are gone before trying to enrich them with our true feelings.

I think it would be nice if we'd been created with a purr-gland, like a cat, so people would be alerted to the fact that we were content, there would be no confusion. The beauty of it would be, it would be instinctive, sincere compliments would trigger a purr, but when someone smarmed up to you there would only be silence.

Actually, you do get it very occasionally in schools - have you ever been in a lesson when everyone starts humming while they're doing their work? Or, most teachers have had times when even a secondary kid might call them mum or dad by mistake. Rare giveaway signs of contentment.

A form of writing that is very agreeable, but only works with classes that have a friendly spirit, is the chain writing in each others' books I mentioned in chapter ten. With reasonably motivated classes I found that kids enjoyed this and their writing was more careful than usual, being in other people's books - it was actually communicating for a change; I enjoyed marking them and they were interested to read them. Quite often I would dip in and out and jot down observations too.

Here is a typical sample, this time from year-eights:

THE RULES OF LIFE

'The rules of life are things like everything rarely goes the way you want. If things do go your way it is not for long. If you do something good and try to make it better it will fail. Sometimes if you give a little you get a little, and if you give a lot you get a lot. But this doesn't always apply. Sometimes you give a lot and get nothing back. Life is strange and if you are kind people can be horrible back, or if you are horrible people can be nice back. The reality is there are no rules to life. It is such a wide subject.'

'I agree. Rules are there to help you but aren't always helpful. You can't keep to every single rule there is, because no-one is perfect. Rules are there, but people just don't abide by them thoroughly. I agree with the part that if you give something you don't get anything but sometimes you do.'

'I think there is one rule, do whatever you want - if it goes bad, so what. Don't try and please other people, try and please yourself and your family.'

'Since reading other people's I think that there are no rules to life. People make rules for other people but who are they to tell you what you can and can't do? Sometimes there are times when you must obey rules or you will put your life and other people's in danger. Example - firemen and police officers.'

'The sad truth is, nowadays people's lives are ruled by money. Life isn't fair, and that's a fact that we just have to accept. "If there wasn't any money on this earth we would all be happy and live in peace" is something people might say. Yeah? Get real. What would people work for? For example, people in car factories wouldn't work for nothing, then there wouldn't be any cars. The consequences would be disastrous. Doctors and nurses wouldn't work for nothing.'

'I completely agree with what you're saying. Where would we be without money? Not a lot of people I know are prepared to work for nothing. I, for one, certainly don't intend to work for peanuts when I'm older, no way! People's lives can be ruled by money and that's pretty sad...'

'Since doing this, and reading other people's work, it makes me think, for example, children don't often disobey rules, but as we grow older we start to rebel. People make rules, most are simple and must be kept, for example: don't kill. But other rules are plain daft. For example it is illegal in New York for women to smoke in public (this law may have now been changed). If we break laws we are punished. But sometimes if we break laws we instantly gain a bad reputation. Some people refuse to look behind what they see as guilty faces, to ask why they broke the law in the first place. For example, they may have killed someone in self-defence, or stolen to feed their family. As soon as you're in that court and the jury say 'Guilty' and the judge hands out your sentence you are instantly recognisable as a convict, criminal, things you can never live down no matter how much you try to hide them.'

'I don't think there are any rules in life. There are, sort of, rules though, like not killing people and things like that, although this rule has been broken. In fact, if there were any rules to life they've probably all been broken by now. There are a lot of things that you shouldn't do in life like murdering, stealing, etc., but this doesn't mean that people don't do it. I suppose you should have rules in your life if you are a teacher, policeman/woman, etc. I'm just a child though, so if I had rules they'd be, keep out of trouble, do my best in work, etc., and obey the teachers and staff in my school. This is the rules that probably apply to most of the children of my age but even some of us don't keep them. A lot of rules are broken.'

'I really agree with what you said. Life is so big that there can't be any rules. The law can make laws and set punishments, but who are they to say what we can and can't do? They are people like us. In life, if you break the rules of life (if there are some), what would be the punishment? I like what you said about the rules for people like policemen. They must stick to those rules and if they don't, they are putting people's lives at risk.'

'You say that there are no rules of life. I think they are real because the law and the Ten Commandments are rules, and a lot of people lead their lives by them. There will always be someone who will break a rule. Life is what you make of it.'

'After reading these point of views I have realised about the people in other countries, I never thought about their lives and rules. For example, you get in trouble for something you didn't do. But that doesn't happen all the time. In other countries it could be very unfair because they're at war and starving with no homes. I'm quite lucky though and I'm trying to enjoy every bit of it. Life for me is great because I'm not treated unfairly and I enjoy it.'

'I agree that it's unfair that the war-stricken countries populations have to starve and get killed. But sometimes even people in this country get treated unfairly, for example if you're a black young person in an expensive car the police most of the time will stop you and not a white person.'

'I actually never thought about the unfairness in this country, for example the racism, class distinction and prejudice towards people in this country.'

'Life is full of murder, people missing, and then other people assaulting and breaking the law. If you watch the news, most of the time the news is just full of people breaking the law, wars breaking out in other countries. Not much of the news is of older and younger people getting married or winning money or having a good time, it's full of people breaking the law. A lot of the world is full of crime.'

'The world is not full of crime. I think you have been watching the news too much. You said it like the news was on every minute of the day just saying about crimes and murder. Next time the news is on flick the channel over and you might get a holiday programme. I don't see people in that murdering and assaulting each other. Most, no not most, few countries have wars in. Say 10% of the world is at war with another country, but it's not all like this. Think of Sweden, the cleanest country in the world. They also have the lowest crime rate in the world (probably). There might be a lot of crime but it isn't all like this.'

'The rules in my life are quite strict. These rules are probably in everyone's life. The one I hate the most is "No, you can't go there or do that, you're too young, Becky never done that when she was young." Then there's this one: "Now as we've decided, every week you have to do one job or more."'

'I agree with what Helen has said. I did not think about the rules that my family has got. I don't like it when my mum compares me with my older brothers and sisters, and makes rules for me judging by what they did when they were my age.'

'I agree with you entirely, but you've got to put about other things, like law and stuff. If you asked your mum, can I go to the club tonight? and the club is full of drug addicts, your mum's got a point that you can't go till you're older.'

'Life is very tiring if you go to school or work because after five one-hour lessons on a different subject each hour it is very tiring for your brain. For example, after R.E., history, music, maths and P.E., all you want to do is go to sleep.'

'Life's not always tiring, it depends what kind of day you have. For example, if you have all your favourite lessons in one day then you may not be tired when you get home. When I get home after school I don't feel as if I want to go straight to sleep.'

'Life is what you make of it, it doesn't have to be full of rules and complications, just make the most of it. Sometimes it might not be fair but that is the way life is. If you have a great chance in life don't miss it or you'll always be wondering what could have been. Life is full of different opportunities, so just relax about life and have some fun.'

* * * * *

This piece of writing on friendship was written by a year-eight girl (I'm not sure how strong she is on religious symbols):

I did not worship her like an Indian worships the sun or the moon nor as a Hindu worships a cow. I worshipped her as much as in I respected her and I could even say I loved her in my own way, but it was only when she mounted those unpredictable beasts that she towered over me in both knowledge and sense.

I woke up with a start at the sound of the telephone ringing in my ears. I quickly got up and ran downstairs and answered it. It was Saturday morning and Sue was asking if I was ready to go riding, I told her that I would be over in 10 minutes. I ran upstairs and looked out of the window, it was a cold, foggy morning and the roofs and streets were covered in a thin glistening blanket of frost.

I walked over to the chest of drawers and pulled out the thermal vest and long johns my grandma had bought for me and the thick woolly socks she had knitted for my birthday. I then looked around for my jodphurs which I found in the bottom of my wardrobe, as usual, creased up. I pulled them over my feet, then dragged them up over my legs and fastened them. They were so tight there was hardly a crease left.

As we climbed over the stile and made our way to the big green gate at the far end of the field, we called out to the ponies "Charlie; Star..." I tried to undo the latch on the gate but it was so cold that when I touched it, it seemed to burn my fingers. As we fought our way through the thick river of mud trying not to lose our wellies, the smell of the muck heap overcame us. It was kind of sweet-smelling in the coldness of the early morning air.

Sue and I decided it would be better to go over the top of the muck heap rather than go through the muddy swamp that lay before us. As we made our way over the top of it, the smell seemed to comfort us on this cold December morning and reminded us of the times we used to fight in it on those far away hot sunny days. As we climbed down the steep slope and onto the concrete slabs, I looked back and saw the steam rise off it like a volcano.

We collected the ponies from the field and took them into the stable. Sue told me what had to be done. "First take their rugs off." I'd only just learnt how to do this properly, before I kept getting muddled with all the different straps. Then I had to brush Charlie. This was a lot harder than it sounded because Charlie did not like getting brushed - he knew that I loved to fuss him so he would lean his head over my shoulder and lick my hand, his tongue was so soft it had a very gentle and soothing effect on me, and I could have stood there with him like that for hours.

As Sue and I used to trot up the winding road to Clent we would sing out of tune and tell each other who we were in love with at the time - it seemed to change every day. When we came to the top of Clent, we would feel the horses under us they were like fire and it felt that if we held them back any longer, they would burn us up. We would then go thundering down the hills, by the time we came to a stop the horses would be gasping for air and so would we. Our eyes would be full of tears with the force of the wind in our faces.

On the following Saturday morning, Sue was late ringing me. I had on my riding clothes and was waiting for her to call. When I went up to the stables, she seemed really excited. She kept asking me what she should wear and going on. Finally I seemed to blow up inside and I practically screamed at her, "For God's sake Sue, shut up," then I realised what I had said. She had a right to be excited and was just trying to share her excitement with me. I realised how awful I had been and quickly made the excuse that I had a headache and was feeling a bit queasy.

Sue apologised and said that she was sorry and that she shouldn't have gone on so much. I then wished she had had a go back at me, at least I wouldn't have felt so guilty. I was the one that should have been apologising.

The time we spent at the stables seemed to be less and less and when we did go up we never had as much fun as before. There was no talking and giggling or having fun, not even fights in the muck heap.

Sue often used to go out with Mark to the pictures or disco's, but whenever I had the chance I would go over to Sue's house, even if it did mean being a gooseberry all night. I was jealous of Mark, very jealous, but he was a nice boy and I found it easy to talk to him.

On one Tuesday evening when I was over at Sue's, I asked if they were going out on Friday. She said, "I thought we might go to the pictures." Mark looked at me and smiled and asked if I would like to go with them. I saw Sue glare at him and I realised that she didn't want me to go, so I said that I didn't want to play gooseberry, but Mark quickly said I could bring Kirsty my friend, so it was all settled.

I thought Friday night went well. It was that night I realised I fancied Mark. He seemed to take a big interest in me. We talked a lot, mostly about Kirsty my friend, he said she was nice and asked me if she had a boyfriend, amongst other questions. I began to see more of Sue and Mark and go out with them. I always took Kirsty and we all seemed to get on well, that was apart from Sue. She hated Mark talking to Kirsty and me. Mark seemed to take less and less notice of Sue and they slowly began to fall out. It started with just a few arguments and then they seemed to be at each other's throats all the time.

It was Wednesday evening and I was ready for bed. The door bell rang and as I opened the door, my heart jumped - it was Mark. I made him a cup of coffee and he told me that he didn't want to go out with Sue any more and asked if I would ring and tell her. I jumped at the chance and hated myself for doing so because I knew how upset she would be. As I rang the number my fingers started to shake with excitement as did my voice when I spoke to her. I felt so guilty, I could tell in her voice that she had a lump in her throat and she had a problem speaking, then suddenly she burst into tears. I quickly told her that I had to go and put the phone down.

It was now Saturday night and I had managed to avoid Sue for the past few days, although I had heard nothing from Mark. I decided to take the dog for a walk to his usual hangout down at the park.

As I went through the clearing of trees I saw a line of figures, then I saw Mark. He had just got a light for his cigarette off a friend, now he was walking back towards the silhouette sitting on the bench - he then put his arm around the figure, it wasn't until I heard them laugh that I knew it was Kirsty.

I clenched my fists and felt my eyes sting with tears, my throat was dry. I ran all the way home and cried myself to sleep. I realised how I had been used and that he had only been friendly with me so he could get to know Kirsty - how stupid and naive I had been.

I had filled my head with so many romantic notions that I believed he loved me as much as I did him.

I took the dog for a walk in the park and saw Sue in the distance riding that magnificent beast of hers, ploughing through the earth further and further away. It was only then that I realised that she was really gone out of my life and we could never be friends again.

Sheryl Caine

*   *   *   *   *

And so, as we reach the end of this book, I would like to pay my respects to some of the friends who saw me through.

To Conway, the Baggies fan: one season he bet me his Albion would finish higher in the league than mine. I lost, and sellotaped his tenner in an endless tail of five p's, stuffing it in a dirty sock along with a couple of pickled onions and some rancid cheese; whenever tea-money time came round he would go to his locker, pull out a couple of feet of five p's, nip them off and drop them in the tin.

To Jenko, who would have walked the auditions for Men Behaving Worse Than Badly - when he left we put a bucket in the staffroom for people to put donations in; there were bags of crisps, washers, holiday brochures, loose tea-bags, the joke was so perfectly guaged at his level that he came in on several separate days with his camera and took pictures of it. He was a legendary cheap-skate, and a colleague found a four-pack of 'Rustic' 2.1% bitter for £1.17 and dropped it in the bucket, leaving the price on. He fetched it out, and in triumph said, 'I can get it cheaper than that!'. To McCormack, who appeared on the cover of 'Rugby World', having run on the field after a game at Cardiff Arms Park to scrag the players. One term he came across a second year who studied racing form and had tipped him the winner of the Melbourne Gold Cup, so he got him scouring the race cards in his lunch-hours, and came to the staffroom to raise a kitty. The boy got community service when the bets went down.

To Wendy, the smallest P.E. teacher I ever met, but massive in talent: her netball team went five years undefeated in all competitions, winning the league and cup each time; on one occasion she asked at the briefing if staff could spare them for five minutes for a photo, and the head enquired whether they'd achieved anything we should know about.

To John, unrepentant Marxist, tireless NASUWT rep and wit without equal. He was contemptuous of people who took time off, and never did so himself. Once, however, the trains came to a stop, and his first lesson had to be covered; I got the job. I got into his classroom and sent for my friend in the art department who always had a camera; we wrote the slogan 'CONSERVATIVE VALUES - DISCIPLINE / DAILY WORSHIP / LOYALTY TO THE QUEEN' on the board, got all the kids with their hands up as if eagerly answering questions on the subject, took the shot, printed it and had it up on his wall by the time he came in.

To Ted, the staff homophobe, who wrecked my Brighton & Hove Albion christmas card signed by all the playing staff by pasting a pink triangle across it: Brighton's gay profile was a source of extreme fascination and aversion for him. Ted had a very short fuse, and was sensitive about the car he drove; when he did bus duties the kids used to bait him by shouting 'Skoda!' out of the top windows just as their bus was moving off, and he would periodically chase after one and make the driver stop so he could dash up the stairs and harangue them. At a trip to Chester Zoo one year, he spotted a child spitting from a pedestrian bridge onto the people below, slapped him, and threatened to ban him from future trips. It was only when we got back to the coach he realised the boy wasn't with our party.

Joe, the man who used to phone Severn-Trent Water and rant at them about their purity levels, knackered his suspension fetching spring water from Malvern to brew his beer with, Joe's 'Fat Bastard' bitter, A.B.V. 5.0%. Joe was a rear gunner at the Normandy landings and told me the only war joke I've ever laughed at. The forces used to be issued with cigarettes, but had no say over what they would receive - it might be Players Weights, Senior Service, whatever, or a brand called Pashas which they all detested. A British infantryman is hit, and a French field doctor is brought over; he pushes a thermometer into his rectum, checks, and pronounces him dead. But he has to be seen by a British medic for confirmation. They find one - he takes the thermometer out of the chap's rectum and puts it under his tongue. The Tommy wakes up, spits it out and says, 'Christ, bloody Pashas again.'

I have been lucky to meet with two magi in life - one is David Hart who you've met in previous chapters, he is clearly recognisable as a man of the spirit by his unkempt beard and duffle coats; the other, Richard, has the disguise of a formal head of department, yet is the most soulful person I know. In his house all things are equal - if you should go to sit down and there is a tortoise, dog, cat or hen on the settee, you sit somewhere else. I once called round because I needed a lift with him, and he was running late. He was a very correct head of department, and when he let the dogs out I thought it would just be a question of their wetting the nearest tree and back in so we could make up some time, but he did the full walk, at their pace, communicating with them all the way.

I give praise to Barbara and Margaret, matriarchs of the reprographics room - the outstanding sanctuary for knackered teachers in the midlands. They were the best team since Pearl Carr and Teddy Johnstone: Barbara the stretcher-bearer, wearing her Cliff Richard T-shirt inside-out under her blouse so she always had him next to her bosom, Margaret the warrior, but soft as a marshmallow underneath it.

Chris, my fellow writer on the staff for many years and fanatical devotee of the English Electric Lightning fighter plane, he even has shares in one. His books have titles like 'Lightning Love' and 'Lucky Fiver', a reference to Lancaster bomber crews in the Second World War. Chris's idea of the sublime weekend is to pass it in the pissing rain at the end of a runway, not necessarily seeing them bring the Lightnings out, but having a conversation with a chap who saw them come out the previous week.

To Lomax, Barnsley boot-boy, self-styled child-hater, but revered by the kids. Before Ofsted he primed his fifth-year dossers; they said, 'Sir, it's O.K., we'll all put our hands up, but if we know the answer we'll put the right one up and if we don't we'll put the left.' Yes, he said, only one small problem comes to mind... He stood for parliament, and used to bring in boxes of leaflets which a crowd of us enveloped in our lunch-hours, whistling the Red Flag together like the seven dwarves.

Annie Hollis, the best deputy that never was, who took a group of kids to Germany with me when the department people couldn't go, and sorted every problem with a wave of dismissal and a hug, even though she spoke not a word of German. Another one who was absolutely in tune with the rebellious kids - one year she had to witness a deputy head deliver a spiteful tirade nose to nose with one of her fifth years (year elevens), and cried with humiliation for him when it was over; he put his arm round her and said, 'It's O.K. miss, don't upset yourself, we can handle him.'

To Dave, our madman, tea-money merchant and former serial fondler of the younger teachers ('Ere, cum rand the back an give us a pull o yer pigtail..'). Dave pestered our staff politician for years about petty decisions such as the introduction of traffic calmers to one of his favourite cut-throughs, even though he never voted for him - 'Right then Carncillor, abart them there bollard things..' As time wore on Dave mellowed, first becoming a devotee of vitamin pills and supplements, which he would take out of a carrier bag and cover the table with at lunch-times (I would lean over and take a brazil from the mixed nuts; 'Ere, gi' that back, it's me last one, ave one a them peanut whatsits'), then turning to the Lord, and reading us passages from the Old Testament whenever our conversations descended into bad taste.

To Chopper, perfect gentleman but staff five-a-side psycho, who had in his room the best poster I ever saw, designed by a young pupil after his form had collected a few pounds for an environmental charity in India: 'We Have Cleaned The Ganges'. Hell, and I thought going down the tip at weekends was hard work. Chopper used to play five-a-side with an imaginary ref by his side, who he would constantly appeal to: ''ead 'igh ref', 'come on ref, what about the four-second rule*'; he was very even-handed, though - on one occasion he hacked a colleague too enthusiastically and sent himself off ('No no, fair play, I deserved it...').

*[A rule invented by him to give himself time to get back into position after a goal had been scored.]

But last, I pay respects to Pete Behan, our moral head for two decades, the most respected and professional teacher I ever met. Pete never shirked from any situation, but never broke off communication with any child or parent, never set up in opposition to them, never failed to tell it exactly how it was. I helped a friend take a trip abroad one year, and at the Shuttle terminus decided to get a case of duty-free beer; it was my friend's trip, but when I took a couple out of the pack for us to drink on the coach, I found myself hiding them from Pete, like a kid. I was having a laugh about this one lunch-break, and another friend said he had been sharing a room with him on a ski-trip, and had stopped at the bar last thing to get a short to take up to the room; he said, 'I crept in that quiet, I couldn't hear myself.' A man of absolute authority.

To all those people, to the kids and their indomitable spirit: Gerard who pushed his head, arms and shoulders through a black-out curtain during a showing of King Lear to a sixth-form, blanking the picture, sniffed, said to the teacher, 'Shakespeare miss - load of crap, ay miss', and strolled off; Bones, who came to me on the last day before the christmas break with a busted single twig of mistletoe, one leaf and a couple of berries loose in his hand, and asked if he could borrow the Prit-Stick; to Andrew, who after I'd read Yeats' Easter 1916 as passionately as I've read any poem and asked him for a response to it, sniffed, flicked the page, looked up and said, 'Load of old bollocks really, ain't it..'; to all the jokers and piss-takers I've taught, to the friends and confidants, to the seekers and searchers, the thinkers, the probers, the dreamers - and lastly, to the writers...

To all of you: I bow down and give thanks.

CHAPTER 16

Finale

This book has been about teenage writing, and as I've reread pieces before placing them in chapters I've experienced again the excitement I remember when they first sprang out at me. I have tried to link them by flagging up the subjective mind as an exact counterweight to the objective mind. The objective, pinning down facts, nailing lies, narrowing things down to the point where they can be proved to be one or the other; the subjective, trying on the lies, moving among fantasies and suppositions sniffing out the ones that are the least untrue.

I would say that the creative mind is not a responsible one - it is, in the best sense of the word, irresponsible. I think of its work as the equivalent of rot: it breaks down what is dead and delivers it back into the cycle of life. How does it know what is dead and what is not? It attacks everything: what is healthy survives and is made stronger by the attack. Well, it is also - especially - a loving thing, an affirmation: what I mean is it attacks old forms and clichés, and constantly seeks new and unthought ways of expressing itself. Man doesn't make the rules of life, nature does; art attacks man's rules and the healthy survive. Not the pirannah fish keeping the tank clean, more like the parrot fish which, by eating at healthy coral keeps the coral healthy.

I had no right to produce the book - I'm neither a successful teacher, nor writer. I just had these stunning pieces, collected over a decade or two because I couldn't bring myself to let them become nothing, which I have always wanted to share. And now I've done it.

Please use the contacts at the very front to give feedback. I am excited to know how people, young and older, react to what is here - and if more pieces of quality come in, it would give me immeasurable pleasure to bring out another volume.

P.H. July 2000

Books referred to:

I haven't got a researcher, but these notes might give you a start.

Chapter 1. The H.M.I. report appeared 1979 - I don't have any more details.
'A Game of Dark' William Mayne Hamish Hamilton 71 [0241020506] O/P?
'Gideon Ahoy!' William Mayne Penguin Plus 89 [0140321292]

Chapter 2. 'Goldengrove' Jill Paton Walsh Corgi 97 [0552996556]
'Unleaving' Jill Paton Walsh Red Fox 90 [0099753200]
'A Parcel of Patterns' Jill Paton Walsh Penguin 88 [0140326278]

Chapter 3. 'Song of the City' Gareth Owen Fontana Lions 85 [0006724108] O/P?
'Red Shift' Alan Garner Collins 95 [0006742955]

Chapter 4. 'The Ennead' Jan Mark Kestrel 78 [0722654774]
'Divide and Rule' Jan Mark Penguin Plus 90 [0140343857]
'Feet and Other Stories' Jan Mark Puffin 97 [0140378227]

Chapter 5. 'The Mouse and His Child' Russell Hoban Puffin 93 [0140364552]
'Turtle Diary' Russell Hoban Picador 82 [0330266454]
'Ridley Walker' Russell Hoban Pan 77 [0330250507]
'The Intelligence of Feeling' R.J. Witkin Heinemann 74 [0435809385] O/P?

Chapter 6. 'Goggle Eyes' Anne Fine Penguin 90 [0140365125]

Chapter 7. 'Border Country' David Hart - contact Woodwind Publications, 42 All Saints Road, Birmingham B14 7LL
'setting the poem to words' David Hart Five Seasons Press 98 [0947960198]
'Poetry in the Making' Ted Hughes Faber 67 [0571090761] O/P?

Chapter 8. 'The Act of Creation' Arthur Koestler Arkana 89 [0140191917]
'The Earthsea Quartet' Ursula Le Guin Penguin 93 [0140154272]

Chapter 9. 'Bilgewater' Jane Gardam Abacus 85 [0349114021]
'A Long Way from Verona' Jane Gardam Abacus 97 [0349114056]
'The Hollow Land' Jane Gardam Walker 98 [0744560659]

Chapter 10. 'Animal Heroes' Ernest Thompson Seton 1905 Whitefriars Press
'Best of Ernest Thompson Seton' ed Richard Adams Fontana 82 [0006164528].

Chapter 12. 'Lord of the Flies' William Golding Faber 54 [0571176534]
'A Prayer for Owen Meany' John Irving Black Swan 90 [0552993697]
'The Coral Island' R.M. Ballantyne Puffin 82 [0140367616] (abridged)
'Blue Remembered Hills' Dennis Potter Faber 84 [057113081X]

Chapter 13. 'Tough Luck' Berlie Doherty Collins Lions 89 [0006732194]
'The Cider House Rules' John Irving Black Swan [0552992046]
'Setting Free the Bears' John Irving Black Swan 86 [0552992062]
'A Midsummer Night's Death' K.M. Peyton O.U.P. 99 [019271774X]

Chapter 14. 'Selected Poems' Dannie Abse Hutchinson 70 [0091012015] O/P?
'Air and Chill Earth' Mollie Holden Hogarth Press 71 [0701118318] O/P?
Brambles Trust: Bannut Tree House, Lye Head, Bewdley, Worcs DY12 2UW

I realise this is not the most up-to-date information; please contact me if you can update, and I will put it in the next printing.
If you are curious to read any of my books which never made it to print, send a cheque for £7 to Crazy Horse Press and I'll get the script photocopied for you.

"And Smith Must Score…"
Peter Hayden

Pub: Crazy Horse Press
Published Sept. 1999

ISBN 1871870089
1st Reprint Nov. 1999

LATEST REVIEWS

"'*And Smith Must Score…*' is quite wonderful. Yes, '*Catcher In The Rye*' and '*Fever Pitch*' joined together for kids: I thought it was tremendous. The football scenes are unmatchable, especially the semi-final. I shall make a lot of people read this. I wish I could catch that note. They say Pete Johnson is best at catching actual voices and thought processes of that age group… but about you doing it I have no doubt. IT IS REAL."
Dennis Hamley (author of Death Penalty, Haunted United, Ryans United, &c.)

"I cannot praise it highly enough. It is a great read from cover to cover… A witty and well-written story that will appeal to all young at heart fans."
'Peeping Tom' (Coventry City fanzine)

"Hayden blends some '*Fever Pitch*'-style observations about football and identity crisis with a well structured plot and deft characterisations and comes up with an exciting and poignant book."
Independent on Sunday

"More than just a football book… The writing is a cross between Nick Hornby meets Adrian Mole, but it far better describes the feelings and emotions of an ordinary fan."
'Black Arab' (Bristol Rovers fanzine)

"It is a book which gripped me immediately, and it's rare to get a review copy which isn't a chore to plough through; I literally couldn't put it down."
'Mr Harry Urz' (Kidderminster Harriers fanzine)

"'And Smith Must Score' got me intrigued from the off and once I had finished the first page I was hooked and just had to read on… The book is charmingly funny and exemplifies the exploits of a teenage boy with unerring accuracy. It will appeal to just about everyone whether you are young or old, footy fans or not, a super story and a compelling read."
'Those Were The Days' (Huddersfield Town fanzine)

"It is simply an excellent read."
'Grorty Dick' (W.B.A. fanzine)

"Loved it. It's an easy thing to say but sometimes your mood catches the book you're reading and this was one of those rare occasions."
Covering letter - 'Grorty Dick'

"It's hard to do it justice, as there is so much packed into this book to make it so witty yet serious that it just can't be done… I can't recommend it enough. It will appeal to everybody from teenage years upwards, and will guarantee you not only a good read but a great laugh as well. Excellent stuff."
'We Are Crewe' (Crewe Alexandra fanzine)

In-School Days
with Peter Hayden

PRIMARY
Primary School visits involve talks, readings, workshops, follow-up service (written comment on work done as a result of the visit), and signing session. There is a single fee, no extras, which includes presentation of books to the schools library.

All books at signing sessions are well below cover-price.

SECONDARY
The visits involve talks and readings from 'The Day Trip', 'The Headmaster's Daughter' and other writing, including published work by teenagers. Writing workshops are geared towards exam and coursework needs if desired. The one-off fee includes signing session, follow-up service (see primary notes) and presentation of books to the school library.

All books at signing are well below cover-price.

INSET
Talks, demonstrations and workshops from the perspective of the child, teacher, and examiner, based on the book 'The Poppy Factory Takeover: Teenage Writing'.

'I loved it, I want you to come again.'
'You are a kind person.'
(Yr 3 pupils, Valley Rd Junior Sch., Sunderland)
'Best day ever.'
'I wish you worked here.' *(Yr 4 pupils, Bloemfontein Primary, Durham)*
'He's cool.'
'His stories were the best.' *(Yr 8 pupils, Ysgol Llangefni, Anglesea)*
'I think everything was brilliant.' *(Yr 5 pupil, St Godric's Prim., Durham)*

[originals available]

BOOKINGS
For bookings phone Peter Hayden on 01299 824858 or e-mail Crazy Horse (details page ii).

For illustrator days, contact Clinton Banbury on 01277 630421.

Or contact Crazy Horse Press direct.

Photocopy

Publications available from Crazy Horse Press

no p&p, delivery by return, order form overleaf:

The Adventures of Stringy Simon – Peter Hayden

Book 1: Sampler Edition 7 – 12 yrs   ISBN 1 871870 07 0   £4.99
Book 2: The Willy Enlarging Elixir 9 – 13 yrs   ISBN 1 871870 10 0   £4.99
Book 3: The Sneeze & Other Stories 7 – 12 yrs   ISBN 1 871870 11 9   £4.99

'You are my favourite author and I enjoy your books. They are funny.'
'I really like your books, especially Stringy Simon, it is fantastic.'
'I think your book about Stringy Simon and his willy is great.'
'I have not heard of a children's book writer or adult book writer as good as you.'   (Junior readers – originals available)

The Day Trip – Peter Hayden
'Gripped by the pace and realism of the writing we join the school outing and are bussed, sailed and decanted onto French soil. From now on, in spite of their luckless teachers, the kids are on their own, our lot rather more than the rest. Lost and late, they board the wrong boat home, merge with another school, and end up on the wrong side of the Watford Gap. Ah - but Mike and Lee have declared their love; and what a day they've all had. Hayden's an invigorating new talent to watch.'
     (The Guardian)   Teens   ISBN 0 19 271 510 0   £4.95

And Smith Must Score... – Peter Hayden
'I recommend it to anyone looking for a good footy read.'   (Nick Hornby)
'A wonderful, charming and witty dose of escapist fiction.'
     (Derby Co. F.C. fanzine)
'A football supporter's dream of a book.'   (Middlesbrough F.C. fanzine)
'If you're a footy fan counting down the weeks to the new season, then this is the book for you.'
     (Observer)   Adults & teens   ISBN 1 871870 08 9   £6.99

The Headmaster's Daughter – Peter Hayden
'I really enjoyed reading it. It was like listening in on a girls' cloakroom gossip.'
     (Berlie Doherty)
'We didn't think you were the type who knew about the words snogging, getting-off, or swearing. Me and Donna thought you were the innocent type (speaking-wise)... We thoroughly enjoyed reading it (we are being serious).'
'It's the kind of book that you would be sort of drifting with when you start reading it but when you'd finished you'd read it again because you realise how it fits together and appreciate the detail given at the beginning.'
     (Teenage readers - originals available)
     Older teens   ISBN 1 871870 09 7   £5.99

Catch & Other Stories – Steve Bowkett
Tales of horror, fantasy and science fiction. Steve Bowkett has 22 teen horror and fantasy titles to his credit, including the popular Dreamcatcher series. His books have been translated into five languages.

'Stephen Bowkett has a rare flair for creating an atmosphere of fear and horror out of the most prosaic of situations. Edgar Allen Poe would have been proud.'
(Junior Bookshelf)

Bowkett 'catches the stuff of adolescence.'   (Observer)
9 – 12 yrs   ISBN 1 871870 13 5   £5.99

The Poppy Factory Takeover & Other Stories – Peter Hayden
Observations and stunning examples from three decades of writing with the young.

"There is about the whole book a trustworthiness which carries it all – i.e. I like the sound of this ex-teacher writer, he's got experience worth learning from, and you don't lay the learning on heavy man, only say what you believe passionately. I hope this book gets reviewed at length in the right places."
(David Hart, Birmingham Poet Laureate)
Parents, adults and teens   ISBN 1 871870 12 7   £6.99

Against The Odds	ISBN 1 871870 02 X
George's Mechanical Sledge	ISBN 1 871870 03 8
I'm Seeing Stars	ISBN 1 871870 01 1
Man's Best Enemy	ISBN 1 871870 00 3

Four humorous stories written and illustrated by teenagers.
9 - 12 yrs   £5.99 - set of four.

'The Keeper Looks Like Elvis'
[Not really a Crazy Horse production - five football sit-com episodes, each in a staple-bound booklet, featuring a non-league team and their fanzine. Written by Peter Hayden & Robert Pant.]
Adults   £5 set of five.

[Order form overleaf]

Photocopy

ORDER FORM

Photocopy and send to: **Crazy Horse Press**,
116 Bewdley Road, Stourport, Worcs DY13 8XH.
Please send me the following books by return:

....	copies of 'The Adventures of Stringy Simon' @ £4.99	= £ ....
....	copies of 'The Willy Enlarging Elixir' @ £4.99	= £ ....
....	copies of 'The Sneeze & Other Stories' @ £4.99	= £ ....
....	copies of 'The Headmaster's Daughter' @ £5.99	= £ ....
....	copies of 'The Day Trip' @ £4.95	= £ ....
....	copies of 'And Smith Must Score...' @ £6.99	= £ ....
....	copies of 'The Poppy Factory Takeover' @ £6.99	= £ ....
....	copies of 'Catch & Other Stories' @ £5.99	= £ ....
....	sets of 'Against The Odds', &c. @ £5.99	= £ ....
....	sets of 'The Keeper Looks Like Elvis' sit-com @ £5.00	= £ ....
	TOTAL [no p&p required]	= £ ....

NAME ....

ADDRESS ....

....POSTCODE ....

PHONE ....

I enclose a cheque for £..

Signed:..